VISUAL QUICKSTART GUIDE

MICROSOFT OFFICE EXCEL 2003 FOR WINDOWS

Maria Langer

 Peachpit Press

Visual QuickStart Guide
Microsoft Office Excel 2003 for Windows
Maria Langer

Peachpit Press
1249 Eighth Street
Berkeley, CA 94710
510-524-2178 • 800-283-9444
510-524-2221 (fax)

Find us on the World Wide Web at: http://www.peachpit.com/

Peachpit Press is a division of Pearson Education

Editor: Nancy Davis
Indexer: Emily Glossbrenner
Cover Design: Peachpit Press
Production: Maria Langer, David Van Ness

Colophon

This book was produced with Adobe InDesign 2.0 and Adobe Photoshop 7 on a Power Macintosh G4 running Mac OS X 10.2. The fonts used were Utopia, Meta Plus, PIXymbols Command, and ITC Zapf Dingbats. Screenshots were created using IMSI Capture and Collage Capture on a Dell Dimension L933r.

Notice of Rights

Notice of Liability

Trademarks

ISBN 0-321-20038-1

9 8 7 6 5 4

Printed and bound in the United States of America.

Dedication

To Tristan Charney
with best wishes for the future.

Thanks!

To Nancy Davis, for her thorough editing and fast turnaround.

To David Van Ness, for doing a good job on production editing.

To Emily Glossbrenner, for preparing another great index.

To Microsoft Corporation, for continuing to revise and improve the best spreadsheet program on earth.

And to Mike, for the usual reasons.

The Flying M

www.marialanger.com

Table of Contents

TABLE OF CONTENTS

Introduction

Introduction

Microsoft Excel 2003, a component of Microsoft Office 2003, is a powerful spreadsheet software package. With it, you can create picture-perfect worksheets, charts, and lists based on just about any data you can enter.

This *Visual QuickStart Guide* will help you take control of Excel by providing step-by-step instructions, plenty of illustrations, and a generous helping of tips. On these pages, you'll find what you need to know to get up and running quickly with Excel 2003—and more!

This book was designed for page flipping. Use the thumb tabs, index, or table of contents to find the topics for which you need help. If you're brand new to Excel or spreadsheets, however, I recommend that you begin by reading at least the first two chapters. **Chapter 1** provides basic information about Excel's interface. **Chapter 2** introduces spreadsheet concepts and explains exactly how they work in Excel.

If you've used other versions of Excel and are interested in information about new Excel 2003 features, be sure to browse through this **Introduction**. It'll give you a good idea of the new things Excel has in store for you.

One word of advice: don't let Excel intimidate you! Sure, it's big, and yes, it has lots of commands. But as you work with Excel, you'll learn the techniques you need to get your work done. That's when you'll be on your way to harnessing the real power of Excel.

New & Improved Features in Excel 2003

Excel 2003 includes some brand new features, as well as improvements to some existing features. Here's a list.

◆ The Microsoft Office interface has been revised to look brighter and "more energetic" (in Microsoft's words).

◆ The list feature has been improved to make it easier to work with data in designated lists. In addition, list data can now be shared with others via Microsoft Windows Sharepoint Services.

◆ A number of statistical functions have been improved to make them more precise.

◆ The new Compare Workbooks Side by Side command makes it easier to see the differences between two workbook files.

◆ Excel now supports XML for importing and exporting data.

◆ The new Research task pane enables you to get information about topics, right from within Excel.

◆ The new Document Workspaces feature enables multiple people to collaborate on a document in real-time via Microsoft Windows Sharepoint Services.

◆ The new smart documents feature makes it possible to associate Excel worksheet files with databases to automate data entry.

◆ The new Information Rights Management (IRM) feature helps protect sensitive information from unauthorized access, using flexible permissions options.

◆ Excel can now accept input from a Tablet PC.

The Excel Workplace

Meet Microsoft Excel

Microsoft Excel is a full-featured spreadsheet program that you can use to create worksheets, charts, lists, and even Web pages.

Excel's interface combines common Windows screen elements with buttons, commands, and controls that are specific to Excel. To use Excel effectively, you must have at least a basic understanding of these elements.

This chapter introduces the Excel workplace by illustrating and describing the following elements:

◆ The Excel screen, including window elements

◆ Menus, shortcut keys, toolbars, dialogs, and task panes

◆ Document scrolling techniques

◆ Excel's Help feature

✔ Tips

■ If you're brand new to Windows, don't skip this chapter. Many of the interface elements discussed in this chapter apply to all Windows programs, not just Excel.

■ If you've used previous versions of Excel, browse through this chapter to learn about some of the interface elements that are new to this version of Excel.

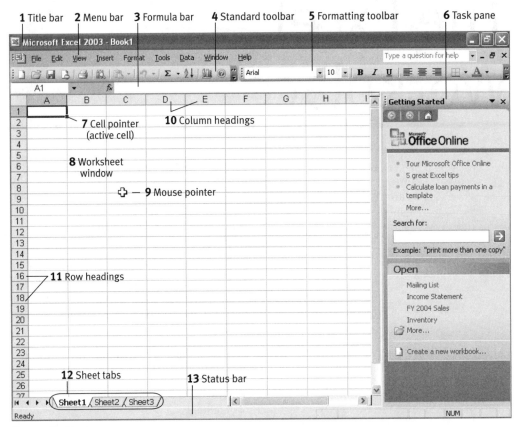

Figure 1 The Excel screen.

Key to the Excel screen

1 Title bar

The title bar displays the document's title. You can drag the title bar to move the window.

2 Menu bar

The menu bar appears at the top of the screen and offers access to Excel's commands.

3 Formula bar

The formula bar displays the contents of the active cell, as well as that cell's address or reference.

4 Standard toolbar

The Standard toolbar offers buttons for many basic Excel commands. This toolbar is similar in other Microsoft Office 2003 programs.

5 Formatting toolbar

The Formatting toolbar offers buttons for formatting commands.

6 Task pane

The task pane offers a convenient way to access common Excel tasks.

7 Cell pointer (active cell)

The cell pointer is a heavy or colored border surrounding the active cell. The active cell is the cell in which text and numbers appear when you type.

8 Worksheet window

The worksheet window is where you'll do most of your work with Excel. This window has columns and rows which intersect at cells. You enter data and formulas in the cells to build your spreadsheet.

9 Mouse pointer

When positioned within the worksheet window, the mouse pointer appears as a hollow plus sign. You can use the mouse pointer to select cells, enter data, choose menu commands, and click buttons.

10 Column headings

Column headings are the alphabetical labels that appear at the top of each column.

11 Row headings

Row headings are the numbered labels that appear on the left side of each row.

12 Sheet tabs

Each Excel document has one or more sheets combined together in a workbook. The sheet tabs let you move from one sheet to another within the workbook. To use the sheet tabs, just click on the tab for the sheet that you want to view.

13 Status bar

The status bar displays information about the document.

✔ Tip

- Standard Windows window elements are not discussed in detail in this book. For more information about how to use standard window elements such as the Close button, Minimize button, Maximize button, Restore button, and scroll bars, consult the documentation that came with your computer or Windows online help.

THE EXCEL SCREEN

The Mouse

As with most Windows programs, you use the mouse to select text, activate buttons, and choose menu commands.

Figure 2
The mouse pointer looks like an arrow when pointing to a menu name or command.

Mouse pointer appearance

The appearance of the mouse pointer varies depending on its location and the item to which it is pointing. Here are some examples:

Figure 3 The mouse pointer looks like an I-beam pointer when positioned over the formula bar ...

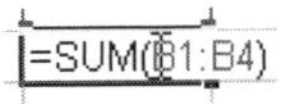

- ◆ In the document window, the mouse pointer usually looks like a hollow plus sign (**Figure 1**).

- ◆ On a menu name (**Figure 2**), the mouse pointer appears as an arrow pointing up and to the left.

Figure 4 ... or over the contents of a cell being edited.

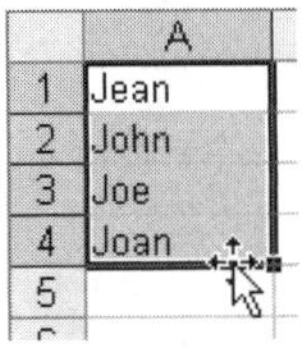

- ◆ In the formula bar (**Figure 3**) or when positioned over a cell being edited (**Figure 4**), the mouse pointer appears as an I-beam pointer.

- ◆ On a selection border, the mouse pointer looks like a standard pointer with a four-headed arrow (**Figure 5**).

Figure 5
The mouse pointer looks like a standard pointer with a four-headed arrow when positioned over a selection border.

To use the mouse

There are four basic mouse techniques:

- ◆ **Pointing** means to position the mouse pointer so that its tip is on the item to which you are pointing (**Figure 2**).

- ◆ **Clicking** means to press the mouse button once and release it. You click to make a cell active, position the insertion point, or choose a toolbar button.

- ◆ **Double-clicking** means to press the mouse button twice in rapid succession. You double-click to open an item or to select a word for editing.

- ◆ **Dragging** means to press the mouse button down and hold it while moving the mouse. You drag to resize a window, select multiple cells, or draw shapes.

✔ Tip

- ■ Throughout this book, when I instruct you to simply *click*, press the left mouse button. When I instruct you to *right-click*, press the right mouse button.

Figure 6 A personalized version of the Edit menu.

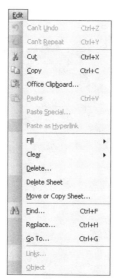

Figure 7 The full version of the Edit menu.

Figure 8 The Fill submenu under the Edit menu.

✔ Tips

- The above menu rules apply to the menus of most Windows programs, not just Excel.

- Dialogs and shortcut keys are discussed later in this chapter.

Menus

All of Excel's commands are accessible through its menus. Excel has three types of menus:

- **Personalized menus** appear on the menu bar near the top of the window. These menus automatically track and display only the commands you use most (**Figure 6**).

- **Full menus** also appear on the menu bar at the top of the window, but only when you either double-click the menu name, pause while displaying the menu, or click the arrows at the bottom of the menu. **Figure 7** shows the menu in **Figure 6** with all commands displayed.

- **Shortcut menus** appear at the mouse pointer when you right-click on an item (**Figure 11**).

Here are some rules to keep in mind when working with menus:

- A menu command that appears in gray (**Figure 6**) cannot be selected.

- A menu command followed by an ellipsis (…) (**Figures 6** and **7**) displays a dialog.

- A menu command followed by a triangle has a submenu (**Figure 8**). The submenu displays additional commands when the main command is selected.

- A menu command followed by one or more keyboard symbols and a letter or number (**Figures 6** and **7**) can be chosen with a shortcut key.

- A menu command preceded by a check mark is "turned on." To toggle the command from on to off or off to on, choose it from the menu.

To choose a menu command

1. Point to the menu from which you want to choose the command.

2. Click on the menu name to display the menu (**Figure 6**).

3. Click the command you want (**Figure 9**).

   or

   If the command is on a submenu, click on the name of the submenu to display it (**Figure 8**) and then click on the command you want (**Figure 10**).

   The command may blink before the menu disappears, confirming that it has been successfully selected.

✔ Tip

■ Throughout this book, I use the following shorthand to refer to menu choices: *Menu Name > Command Name* or *Menu Name > Submenu Name > Command Name*. For example, to instruct you to choose the Copy command from the Edit menu, I'll write "Choose Edit > Copy."

To use a shortcut menu

1. Right-click on the item for which you want to display the shortcut menu. The shortcut menu appears (**Figure 11**).

2. Click to choose the command you want.

✔ Tips

■ The shortcut menu only displays the commands that can be applied to the item to which you are pointing.

■ Shortcut menus are often referred to as *contextual menus*.

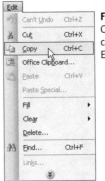

Figure 9
Choosing the Copy command from the Edit menu.

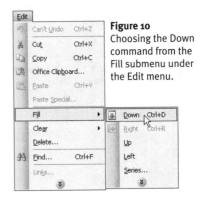

Figure 10
Choosing the Down command from the Fill submenu under the Edit menu.

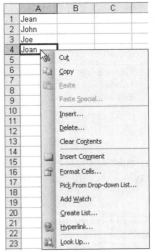

Figure 11
A shortcut menu for a selected cell.

USING MENUS

Shortcut Keys

Shortcut keys are combinations of keyboard keys that, when pressed, choose a menu command without displaying the menu. For example, the shortcut key for the Copy command on the Edit menu (**Figure 9**) is Ctrl C. Pressing this key combination chooses the command.

✔ Tips

■ All shortcut keys use at least one of the following modifier keys:

Key Name	Keyboard Key
Control	Ctrl
Shift	Shift
Alt	Alt

■ A menu command's shortcut key is displayed to its right on the menu (**Figure 9**).

■ Many shortcut keys are standardized from one program to another. The Save and Print commands are two good examples; they're usually Ctrl S and Ctrl P.

■ **Appendix A** includes a list of shortcut keys.

To use a shortcut key

1. Hold down the modifier key for the shortcut (normally Ctrl).

2. Press the letter or number key for the shortcut.

For example, to choose the Copy command, hold down Ctrl and press C.

Toolbars

Excel includes a number of toolbars for various purposes. Each one includes buttons or menus that activate menu commands or set options.

By default, Excel automatically displays two toolbars when you launch it:

◆ The Standard toolbar (**Figure 12**) offers buttons for a wide range of commonly used commands.

◆ The Formatting toolbar (**Figure 13**) offers buttons and menus for formatting selected items.

When all of a toolbar's buttons cannot fit in the window, Excel displays the toolbar using its personalized toolbar feature. This feature keeps track of the buttons and options you use and displays the ones you use most on the toolbar. The other toolbar buttons are hidden; you can display them by clicking the More Buttons button at the end of the toolbar (**Figures 12** and **13**).

✔ Tips

■ Other toolbars may appear automatically depending on the task you are performing with Excel.

■ Toolbar buttons with faint icon images (for example, Undo in **Figure 12**) cannot be selected.

■ Toolbar buttons with a blue border around them are "turned on."

■ A toolbar button that includes a triangle (for example, AutoSum and Zoom in **Figure 12**), displays a menu (**Figure 17**).

More Buttons

Figure 12 The Standard Toolbar, with all buttons displayed.

More Buttons

Figure 13 The Formatting toolbar, with all buttons displayed.

■ You can identify a button by its ScreenTip (**Figure 14**).

■ A toolbar can be *docked* or *floating*. A docked toolbar (**Figures 12** and **13**) is positioned against any edge of the screen. A floating toolbar can be moved anywhere on the screen.

Figure 14
A ScreenTip appears when you point to a button.

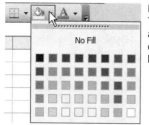

Figure 15
The Fill Color menu appears when you click the Fill Color button.

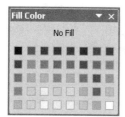

Figure 16
Drag a menu away from the toolbar to display it as a floating palette.

Figure 17
Click the triangle beside the menu to display the menu.

Figure 18 Click to select the value in the box.

Figure 19 Enter a new value and press (Enter).

To view more buttons

Click the More Buttons button at the far right end of the toolbar. Additional buttons for the toolbar appear (**Figures 12** and **13**).

To view ScreenTips

Point to a toolbar or palette button. A tiny box containing the name of the button appears (**Figure 14**).

To use a toolbar button

1. Point to the button for the command or option that you want (**Figure 14**).

2. Click once.

To use a toolbar menu

1. Click on the triangle beside the menu to display the menu and its commands (**Figures 15** and **17**).

2. Click a command or option to select it.

✔ Tips

■ Button menus that display a dotted move handle along the top edge (**Figure 15**) can be "torn off" and used as floating menus or palettes. Simply display the menu and drag the move handle away from the toolbar. When the palette appears, release the mouse button. The menu is displayed as a floating menu with a title bar that displays its name (**Figure 16**).

■ Menus that display text boxes (**Figure 17**) can be changed by typing a new value into the box. Just click the contents of the box to select it (**Figure 18**), then type in the new value and press (Enter) (**Figure 19**).

To display or hide a toolbar

From the Toolbars submenu under the View menu (**Figure 20**), choose the name of the toolbar that you want to display or hide.

If the toolbar name has a check mark beside it, it is displayed and will be hidden.

Or

If the toolbar name does not have a check mark beside it, it is hidden and will be displayed.

✔ Tip

■ You can also hide a floating toolbar by clicking its close button.

To float a docked toolbar

Drag the toolbar's move handle (**Figure 21**) away from the toolbar's docked position (**Figure 22**).

✔ Tip

■ Floating a docked toolbar will change the appearance and position of other tool- bars docked in the same row (**Figure 22**).

To dock a floating toolbar

Drag the toolbar's titled bar to the edge of the screen.

✔ Tip

■ You can dock a toolbar against the top (**Figure 22**), either side, or the bottom of the screen. Buttons may change appear- ance when the toolbar is docked on the side of the screen.

To move a floating toolbar

Drag the title bar for the toolbar to reposition it on screen.

To resize a floating toolbar

Drag the edge of the toolbar (**Figure 23**).

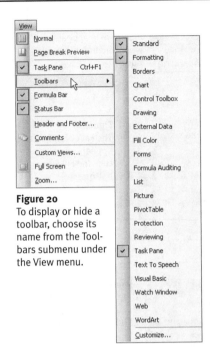

Figure 20
To display or hide a toolbar, choose its name from the Tool- bars submenu under the View menu.

Move handle

Figure 21 Each docked toolbar has a move handle on its end.

Figure 22 Drag the toolbar into the document window to float it. When you float the Formatting toolbar, the Standard toolbar expands to occupy some of the vacated space.

Figure 23 Drag the edge of a toolbar to resize it.

Figure 24
The Getting Started
task pane.

The Task Pane

Task panes, which appear in all Office applications, include clickable links and other options to perform common tasks. For example, the Getting Started task pane (**Figure 24**), which appears when you run Excel, offers options you might find helpful when you start Excel.

Excel includes 11 different task panes:

- **Getting Started** (**Figure 24**) enables you to learn more about using Excel, open recently opened workbooks, and create new workbooks.

- **Help** enables you to search Excel's internal and online help. I discuss the Help task pane later in this chapter.

- **Search Results** enables you to view the results of a search of Microsoft.com. I discuss the Search Results task pane later in this chapter.

- **Clip Art** enables you to search for clip art items and insert them in your workbooks. I discuss the Clip Art task pane in **Chapter 7**.

- **Research** enables you to search a number of online resources for information about a topic.

- **Clipboard** displays the Microsoft Office Clipboard, which you can use to store multiple items to paste into Office documents. I tell you how to use the Office Clipboard in **Chapter 3**.

- **New Workbook** enables you to create a new workbook from scratch or based on a template. I tell you more about the New Workbook task pane in **Chapter 2**.

Continued on next page...

THE TASK PANE

Continued from previous page.

- **Template Help** provides custom help for using the current template. I tell you more about templates in **Chapter 2**.

- **Shared Workspace** enables you to set up and manage a document to be shared by multiple users on a network or over the Internet.

- **Document Updates** enables you to manage updates to documents with a copy stored in a shared workspace.

- **XML Source** enables you to work with XML source code for an Excel workbook.

✔ Tip

- Although the task pane is a handy way to access commonly used commands and features without the use of dialogs that block your work, you may find that it takes up too much space on screen. If you prefer to use all screen real estate for your documents, you can close the task pane, as discussed in this section.

To perform a task pane task

Click the link or button for the task you want to perform.

To display a different task pane

Choose the name of the task pane you want to display from the pop-up menu in the task pane's title bar (**Figure 25**).

To close the task pane

Click the task pane's close button (**Figure 25**).

To open the task pane

Choose View > Task Pane (**Figure 26**) or press `Ctrl` `F1`.

Close button

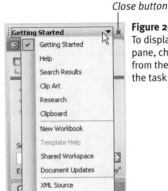

Figure 25
To display a different task pane, choose its name from the pop-up menu in the task pane's title bar.

Figure 26
You can view the task pane by choosing Task Pane from the View menu.

WORKING WITH THE TASK PANE

Figure 27 The dialog that appears at the end of a spelling check just displays information.

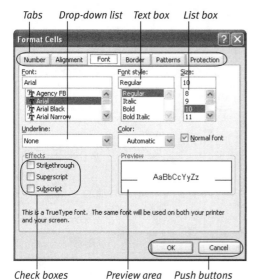

Tabs   Drop-down list   Text box   List box

Check boxes   Preview area   Push buttons
Figure 28 The Font tab of the Format Cells dialog.

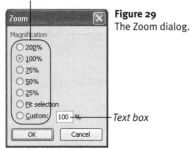

Option buttons

Figure 29
The Zoom dialog.

Text box

Dialogs

Like most other Windows programs, Excel uses *dialogs* to communicate with you.

Excel can display many different dialogs, each with its own purpose. There are two basic types of dialogs:

◆ Dialogs that simply provide information (**Figure 27**).

◆ Dialogs that offer options to select (**Figure 28**) before Excel completes the execution of a command.

✔ Tip

■ Often, when a dialog appears, you must dismiss it by clicking OK or Cancel before you can continue working with Excel.

Anatomy of an Excel dialog

Here are the components of many Excel dialogs, along with information about how they work.

◆ **Tabs** (**Figure 28**), which appear at the top of some dialogs, let you move from one group of dialog options to another. To switch to another group of options, click its tab.

◆ **Text boxes** or **entry fields** (**Figures 28** and **29**) let you enter information from the keyboard. You can press ⟨Tab⟩ to move from one box to the next or click in a box to position the insertion point within it. Then enter a new value.

◆ **List boxes** (**Figure 28**) offer a number of options to choose from. Use the scroll bar to view options that don't fit in the list window. Click an option to select it; it becomes highlighted and appears in the text box.

Continued on next page...

DIALOGS

Continued from previous page.

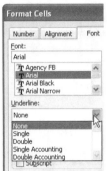

Figure 30
Displaying a drop-down list.

◆ **Check boxes** (**Figure 28**) let you turn options on or off. Click in a check box to toggle it. When a check mark or X appears in the check box, its option is turned on.

◆ **Option buttons** (**Figure 29**) let you select only one option from a group. Click on an option to select it; the option that was selected before you clicked is deselected.

◆ **Drop-down lists** (**Figure 28**) also let you select one option from a group. Display a list as you would a menu (**Figure 30**), then choose the option that you want.

◆ **Preview areas** (**Figure 28**), when available, illustrate the effects of your changes before you finalize them by clicking the OK button.

◆ **Push buttons** (**Figures 27**, **28**, and **29**) let you access other dialogs, accept the changes and close the dialog (OK), or close the dialog without making changes (Cancel). To choose a button, click it once.

✔ Tips

■ When the contents of a text box are selected, whatever you type will replace the selection.

■ Excel often uses text boxes and list boxes together (**Figure 28**). You can use either one to make a selection.

■ In some list boxes, double-clicking an option selects it and dismisses the dialog.

■ You can turn on any number of check boxes in a group, but you can select only one option button in a group.

■ Pressing Enter while a push button is active "clicks" that button.

■ You can usually "click" the Cancel button by pressing Esc.

DIALOGS

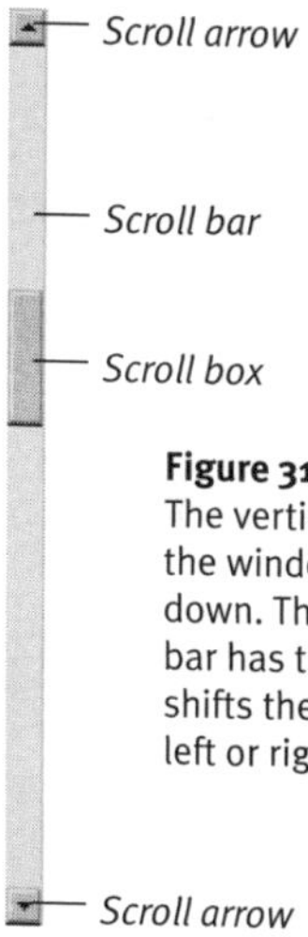

Scroll arrow

Scroll bar

Scroll box

Figure 31
The vertical scroll bar shifts
the window's contents up or
down. The horizontal scroll
bar has the same parts, but
shifts the window's contents
left or right.

Scroll arrow

Scrolling Window Contents

You can use Excel's scroll bars to shift the contents of a document window so you can see items that don't fit in the window.

✔ Tip

■ I tell you more about working with document windows in **Chapter 4**.

To scroll the contents of the document window

Click the scroll arrow (**Figure 31**) for the direction that you want to view. For example, to scroll down to view the end of a document, click the down arrow.

Or

Drag the scroll box (**Figure 31**) in the direction that you want to view. The contents of the window shift accordingly.

Or

Click in the scroll bar above or below the scroll box (**Figure 31**). This shifts the window contents one screenful at a time.

✔ Tips

■ Having trouble remembering which scroll arrow to click? Just remember this: click up to see up, click down to see down, click left to see left, and click right to see right.

■ Although some keyboard keys change the portion of the document being viewed, they also move the cell pointer. I tell you about these keys in **Chapter 2**.

Excel Help

Excel has an extensive onscreen help feature that draws from help files automatically installed with Excel as well as help information available on Microsoft's Web site. This makes it possible to get accurate, up-to-date information for getting assistance and solving problems with Excel.

Most of Excel's help features can be accessed from its Help menu (**Figure 32**). Here's a quick overview of what each command on that menu does.

◆ **Microsoft Office Excel Help** (F1) displays the Excel Help task pane (**Figure 33**), which you can use to access a variety of onscreen and online help features.

◆ **Show the Office Assistant** displays the Office Assistant, an animated character (**Figure 34**) that provides an alternative interface for accessing Excel Help. The Office Assistant may not be automatically installed with Excel; the first time you use this command, a dialog may ask whether you want to install it. Click Yes to install and display it. When the Office Assistant is displayed, this command changes to Hide the Office Assistant.

◆ **Microsoft Office Online** uses your Web browser to display the Microsoft Office home page on the Microsoft Web site (**Figure 35**).

◆ **Contact Us** uses your Web browser to display the Contact Us page on the Microsoft Web site. This page offers options for contacting Microsoft about Office products.

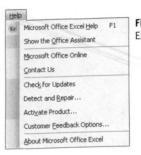

Figure 32
Excel's Help menu.

Figure 33
The Excel Help task pane.

Figure 34
The Office Assistant offers an alternative interface for accessing Excel Help.

Figure 35 The Home page for the Microsoft Office Web site.

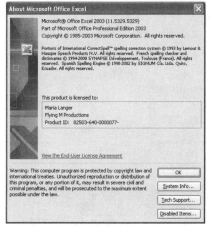

Figure 36 The About Microsoft Office Excel dialog provides version information and more.

◆ **Check for Updates** uses your Web browser to access the Microsoft Office Downloads page on the Microsoft Web site. This is where you can find updates and add-ins for using Microsoft Office products.

◆ **Detect and Repair** runs an internal Office utility that can detect and repair errors in Microsoft Office files. Use this feature if Excel doesn't seem to be running correctly.

◆ **Activate Product** enables you to enter an activation code to activate Excel. If you're a registered Excel or Office user, you should not need to use this command.

◆ **Customer Feedback Options** displays the Service Options dialog, which you can use to set options for sharing information with Microsoft about how you use Excel.

◆ **About Microsoft Office Excel** displays a dialog like the one in **Figure 36** with information about the copy of Excel running on your computer. Buttons in this dialog enable you to get information about your system, technical support, and disabled items that can help you or Microsoft support troubleshoot problems.

This part of the chapter explains how to use the Microsoft Excel Help task pane to get assistance using Excel features. You can explore Excel's other Help menu commands on your own.

ACCESSING EXCEL HELP

To use Excel Help

1. Click in the Type a question for help box at the right end of the menu bar (**Figure 37**). Enter a word, phrase, or question for which you want help (**Figure 38**) and press Enter.

   or

   Choose Help > Microsoft Office Excel Help, press F1, or click the Microsoft Excel Help button 🕮 in the Standard toolbar to display the Excel Help task pane (**Figure 33**). Enter a word, phrase, or question for which you want help in the Search box and click the green Start Searching button or press Enter.

   Excel begins searching and displays the Search Results task pane with topics that may provide the help you need. If you have an active Internet connection, the search results will be from Microsoft's Web site (**Figure 39**). If you don't have an Internet connection, the search results will be from offline help installed with Microsoft Excel.

2. Click a blue topic name in the Search Results task pane. The document window resizes and a Microsoft Office Excel Help window appears to its right (**Figure 40**).

3. Read the information in the Help window to learn about the topic.

   or

   Click links in the Help window to display other topics in the window.

4. Repeat steps 2 and 3 to explore the information in all help topics that interest you.

Figure 37 This box, at the right end of the menu bar, offers one way to ask Excel for help.

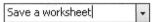

Figure 38 An example of a help request.

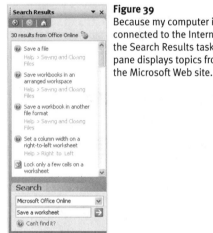

Figure 39
Because my computer is connected to the Internet, the Search Results task pane displays topics from the Microsoft Web site.

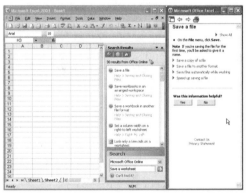

Figure 40 The Microsoft Office Excel Help window appears to the right of the document window when you click a help topic. This is where it pays to have a big, high-resolution monitor!

Figure 41 You can use the drop-down (or should I say "drop-up"?) list at the bottom of the Search Results task pane to tell Excel where to look for help.

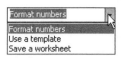

Figure 42 Excel remembers all the things you asked during a work session.

5. When you are finished using Help, click the close button in the far right window to close the Microsoft Office Excel Help window and return the document window to its full size. You can also click the close button in the Search Results task pane to dismiss it.

✔ Tips

- In step 1, if you have already used Excel's help feature, the last help request you entered may appear in the box at the end of the menu bar. Just click in the box and enter a new word, phase, or question.

- After step 1, to instruct the Help feature to display only results from offline help, choose Offline Help from the drop-down list in the search area (**Figure 41**) and click the green Start Searching button.

- After using the help feature several times, you can quickly go back to search results for a help topic by choosing the topic from the drop-down list at the right end of the menu bar (**Figure 42**).

Worksheet Basics

Numeric values

Text values

Formula: =B1–B2

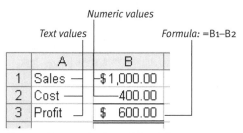

	A	B
1	Sales	$1,000.00
2	Cost	400.00
3	Profit	$ 600.00

Figure 1 This very simple worksheet illustrates how a spreadsheet program like Excel works with values and formulas.

	A	B
1	Sales	$1,150.00
2	Cost	400.00
3	Profit	$ 750.00

Figure 2 When the value for Sales changes from $1,000 to $1,150, the Profit result changes automatically.

How Worksheets Work

Microsoft Excel is most commonly used to create *worksheets*. A worksheet is a collection of information laid out in columns and rows. As illustrated in **Figure 1**, each worksheet cell can contain one of two kinds of input:

◆ A *value* is a piece of information that does not change. Values can be text, numbers, dates, or times. A cell containing a value usually displays the value.

◆ A *formula* is a collection of values, cell references, operators, and predefined functions that, when evaluated by Excel, produces a result. A cell containing a formula displays the results of the formula.

Although any information can be presented in a worksheet, spreadsheet programs like Excel are usually used to organize and calculate numerical or financial information. Why? Well, when properly prepared, a worksheet acts like a super calculator. You enter values and formulas and it calculates and displays the results. If you change one of the values, Excel automatically recalculates the results (**Figure 2**).

How does this work? By using cell *references* rather than actual numbers in formulas, Excel knows that it should use the contents of those cells in its calculations. Thus, changing one or more values affects the results of calculations that include references to the changed cells. As you can imagine, this makes worksheets powerful business planning and analysis tools!

Running Excel

To use Excel, you must run the Excel program. This loads Excel into RAM (random access memory), so your computer can work with it.

To run Excel from the Taskbar

Click Start > All Programs > Microsoft Office > Microsoft Office Excel 2003.

The Excel splash screen appears briefly, then an empty document window named *Book1* and the Getting Started task pane appear (**Figure 3**).

To run Excel by opening an Excel document

1. In Windows, locate the icon for the document that you want to open (**Figure 4**).

2. Double-click the icon.

   The Excel splash screen appears briefly, then a document window containing the document that you opened appears (**Figure 5**).

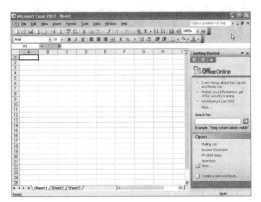

Figure 3 When you run Excel from the Windows Taskbar, it displays an empty document widnow and the Getting Started task pane.

Figure 4
An Excel document icon.

FY 2004 Sales

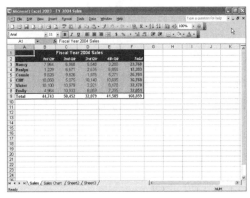

Figure 5 When you run Excel by opening an Excel document file, it displays the document you opened.

RUNNING EXCEL

Figure 6
Excel's File menu.

Exiting Excel

When you're finished using Excel, you should use the Exit command to close the program. This completely clears Excel out of RAM, freeing up RAM for other programs.

✔ Tip

■ Exiting Excel also instructs Excel to save preference settings.

To exit Excel

Choose File > Exit (**Figure 6**). Here's what happens:

◆ If any documents are open, they close.

◆ If an open document contains unsaved changes, a dialog appears (**Figure 7**) so you can save the changes. I explain how to save documents later in this chapter.

◆ The Excel program closes.

✔ Tip

■ As you've probably guessed, Excel automatically exits when you restart or shut down your computer.

Figure 7 A dialog like this appears when a document with unsaved changes is open when you exit Excel.

Creating a New Workbook

The documents you create and save using Excel are *workbook* files. A workbook is an Excel document.

Excel's New Workbook task pane (**Figure 8**) offers three ways to create workbook files:

Figure 8
The New Workbook task pane.

◆ A *blank workbook file* is an empty workbook file with Excel's default settings. You must enter and format all workbook contents.

◆ A workbook file based on an existing workbook. This makes it possible to duplicate a workbook without accidentally overwriting it with new information.

◆ A workbook file based on a *template* contains the values, formulas, formatting, custom toolbars, and macros included in a template file.

✔ Tips

■ Basing a workbook on a template or existing workbook can save a lot of time if you often need to create a standard document—such as a monthly report or invoice—repeatedly. Creating templates is covered in **Chapter 4**.

■ You can find more information about Excel workbook files in **Chapter 4**.

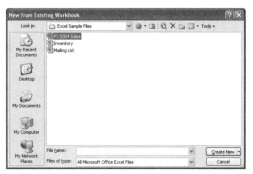

Figure 9 The New from Existing Workbook dialog enables you to select an existing workbook to base a new workbook on.

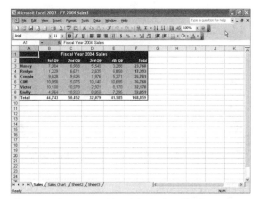

Figure 10 The new workbook looks just like the existing workbook, but its default name includes a number.

To create a blank workbook

1. If the New Workbook task pane is not showing, choose File > New (**Figure 6**) or press Ctrl N to display it.

2. In the New area of the New Workbook task pane (**Figure 8**), click the Blank workbook link.

Or

Click the New button on the Standard toolbar.

A blank workbook window appears (**Figure 3**).

To create a workbook based on an existing workbook

1. If the New Workbook task pane is not showing, choose File > New (**Figure 6**) or press Ctrl N to display it.

2. In the New area of the New Workbook task pane (**Figure 8**), click the From existing workbook link.

3. In the New from Existing Workbook dialog that appears (**Figure 9**), locate and select the workbook you want to base the new workbook on. Then click Create New.

A workbook with the name of the existing workbook followed by a number appears (**Figure 10**). Make changes to the workbook as desired for the new workbook.

✔ Tips

- The New from Existing Workbook dialog (**Figure 9**) is very similar to the Open dialog, which I cover later in this chapter.

- This is the best way to create a new workbook from an existing workbook. If you simply open an existing workbook and make changes to it, you might accidentally overwrite the original workbook when you save the new one.

To create a workbook based on a template

1. If the New Workbook task pane is not showing, choose File > New (**Figure 6**) or press ⌃Ctrl ⌃N to display it.

2. In the Templates area of the New Workbook task pane (**Figure 8**), click the On my computer link.

3. The Templates dialog appears. If necessary, click the Spreadsheet Solutions tab to display its options.

4. Select the icon for the template you want to use (**Figure 11**). A preview of the template may appear in the Preview area.

5. Click OK.

   A workbook based on the template that you selected appears (**Figure 12**). Enter your own values in cells as desired.

✔ Tips

- The New Workbook task pane offers two other options for obtaining templates:
    - ▲ **Templates on Office Online** uses your Web browser to open the Templates page on the Microsoft Office Web site (**Figure 13**).
    - ▲ **On my Web sites** displays a dialog you can use to access templates you may have stored in Network Places.

- Excel comes with several sample templates (**Figure 11**) that you can experiment with. Not all of these templates are installed by default, however. If you select a template that has not been installed, you may be prompted to insert your Excel or Office install disk to install the template.

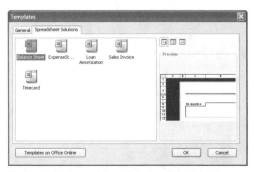

Figure 11 The Spreadsheet Solutions tab of the Templates dialog.

Figure 12 Excel creates a new workbook based on the template you selected.

Figure 13 The Microsoft Office Templates page is a good place to start looking for new templates.

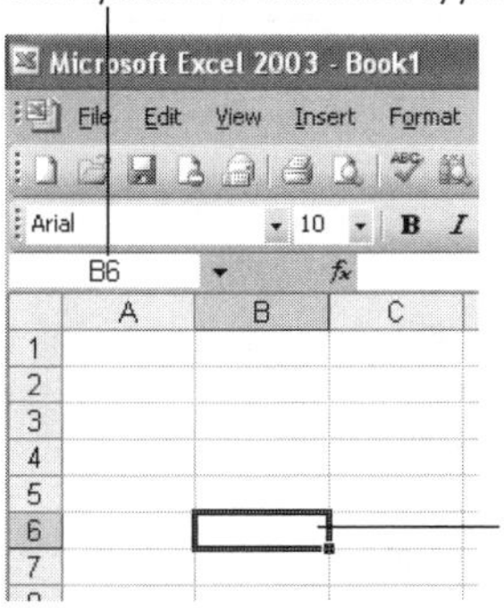

Cell reference in name box of formula bar

Figure 14 The reference for an active cell appears in the formula bar.

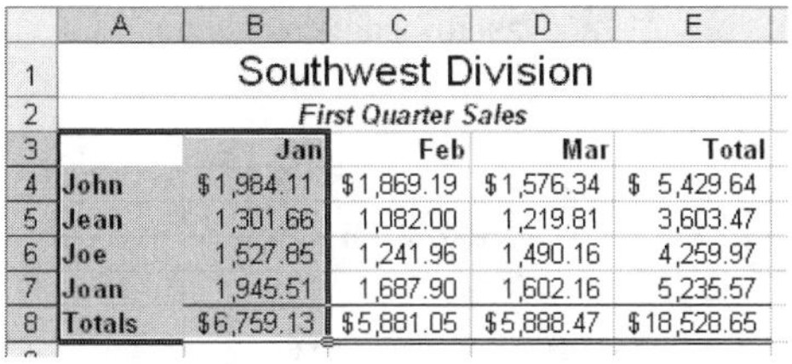

Figure 15 In this illustration, the range *A3:B8* is selected, and cell *A3* is the active cell.

Activating & Selecting Cells

Worksheet information is entered into cells. A *cell* is the intersection of a column and a row. Each little "box" in the worksheet window is a cell.

Each cell has a unique *address* or *reference*. The reference uses the letter(s) of the column and the number of the row. Thus, cell *B6* would be at the intersection of column *B* and row *6*. The reference for the active cell appears in the name box at the left end of the formula bar (**Figure 14**).

To enter information in a cell, you must make that cell *active*. A cell is active when there is a dark or colored border called the *cell pointer* around it. When a cell is active, anything you type is entered into it.

To use Excel commands on a cell or its contents, you must *select* the cell. The active cell is also a selected cell. If desired, however, you can select multiple cells or a *range* of cells. This enables you to use commands on all selected cells at once. A range (**Figure 15**) is a rectangular selection of cells defined by the top-left and bottom-right cell references.

✔ Tips

■ Although the active cell is always part of a selection of multiple cells, it is never highlighted like the rest of the selection. You should, however, see a dark or colored border (the cell pointer) around it (**Figure 15**).

■ Although you can select multiple cells, only one cell—the one referenced in the name box (**Figure 15**)—is active.

■ The column and row headings for selected cells appear colored (**Figures 14** and **15**).

■ Using the scroll bars does not change the active or selected cell(s). It merely changes your view of the worksheet's contents.

ACTIVATING & SELECTING CELLS

27

To activate a cell

Use the mouse pointer to click in the cell.

Or

Press the appropriate keystroke (**Table 1**) to move the cell pointer.

To select a range of cells with the mouse

1. Position the mouse pointer in the first cell you want to select (**Figure 16**).
2. Hold the mouse button down and drag to highlight all the cells in the selection (**Figure 17**).

Or

1. Click in the first cell of the range you want to select.
2. Hold down [Shift] and click in the last cell of the range. Everything between the first and second clicks is selected. (This technique is known as "Shift-Click.")

To go to a cell or range of cells

1. Choose Edit > Go To (**Figure 18**) or press [Ctrl][G] to display the Go To dialog (**Figure 19**).
2. Enter the reference for the cell you want to activate or the range that you want to select in the Reference text box.
3. Click OK. If you entered a single cell reference, the cell is activated. If you entered a range reference, the range is selected.

✔ Tip

- To specify a reference for a range, enter the addresses of the first and last cells of the range, separated with a colon (:). For example, **Figure 15** shows *A3:B8* selected and **Figure 17** shows *A3:E8* selected.

Table 1

Keys for Moving the Cell Pointer

Key	Movement
[↑]	Up one cell
[↓]	Down one cell
[→]	Right one cell
[←]	Left one cell
[Tab]	Right one cell
[Shift][Tab]	Left one cell
[Home]	First cell in row
[Page Up]	Up one window
[Page Down]	Down one window
[Ctrl][Home]	Cell A1
[Ctrl][End]	Cell at intersection of last column and last row containing data

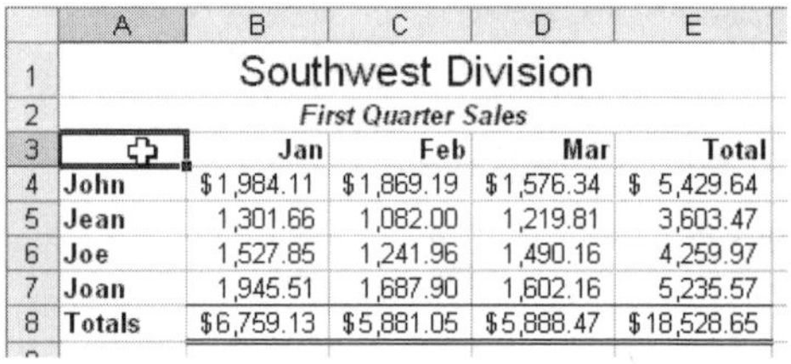

	A	B	C	D	E
1	Southwest Division				
2	First Quarter Sales				
3		Jan	Feb	Mar	Total
4	John	$1,984.11	$1,869.19	$1,576.34	$ 5,429.64
5	Jean	1,301.66	1,082.00	1,219.81	3,603.47
6	Joe	1,527.85	1,241.96	1,490.16	4,259.97
7	Joan	1,945.51	1,687.90	1,602.16	5,235.57
8	Totals	$6,759.13	$5,881.05	$5,888.47	$18,528.65

Figure 16 To select cells, begin in one corner of the range ...

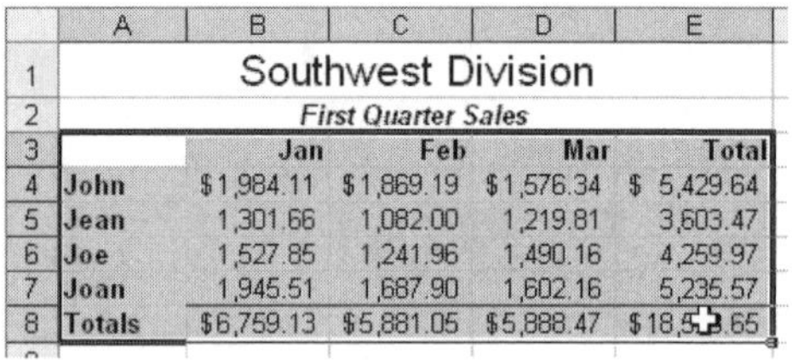

	A	B	C	D	E
1	Southwest Division				
2	First Quarter Sales				
3		Jan	Feb	Mar	Total
4	John	$1,984.11	$1,869.19	$1,576.34	$ 5,429.64
5	Jean	1,301.66	1,082.00	1,219.81	3,603.47
6	Joe	1,527.85	1,241.96	1,490.16	4,259.97
7	Joan	1,945.51	1,687.90	1,602.16	5,235.57
8	Totals	$6,759.13	$5,881.05	$5,888.47	$18,5[illegible]65

Figure 17 ... hold the mouse button down, and drag to the opposite corner of the range.

Figure 18
Choose Go To from the Edit menu.

Figure 19
The Go To dialog lets you move to any cell quickly.

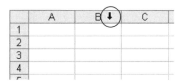

Figure 20
Click a column heading to select the column.

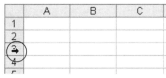

Figure 21
Click a row heading to select the row.

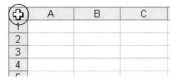

Figure 22
Click the Select All button to select all cells in the worksheet.

To select an entire column

1. Position the mouse pointer on the heading for the column you want to select. The mouse pointer turns into an arrow pointing down (**Figure 20**).

2. Click once. The column is selected.

To select an entire row

1. Position the mouse pointer on the heading for the row you want to select. The mouse pointer turns into an arrow pointing to the right (**Figure 21**).

2. Click once. The row is selected.

To select multiple columns or rows

1. Position the mouse pointer on the first column or row heading.

2. Press the mouse button down, and drag along the headings until all the desired columns or rows are selected.

✔ Tip

■ When selecting multiple columns or rows, be careful to position the mouse pointer on the heading and not between two headings! If you drag the border of two columns, you will change a column's width rather than make a selection.

To select the entire worksheet

1. Position the mouse pointer on the Select All button in the upper-left corner of the worksheet window. The mouse pointer appears as a hollow plus sign (**Figure 22**).

2. Click once.

Or

Press Ctrl A.

The worksheet is selected.

To select multiple ranges

1. Use any selection technique to select the first cell or range of cells (**Figure 23**).
2. Hold down Ctrl and drag to select the second cell or range of cells (**Figure 24**).
3. Repeat step 2 until all desired ranges are selected.

✔ Tips

- Selecting multiple ranges can be tricky. It takes practice. Don't be frustrated if you can't do it on the first few tries!
- To add ranges that are not visible in the worksheet window, be sure to use the scroll bars to view them. Using the keyboard to move to other cells while selecting multiple ranges will remove the selections you've made so far or add undesired selections.
- Do not click in the worksheet window or use the movement keys while multiple ranges are selected unless you are finished working with them. Doing so will deselect all the cells.

To deselect cells

Click anywhere in the worksheet.

Or

Press any of the keys in **Table 1**.

✔ Tip

- Remember, at least one cell must be selected at all times—that's the active cell.

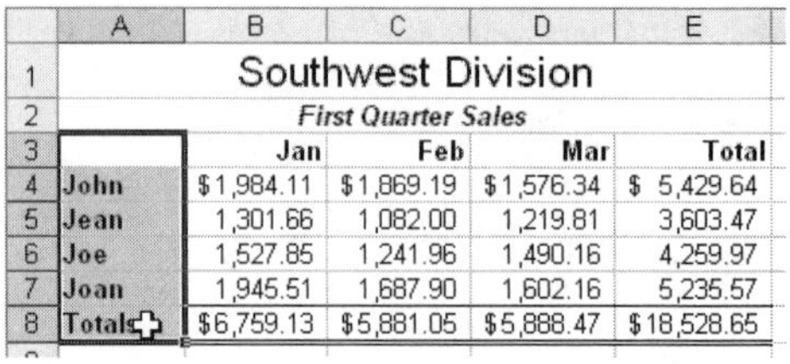

	A	B	C	D	E
1		Southwest Division			
2		First Quarter Sales			
3		Jan	Feb	Mar	Total
4	John	$1,984.11	$1,869.19	$1,576.34	$ 5,429.64
5	Jean	1,301.66	1,082.00	1,219.81	3,603.47
6	Joe	1,527.85	1,241.96	1,490.16	4,259.97
7	Joan	1,945.51	1,687.90	1,602.16	5,235.57
8	Totals	$6,759.13	$5,881.05	$5,888.47	$18,528.65

Figure 23 To select two ranges of cells, start by selecting the first range, ...

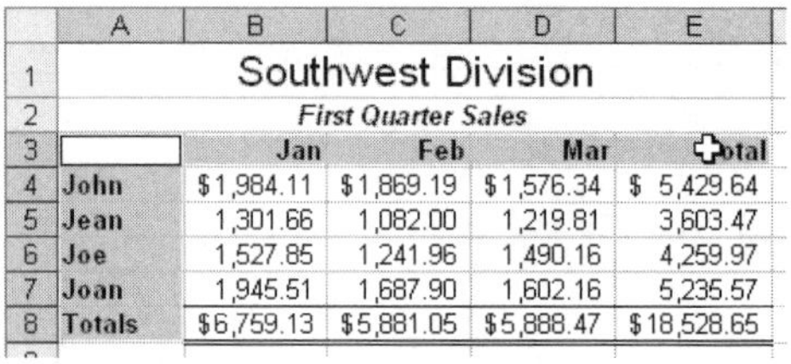

	A	B	C	D	E
1		Southwest Division			
2		First Quarter Sales			
3		Jan	Feb	Mar	Total
4	John	$1,984.11	$1,869.19	$1,576.34	$ 5,429.64
5	Jean	1,301.66	1,082.00	1,219.81	3,603.47
6	Joe	1,527.85	1,241.96	1,490.16	4,259.97
7	Joan	1,945.51	1,687.90	1,602.16	5,235.57
8	Totals	$6,759.13	$5,881.05	$5,888.47	$18,528.65

Figure 24 ... then hold down Ctrl and select the second range.

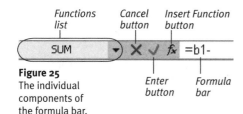

Functions list   *Cancel button*   *Insert Function button*

Enter button   *Formula bar*

Figure 25
The individual components of the formula bar.

Entering Values & Formulas

To enter a value or formula into a cell, begin by making the cell active. As you type or click to enter information, the information appears in both the cell and in the formula bar just above the window's title bar. You complete the entry by pressing Enter or clicking the Enter button ☑ on the formula bar.

While you are entering information into a cell, the formula bar is *active*. You can tell that it's active because the name box on the left end of the formula bar turns into a Functions list and two additional buttons appear between it and the cell contents area (**Figure 25**).

There are two important things to remember when the formula bar is active:

◆ Anything you type or click on may be included in the active cell.

◆ Some Excel options and menu commands are unavailable.

You deactivate the formula bar by accepting or cancelling the current entry.

✔ Tips

■ Pressing Enter to complete a formula entry accepts the entry and moves the cell pointer one cell down. Clicking the Enter button ☑ accepts the entry without moving the cell pointer.

■ To cancel an entry before it has been completed, press Esc or click the Cancel button ☒ on the formula bar. This restores the cell to the way it was before you began.

■ If you include formatting notation such as dollar signs, commas, and percent symbols when you enter numbers, Excel may apply formatting styles. Formatting the contents of cells is discussed in **Chapter 6**.

Values

As discussed at the beginning of this chapter, a value is any text, number, date, or time you enter into a cell. Values are constant—they don't change unless you change them.

To enter a value

1. Activate the cell in which you want to enter the value.

2. Type in the value. As you type, the information appears in two places: the active cell and the formula bar, which becomes active (**Figure 26**).

3. To complete and accept the entry (**Figure 27**), press ⌜Enter⌟ or click the Enter button ☑ on the formula bar.

✔ Tips

- Although you can often use the arrow keys or other movement keys in **Table 1** to complete an entry by moving to another cell, it's a bad habit because it won't always work.

- Pressing ⌜Enter⌟ to complete an entry automatically advances the cell pointer to the next cell.

- By default, Excel aligns text against the left side of the cell and aligns numbers against the right side of the cell. I explain how to change alignment in **Chapter 6**.

- Don't worry if the data you put into a cell doesn't seem to fit. You can always change the column width or use the AutoFit Text feature to make it fit. I explain how in **Chapter 6**.

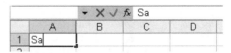

Figure 26 As data is entered into a cell, it appears in the cell and in the formula bar.

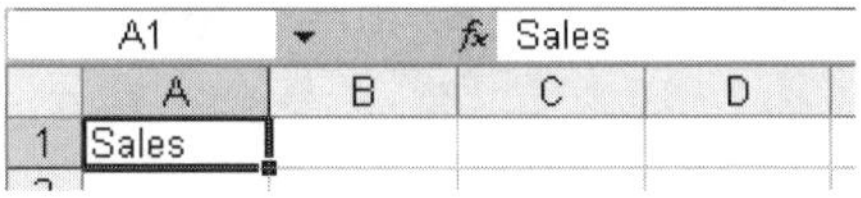

Figure 27 A completed entry. The insertion point is gone.

Table 2

Basic Mathematical Operators Understood by Excel		
Operator	Use	Example
+	Addition	=A1+B10
−	Subtraction	=A1−B10
−	Negation	=−A1
*	Multiplication	=A1*B10
/	Division	=A1/B10
^	Exponential	=A1^3
%	Percentage	=20%

Table 3

How Excel Evaluates Expressions		
Assumptions		
A1=5		
B10=7		
C3=4		
Formula	Evaluation	Result
=A1+B10*C3	=5+7*4	33
=C3*B10+A1	=4*7+5	33
=(A1+B10)*C3	=(5+7)*4	48
=A1+10%	=5+10%	5.1
=(A1+10)%	=(5+10)%	0.15
=A1^2-B10/C3	=5^2-7/4	23.25
=(A1^2-B10)/C3	=(5^2-7)/4	4.5
=A1^(2-B10)/C3	=5^(2-7)/4	0.00008

Formula Basics

Excel makes calculations based on formulas you enter into cells. When you complete the entry of a formula, Excel displays the results of the formula rather than the formula.

Here are some important things to keep in mind when writing formulas:

◆ If a formula uses cell references to refer to other cells and the contents of one or more of those cells changes, the result of the formula changes, too.

◆ All formulas begin with an equal (=) sign. This is how Excel knows that a cell entry is a formula and not a value.

◆ Formulas can contain any combination of values, references, operators (**Table 2**), and functions. I tell you about using operators in formulas in this chapter and about using functions in **Chapter 5**.

◆ Formulas are not case sensitive. This means that =*A1+B10* is the same as =*a1+b10*. Excel automatically converts characters in cell references and functions to uppercase.

When calculating the results of expressions with a variety of operators, Excel makes calculations in the following order:

1. Negation
2. Expressions in parentheses
3. Percentages
4. Exponentials
5. Multiplication or division
6. Addition or subtraction

Table 3 shows some examples of formulas and their results to illustrate this. As you can see, the inclusion of parentheses can really make a difference when you write a formula!

Continued on next page...

Continued from previous page.

✔ Tips

- Do not use the arrow keys or other movement keys to complete an entry by moving to another cell. Doing so may add cells to the formula!

- Whenever possible, use references rather than values in formulas. This way, you won't have to rewrite formulas when values change. **Figures 28** and **29** illustrate this.

- A reference can be a cell reference, a range reference, or a cell or range name. I tell you about name references in **Chapter 13**.

- To add a range of cells to a formula, type the first cell in the range followed by a colon (:) and then the last cell in the range. For example, *B1:B10* references the cells from *B1* straight down through *B10*.

- If you make a syntax error in a formula, Excel tells you (**Figures 30**, **31**, and **32**). If the error is one of the common errors programmed into Excel's Formula Auto-Correct feature, Excel offers to correct the formula for you (**Figure 32**). Otherwise, you will have to troubleshoot the formula and correct it yourself.

- I explain how to edit formulas in **Chapter 3** and how to include functions in formulas in **Chapter 5**.

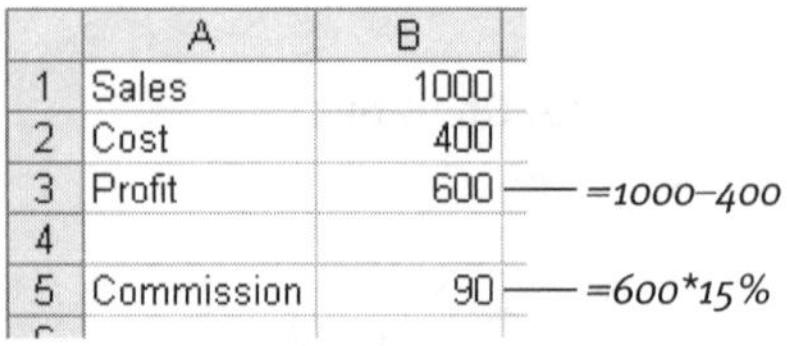

Figure 28 If any of the values change, the formulas will need to be rewritten!

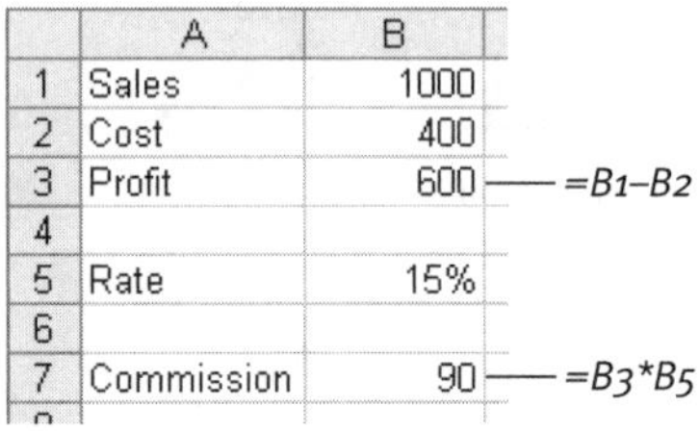

Figure 29 But if the formulas reference cells containing the values, when the values change, the formulas will not need to be rewritten to show correct results.

Figure 30 Excel tells you when a formula has an error and provides information on where you can get help.

Figure 31 This dialog appears when a formula contains a *circular reference*—a reference to its own cell.

Figure 32 If the error is one of the common formula errors Excel knows about, Excel offers to fix it for you.

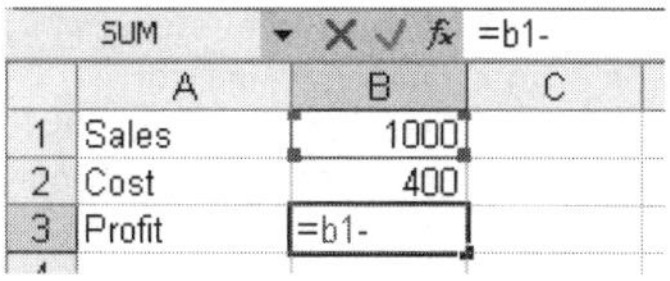

Figure 33 To enter a formula, type it into a cell.

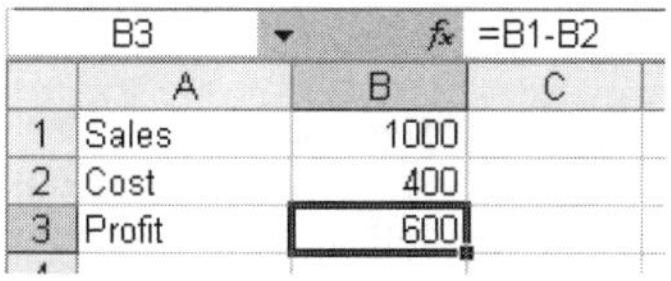

Figure 34 A completed formula entry.

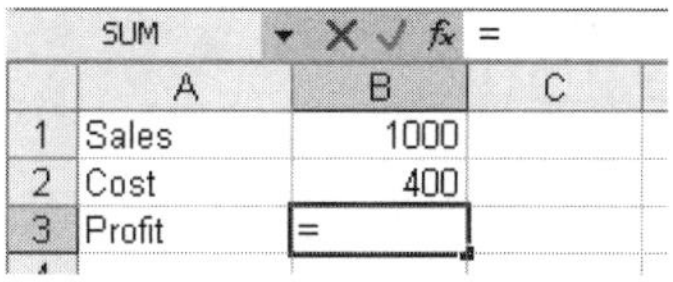

Figure 35 To enter the formula =B1–B2, type = to begin the formula, ...

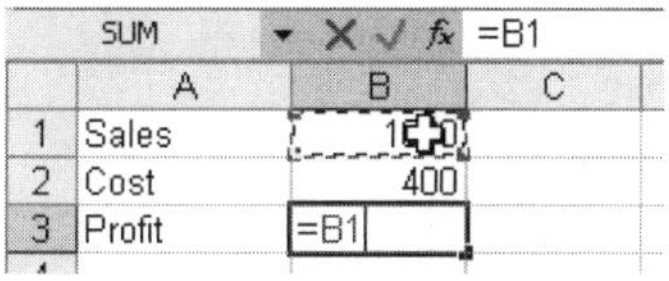

Figure 36 ... click cell B1 to add its reference to the formula, ...

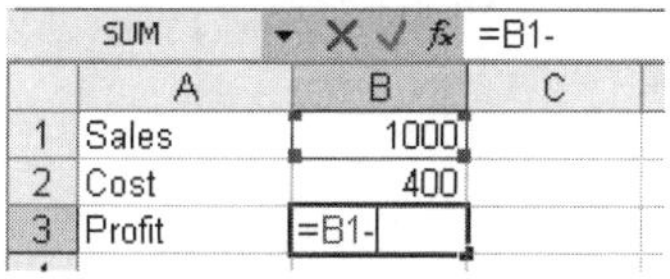

Figure 37 ... type – to tell Excel to subtract, ...

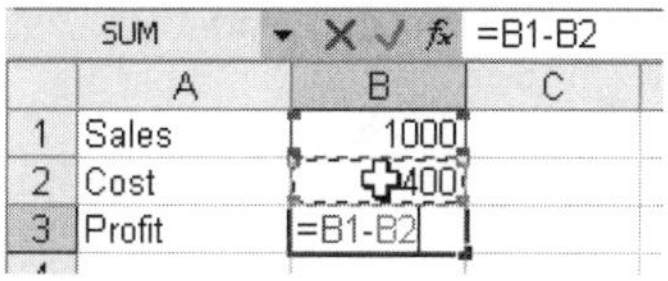

Figure 38 ... click cell B2 to add its reference to the formula, ...

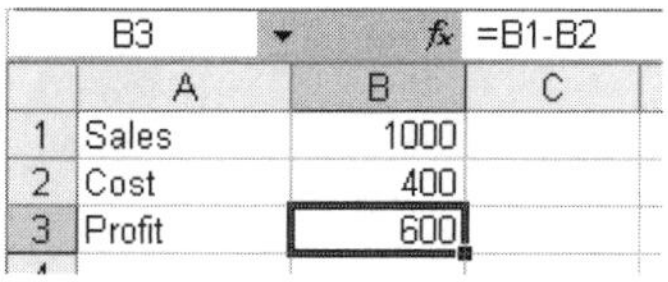

Figure 39 ... and finally, click the Enter button to complete the formula.

To enter a formula by typing

1. Activate the cell in which you want to enter the formula.

2. Type in the formula. As you type, the formula appears in two places: the active cell and the formula bar (**Figure 33**).

3. To complete the entry (**Figure 34**), press [Enter] or click the Enter button ☑ on the formula bar.

To enter a formula by clicking

1. Activate the cell in which you want to enter the formula.

2. Type an equal (=) sign to begin the formula (**Figure 35**).

3. To enter a cell reference, click on the cell you want to reference (**Figures 36** and **38**).

   or

   To enter a constant value or operator, type it in (**Figure 37**).

4. Repeat step 3 until the entire formula appears in the formula bar.

5. To complete the entry (**Figure 39**), press [Enter] or click the Enter button ☑ on the formula bar.

✔ Tips

- If you click a cell reference without typing an operator, Excel assumes you want to add that reference to the formula.

- Be careful where you click when writing a formula! Each click adds a reference to the formula. If you add an incorrect reference, press [Backspace] until it has been deleted or click the Cancel button ☒ on the formula bar to start the entry from scratch. I explain how to edit a cell's contents in **Chapter 3**.

- You can add a range of cells to a formula by dragging over the cells.

ENTERING FORMULAS

35

Error Checking Smart Tags

Excel's Error Checking Smart Tag feature alerts you to possible errors in cells. For example, suppose you write a formula that sums all the numbers in a column, but you leave out the last cell reference for the last cell in the column. Excel assumes this is an error and marks the cell with a small green triangle in the upper-left corner of the cell (**Figure 40**). When you select the cell, a Smart Tag icon appears beside it (**Figure 41**). Clicking the Smart Tag displays a menu of options for correcting, learning more about, or ignoring the possible error (**Figure 42**).

	A	B
1	John	1,533.30
2	Jean	1,305.60
3	Joe	1,872.77
4	Joan	1,598.48
5	Jeff	1,975.65
6	Totals	4,711.67

Figure 40
A tiny green error marker appears in the corner of a cell that contains a possible error.

	A	B
1	John	1,533.30
2	Jean	1,305.60
3	Joe	1,872.77
4	Joan	1,598.48
5	Jeff	1,975.65
6	Total	4,711.67

Figure 41
When you activate a cell with a possible error, the Error Checking Smart Tag icon appears.

✔ Tip

- The green error marker that appears in a cell (**Figure 40**) does not print.

To correct an error with a Smart Tag

1. Click the Smart Tag icon that appears beside a cell with a possible error (**Figure 41**). A menu of options appears (**Figure 42**).

2. Choose the option immediately below the description of the error.

To ignore an error & remove its Smart Tag

1. Click the Smart Tag icon that appears beside a cell with a possible error (**Figure 41**). A menu of options appears (**Figure 42**).

2. Choose Ignore Error. The Smart Tag and green triangle disappear.

Explanation of possible problem

	A	B	C	D
1	John	1,533.30		
2	Jean	1,305.60		
3	Joe	1,872.77		
4	Joan	1,598.48		
5	Jeff	1,975.65		
6	Total	4,711.67		
7				
8		Formula Omits Adjacent Cells		
9		Update Formula to Include Cells		
10				
11		Help on this error		
12		Ignore Error		
13		Edit in Formula Bar		
14				
15		Error Checking Options...		
16		Show Formula Auditing Toolbar		

Figure 42 Choose an option from the Smart Tag menu to resolve the possible error.

Editing
Worksheets

Editing Worksheets

Microsoft Excel offers a number of features and techniques that you can use to modify your worksheets.

◆ Use standard editing techniques and the Clear command to change or clear the contents of cells.

◆ Use Insert and Edit menu commands to insert or delete cells, columns, and rows.

◆ Use Edit menu commands, the fill handle, and drag-and-drop editing to copy cells from one location to another, including cells containing formulas.

◆ Use the fill handle and Fill submenu commands to copy cell contents to multiple cells or create a series.

◆ Modify formulas so they are properly updated by Excel when copied.

◆ Use Edit menu commands and drag-and-drop editing to move cells from one location to another.

◆ Undo, redo, and repeat multiple actions.

This chapter covers all of these techniques.

Editing Cell Contents

You can use standard editing techniques to edit the contents of cells either as you enter values or formulas or after you have completed an entry. You can also clear a cell's contents, leaving the cell empty.

To edit as you enter

1. If necessary, click to position the blinking insertion point cursor in the cell (**Figure 1**) or formula bar (**Figure 2**).

2. Press [Backspace] to delete the character to the left of the insertion point.

   or

   Type the characters that you want to insert at the insertion point.

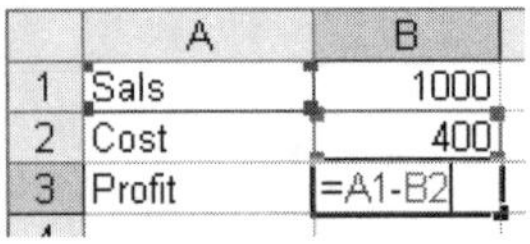

To edit a completed entry

1. Double-click the cell containing the incorrect entry to activate it for editing.

2. If the cell contains a value, follow the instructions in the previous section to insert or delete characters as desired.

   or

   If the cell contains a formula, color-coded Range Finder frames graphically identify cell references (**Figures 3** and **5**). There are three ways to edit cell references:

   ▲ Edit the reference as discussed in the previous section.

   ▲ Drag a frame border to move the frame over another cell. As shown in **Figure 4**, the mouse pointer looks like an arrow as you drag.

   ▲ Drag a frame handle to expand or contract it so the frame includes more or fewer cells. As shown in **Figure 6**, the mouse pointer turns into a two-headed arrow when you position it on a frame handle and drag.

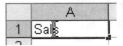

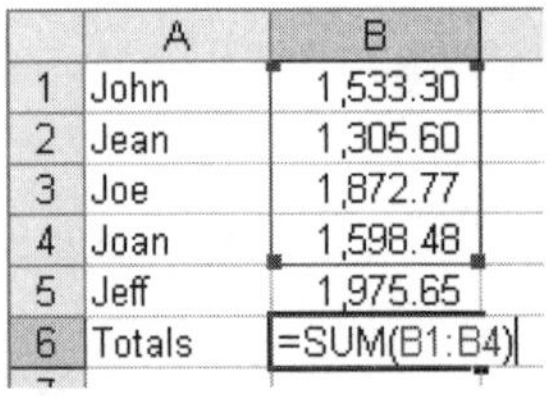

Figure 1 To edit a cell's contents while entering information, click to reposition the insertion point in the cell ...

Figure 2 ... or in the formula bar and make changes as desired.

	A	B
1	Sals	1000
2	Cost	400
3	Profit	=A1-B2

Figure 3 The range Finder frames clearly indicate the problem with this formula.

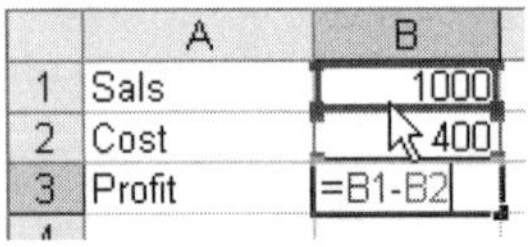

	A	B
1	Sals	1000
2	Cost	400
3	Profit	=B1-B2

Figure 4 You can drag a Range Finder frame to correct the cell reference. In this example, the Range Finder frame on cell A1 is dragged to cell B1.

	A	B
1	John	1,533.30
2	Jean	1,305.60
3	Joe	1,872.77
4	Joan	1,598.48
5	Jeff	1,975.65
6	Totals	=SUM(B1:B4)

Figure 5 In this example, the Range Finder indicates that the range of cells in the formula excludes a cell.

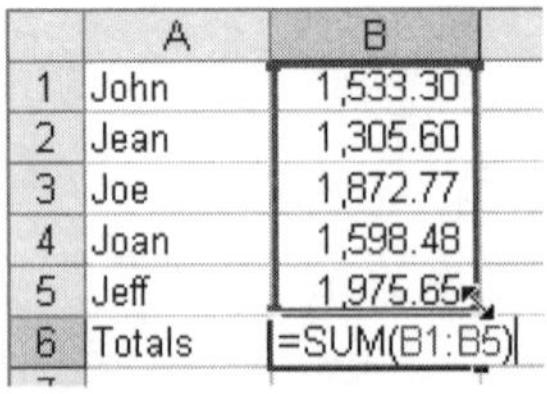

	A	B
1	John	1,533.30
2	Jean	1,305.60
3	Joe	1,872.77
4	Joan	1,598.48
5	Jeff	1,975.65
6	Totals	=SUM(B1:B5)

Figure 6 You can drag a Range Finder frame handle to expand the range and correct the reference in the formula.

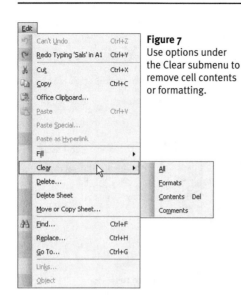

Figure 7
Use options under the Clear submenu to remove cell contents or formatting.

To clear cell contents

1. Select the cell(s) you want to clear.

2. Choose Edit > Clear > Contents (**Figure 7**).

   or

   Press Delete.

✔ Tips

- Another way to clear the contents of just one cell is to select the cell, press Backspace, and then press Enter.

- Do not press Spacebar to clear a cell's contents! Doing so inserts a space character into the cell. Although the contents seem to disappear, they are just replaced by an invisible character.

- Clearing a cell is very different from deleting a cell. When you clear a cell, the cell remains in the worksheet—only its contents are removed. When you delete a cell, the entire cell is removed from the worksheet and other cells shift to fill the gap. I tell you about inserting and deleting cells next.

- The Contents command clears only the values or formulas entered into a cell. The other Clear submenu commands (**Figure 7**) work as follows:

   ▲ **All** clears everything, including formatting and comments.

   ▲ **Formats** clears only cell formatting.

   ▲ **Comments** clears only cell comments.

   I tell you about formatting cells in **Chapter 6** and about adding cell comments in **Chapter 11**.

CLEARING CELL CONTENTS

Inserting & Deleting Cells

Commands under Excel's Insert and Edit menus enable you to insert and delete columns, rows, or cells.

◆ When you Insert cells, Excel shifts cells down or to the right to make room for the new cells.

◆ When you Delete cells, Excel shifts cells up or to the left to fill the gap left by the missing cells.

Figures 9, **11**, **13**, and **15** show examples of how inserting a column or deleting a row in a simple worksheet (**Figure 8**) affects the cells in a worksheet. Fortunately, Excel is smart enough to adjust cell references in formulas so the formulas you write remain correct.

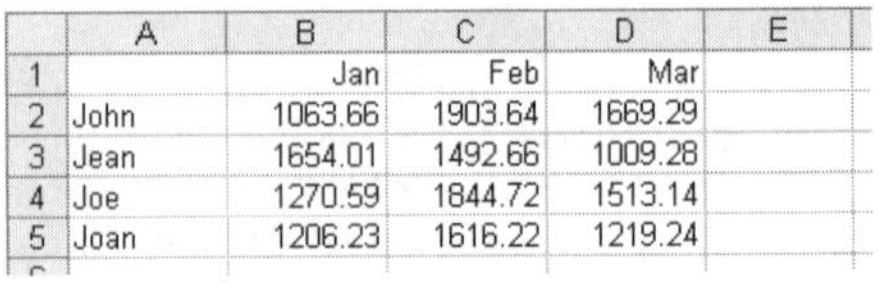

To insert a column or row

1. Select a column or row (**Figure 9**).

2. Choose Insert > Columns, Insert > Rows, or Insert > Cells (**Figure 10**). The column or row is inserted and the Insert Options button appears (**Figure 11**).

3. If desired, choose a formatting option for the inserted column or row from the Insert Options pop-up menu (**Figure 12**).

✔ Tips

■ To insert multiple columns or rows, in step 1, select the number of columns or rows you want to insert. For example, if you want to insert three columns before column *B*, select columns *B*, *C*, and *D*.

■ If a complete column or row is not selected when you choose the Cells command in step 2, the Insert dialog appears (**Figure 18**). Select the appropriate option (Entire row or Entire column) for what you want to insert, then click OK. I tell you about inserting cells a little later in this chapter.

	A	B	C	D	E
1		Jan	Feb	Mar	
2	John	1063.66	1903.64	1669.29	
3	Jean	1654.01	1492.66	1009.28	
4	Joe	1270.59	1844.72	1513.14	
5	Joan	1206.23	1616.22	1219.24	

Figure 8 A simple worksheet.

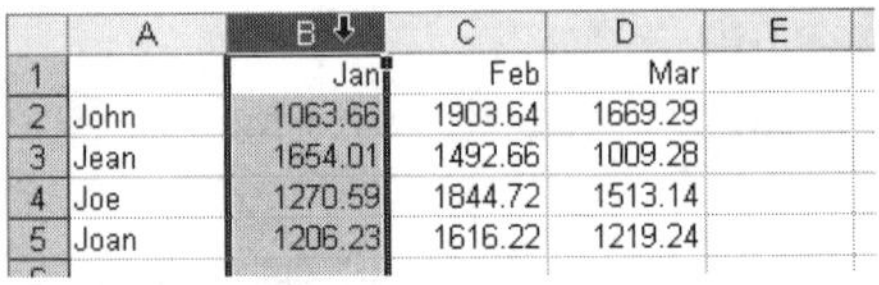

	A	B	C	D	E
1		Jan	Feb	Mar	
2	John	1063.66	1903.64	1669.29	
3	Jean	1654.01	1492.66	1009.28	
4	Joe	1270.59	1844.72	1513.14	
5	Joan	1206.23	1616.22	1219.24	

Figure 9 Selecting a column.

Figure 10
The Insert menu.

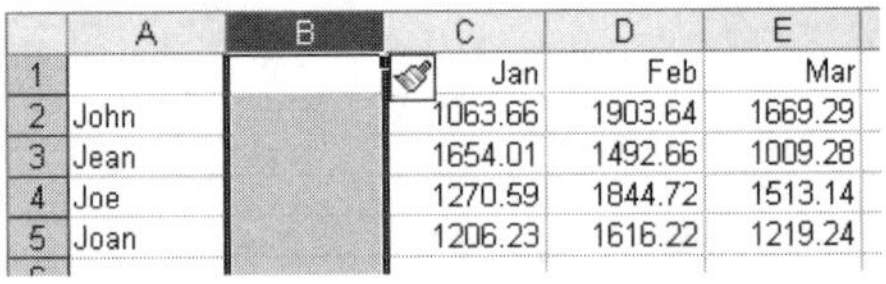

	A	B	C	D	E
1			Jan	Feb	Mar
2	John		1063.66	1903.64	1669.29
3	Jean		1654.01	1492.66	1009.28
4	Joe		1270.59	1844.72	1513.14
5	Joan		1206.23	1616.22	1219.24

Figure 11 An inserted column.

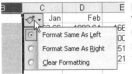

Figure 12
You can use the Insert Options pop-up menu to set formatting options for inserted cells.

INSERTING COLUMNS & ROWS

	A	B	C	D	E
1		Jan	Feb	Mar	
2	John	1063.66	1903.64	1669.29	
3	Jean	1654.01	1492.66	1009.28	
4	Joe	1270.59	1844.72	1513.14	
5	Joan	1206.23	1616.22	1219.24	

Figure 13 Selecting a row.

Figure 14
The Edit menu.

	A	B	C	D	E
1		Jan	Feb	Mar	
2	John	1063.66	1903.64	1669.29	
3	Jean	1654.01	1492.66	1009.28	
4	Joan	1206.23	1616.22	1219.24	

Figure 15 The row selected in **Figure 12** is deleted.

	A	B
1	Sales	1000
2	Cost	400
3	Profit	600
4		
5		
6	Commissions	#REF!

Figure 16 In this example, I deleted a row containing a value referenced in the formula in *B6*. Because Excel can't find one of the references it needs, it displays a *#REF!* error.

To delete a column or row

1. Select a column or row (**Figure 13**).

2. Choose Edit > Delete (**Figure 14**).

   The column or row (**Figure 15**)—along with all of its contents—disappears.

✔ Tips

- To delete more than one column or row at a time, in step 1, select all of the columns or rows you want to delete.

- If a complete column or row is not selected when you choose the Delete command in step 2, the Delete dialog appears (**Figure 20**). Select the appropriate option (Entire row or Entire column) for what you want to delete, then click OK.

- If you delete a column or row that contains referenced cells, the formulas that reference the cells may display a #REF! error message (**Figure 16**). This means that Excel can't find a referenced cell. If this happens, you'll have to rewrite any formulas in cells displaying the error.

DELETING COLUMNS & ROWS

To insert cells

1. Select a cell or range of cells (**Figure 17**).

2. Choose Insert > Cells (**Figure 10**).

3. In the Insert dialog that appears (**Figure 18**), select the appropriate option to tell Excel how to shift the selected cells to make room for new cells—Shift cells right or Shift cells down.

4. Click OK. The cells are inserted and the Insert Options button appears (**Figure 19**).

5. If desired, choose a formatting option for the inserted column or row from the Insert Options pop-up menu.

✔ Tip

- Excel always inserts the number of cells that is selected when you use the Insert command (**Figures 17** and **19**).

To delete cells

1. Select a cell or range of cells to delete (**Figure 17**).

2. Choose Edit > Delete (**Figure 14**).

3. In the Delete dialog that appears (**Figure 20**), select the appropriate option to tell Excel how to shift the other cells when the selected cells are deleted—Shift cells left or Shift cells up.

4. Click OK.

   The cells are deleted (**Figure 21**).

✔ Tip

- If you delete a cell that contains referenced cells, the formulas that reference the cells may display a #REF! error message (**Figure 16**). If this happens, you'll have to rewrite any formulas in cells displaying the error.

	A	B	C	D
1		Jan	Feb	Mar
2	John	1063.66	1903.64	1669.29
3	Jean	1654.01	1492.66	1009.28
4	Joe	1270.59	1844.72	1513.14
5	Joan	1206.23	1616.22	1219.24

Figure 17 Selecting a range of cells.

Figure 18 The Insert dialog.

	A	B	C	D
1		Jan	Feb	Mar
2	John	1063.66	1903.64	1669.29
3	Jean	1654.01	1492.66	1009.28
4	Joe			
5	Joan	1270.59	1844.72	1513.14
6		1206.23	1616.22	1219.24

Figure 19 Here's what happens when you insert cells selected in **Figure 17**, using the Shift cells down option.

Figure 20 The Delete dialog.

	A	B	C	D
1		Jan	Feb	Mar
2	John	1063.66	1903.64	1669.29
3	Jean	1654.01	1492.66	1009.28
4	Joe	1206.23	1616.22	1219.24
5	Joan			

Figure 21 Here's what happens when you delete the cells selected in **Figure 17**, using the Shift cells up option.

John
John
Jean
Jean
Joe
Joe
Joan
Joan

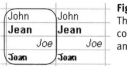

Figure 22 The Copy and Paste commands can make an exact copy.

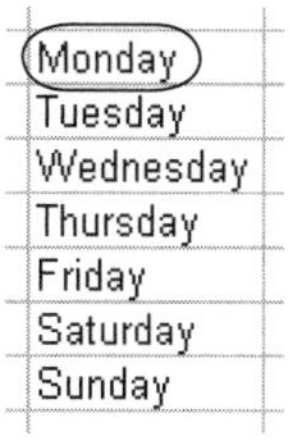

Monday
Tuesday
Wednesday
Thursday
Friday
Saturday
Sunday

Figure 23 Using the Fill handle on a cell containing the word *Monday* generates a list of the days of the week.

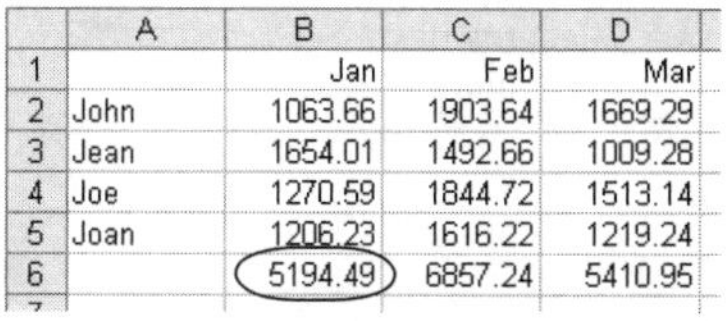

	A	B	C	D
1		Jan	Feb	Mar
2	John	1063.66	1903.64	1669.29
3	Jean	1654.01	1492.66	1009.28
4	Joe	1270.59	1844.72	1513.14
5	Joan	1206.23	1616.22	1219.24
6		5194.49	6857.24	5410.95

Figure 24 Copying a formula that totals a column automatically writes correctly referenced formulas to total similar columns.

Copying Cells

Excel offers several ways to copy the contents of one cell to another: the Copy and Paste commands, the fill handle, and the Fill command.

How Excel copies depends not only on the method used, but on the contents of the cell(s) being copied.

- When you use the Copy and Paste commands to copy a cell containing a value, Excel makes an exact copy of the cell, including any formatting (**Figure 22**). I tell you about formatting cells in **Chapter 6**.
- When you use the fill handle or Fill command to copy a cell containing a value, Excel either makes an exact copy of the cell, including any formatting, or creates a series based on the original cell's contents (**Figure 23**).
- When you copy a cell containing a formula, Excel copies the formula, changing any relative references in the formula so they're relative to the destination cell(s) (**Figure 24**).

✔ Tip

- Copy cells that contain formulas whenever possible to save time and ensure consistency.

Copy & Paste

The Copy and Paste commands in Excel work very much the way they do in other programs. Begin by selecting the source cells and copying them to the Clipboard. Then select the destination cells and paste the Clipboard contents in.

To copy with Copy & Paste

1. Select the cell(s) you want to copy (**Figure 25**).

2. Choose Edit > Copy (**Figure 14**), press Ctrl C, or click the Copy button on the Standard toolbar. An animated marquee appears around the selection (**Figure 26**).

3. Select the cell(s) in which you want to paste the selection (**Figure 27**). If more than one cell has been copied, you can select either the first cell of the destination range or the entire range.

4. Choose Edit > Paste (**Figure 14**), press Ctrl V or Enter, or click the Paste button on the Standard toolbar. The originally selected cells are copied to the new location and the Paste Options button appears (**Figure 28**).

5. If desired, choose an option for the pasted cell(s) from the Paste Options pop-up menu (**Figure 29**).

Figure 25
Begin by selecting the cell(s) you want to copy.

Figure 26
A marquee appears around the selection when it has been copied to the Clipboard.

Figure 27
Select the destination cell(s).

Figure 28
The contents of the copied cells appear in the destination cells.

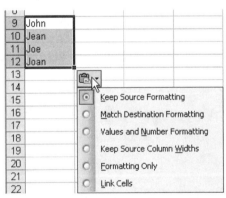

Figure 29 You can set formatting for pasted in cells by choosing an option from the Paste Options pop-up menu.

COPYING WITH COPY & PASTE

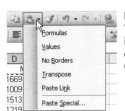

Figure 30
The Paste button includes a menu of options for pasting Clipboard contents.

✔ Tips

- If the destination cells contain information, Excel may overwrite them without warning you.

- If you choose the Paste command, press Ctrl V, or click the Paste button ⬚, the marquee remains around the copied range, indicating that it is still in the Clipboard and may be pasted elsewhere. The marquee disappears automatically as you work, but if you want to remove it manually, press Esc.

- The Paste Options button will not appear if you press Enter in step 4.

- The Edit menu's Paste Special command (**Figure 14**) and the Paste button's pop-up menu (**Figure 30**) offer additional options over the regular Paste command. For example, you can paste only the formatting of a copied selection, convert formulas in the selection into values, or add the contents of the source cells to the destination cells.

COPYING WITH COPY & PASTE

The Fill Handle

The *fill handle* is a small black or colored box in the lower-right corner of the cell pointer (**Figure 31**) or selection (**Figure 32**). You can use the fill handle to copy the contents of one or more cells to adjacent cells.

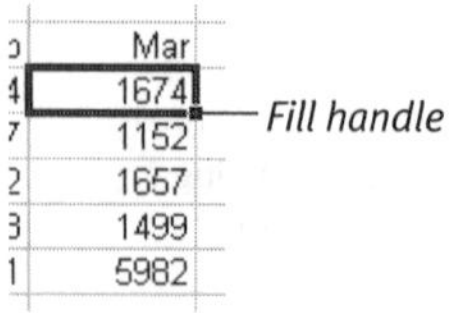

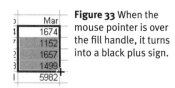

Figure 31 The fill handle on a single cell.

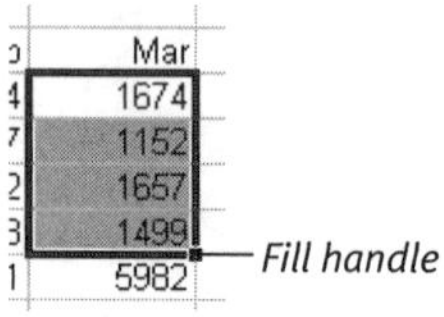

To copy with the fill handle

1. Select the cell(s) containing the information you want to copy (**Figure 32**).

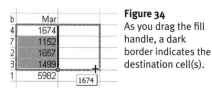

Figure 32 The fill handle on a range of cells.

2. Position the mouse pointer on the fill handle. The mouse pointer turns into a black plus sign (**Figure 33**).

3. Press the mouse button down and drag to the adjacent cells. A gray border surrounds the source and destination cells (**Figure 34**).

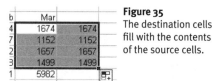

Figure 33 When the mouse pointer is over the fill handle, it turns into a black plus sign.

4. When all the destination cells are surrounded by the gray border, release the mouse button. The cells are filled and the Fill Options button appears (**Figure 35**).

5. If desired, choose an option for the filled cell(s) from the Fill Options pop-up menu (**Figure 36**).

✔ Tips

- You can use the fill handle to copy any number of cells. The destination cells, however, must be adjacent to the original cells.

- When using the fill handle, you can only copy in one direction (up, down, left, or right) at a time.

- If the destination cells contain information, Excel may overwrite them without warning you.

Figure 34 As you drag the fill handle, a dark border indicates the destination cell(s).

Figure 35 The destination cells fill with the contents of the source cells.

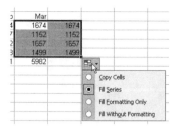

Figure 36 Use the Fill Options pop-up menu to set options for the filled in cells.

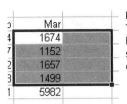

Figure 37
To use the Fill command, begin by selecting the source and destination cells.

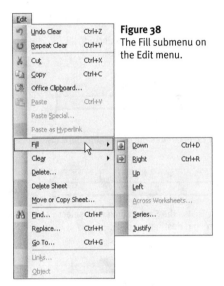

Figure 38
The Fill submenu on the Edit menu.

The Fill Command

The Fill command works a lot like the fill handle in that it copies information to adjacent cells. But rather than dragging to copy, you select the source and destination cells at the same time and then use the Fill command to complete the copy. The Fill submenu offers several options for copying to adjacent selected cells:

◆ **Down** copies the contents of the top cell(s) in the selection to the selected cells beneath it.

◆ **Right** copies the contents of the left cell(s) in the selection to the selected cells to the right of it.

◆ **Up** copies the contents of the bottom cell(s) in the selection to the selected cells above it.

◆ **Left** copies the contents of the right cell(s) in the selection to the selected cells to the left of it.

To copy with the Fill command

1. Select the cell(s) you want to copy along with the adjacent destination cell(s) (**Figure 37**).

2. Choose the appropriate command from the Fill submenu under the Edit menu (**Figure 38**): Down, Right, Up, Left. The cells are filled as specified (**Figure 35**).

   or

   To fill down, press Ctrl D or to fill right, press Ctrl R.

✔ Tip

■ You must select both the source and destination cells when using the Fill command. If you select just the destination cells, Excel won't copy the correct cells.

COPYING WITH THE FILL COMMAND

Series & AutoFill

A *series* is a sequence of cells that forms a logical progression. Excel's AutoFill feature can generate a series of numbers, months, days, dates, and quarters.

To create a series with the fill handle

1. Enter the first item of the series in a cell (**Figure 39**). Be sure to complete the entry by pressing (Enter) or clicking the Enter button ☑ on the formula bar.

2. Position your mouse pointer on the fill handle and drag. All the cells that will be part of the series are surrounded by a gray border and a yellow box indicates the value that will be in the last cell in the range (**Figure 40**).

3. Release the mouse button to complete the series (**Figure 41**).

To create a series with the Series command

1. Enter the first item in the series in a cell (**Figure 39**).

2. Select all cells that will be part of the series, including the first cell (**Figure 42**).

3. Choose Edit > Fill > Series (**Figure 38**).

4. In the Series dialog that appears (**Figure 43**), select the AutoFill option.

5. Click OK to complete the series (**Figure 41**).

✔ Tip

- To generate a series that skips values, enter the first two values of the series in adjoining cells, then use the fill handle or Series command to create the series, including both cells as part of the source (**Figures 44** and **45**).

Figure 39 To create an AutoFill series, start by entering the first value in a cell.

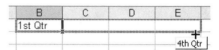

Figure 40 Drag the fill handle to include all cells that will be part of the series.

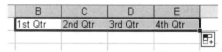

Figure 41 Excel creates the series automatically.

Figure 42 To use the Series command, select the source and destination cells.

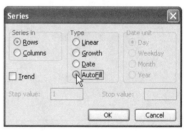

Figure 43 Select the AutoFill option in the Series dialog.

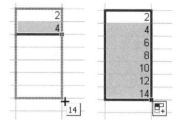

Figures 44 & 45 Enter the first two values in the series, then select both cells and drag the fill handle (left) to complete the series (right).

	A	B	C	D
1	Item	Price	Cost	Markup
2	Product A	54.99	16.24	=(B2-C2)/C2
3	Product B	24.99	10.94	
4	Product C	16.99	3.29	
5	Product D	29.99	4.84	

Figure 46 Here's a formula to calculate markup percentage. If the company has 763 products, would you want to write the same basic formula 762 more times? Of course not!

	A	B	C	D
1	Item	Price	Cost	Markup
2	Product A	54.99	16.24	238.61%
3	Product B	24.99	10.94	128.43%
4	Product C	16.99	3.29	416.41%
5	Product D	29.99	4.84	519.63%

Figure 47 Copying formulas can save time. If the original formula is properly written, the results of the copied formula should also be correct.

$$=(B2–C2)/C2$$
$$=(B3–C3)/C3$$
$$=(B4–C4)/C4$$
$$=(B5–C5)/C5$$

	A	B	C	D	E	F
1			January	February	March	
2		Sales	1000	1250	1485	
3		Cost	400	395	412	
4		Profit	600	855	1073	
5						
6	Owner	Percent	Jan Share	Feb Share	Mar Share	Total
7	John	50%	300	427.5	536.5	
8	Jean	20%	120	171	214.6	
9	Joe	15%	90	128.25	160.95	
10	Joan	15%	90	128.25	160.95	
11		100%	600	855	1073	

$$=SUM(C7:C10) \qquad =SUM(F3:F6)$$

Figure 48 In this illustration, the formula in cell *C11* was copied to cell *F7*. This doesn't work because the two cells don't add up similar ranges. The formula in cell *F7* would have to be rewritten from scratch. It could then be copied to *F8* through *F10*. (I tell you about the SUM function in **Chapter 5**.)

Copying Formulas

You copy a cell containing a formula the same way you copy any other cell in Excel: with the Copy and Paste commands, with the fill handle, or with the Fill command. These methods are discussed earlier in this chapter.

Generally speaking, Excel does not make an exact copy of a formula. Instead, it copies the formula based on the kinds of references used within it. If relative references are used, Excel changes them based on the location of the destination cell in relation to the source cell. You can see an example of this in **Figures 46** and **47**.

✔ Tips

- You'll find it much quicker to copy formulas rather than to write each and every formula from scratch.

- Not all formulas can be copied with accurate results. For example, you can't copy a formula that sums up a column of numbers to a cell that should represent a sum of cells in a row (**Figure 48**).

- I explain the various types of cell references—relative, absolute, and mixed—beginning on the next page.

Relative vs. Absolute Cell References

There are two primary types of cell references:

- A *relative cell reference* is the address of a cell relative to the cell the reference is in. For example, a reference to cell *B1* in cell *B3*, tells Excel to look at the cell two cells above *B3*. Most of the references you use in Excel are relative references.

- An *absolute cell reference* is the exact location of a cell. To indicate an absolute reference, enter a dollar sign ($) in front of the column letter(s) and row number(s) of the reference. An absolute reference to cell *B1*, for example, would be written *$B$1*.

As **Figures 49** and **50** illustrate, relative cell references change when you copy them to other cells. Although in many cases, you might want the references to change, sometimes you don't. That's when you use absolute references (**Figures 51** and **52**).

✔ Tips

- Here's a trick for remembering the meaning of the notation for absolute cell references: in your mind, replace the dollar sign with the word *always*. Then you'll read *$B$1* as *always B always 1—always B1*!

- If you're having trouble understanding how these two kinds of references work and differ, don't worry. This is one of the most difficult spreadsheet concepts you'll encounter. Try creating a worksheet like the one illustrated on this page and working your way through the figures one at a time. Pay close attention to how Excel copies the formulas you write!

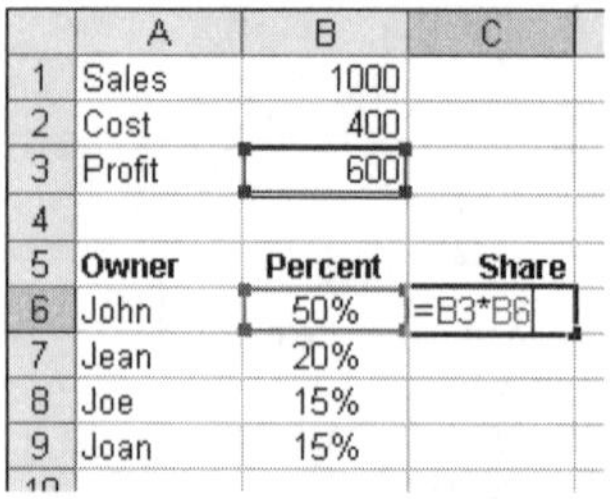

Figure 49 This formula correctly calculates a partner's share of profit.

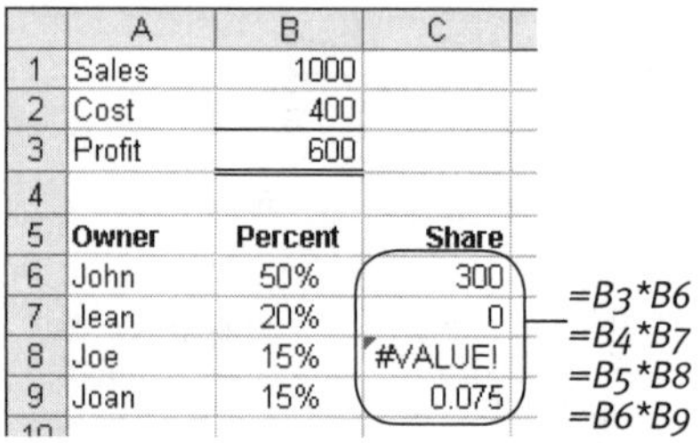

Figure 50 But when the formula is copied for the other partners, the relative reference to cell *B3* is changed, causing incorrect results and an error message!

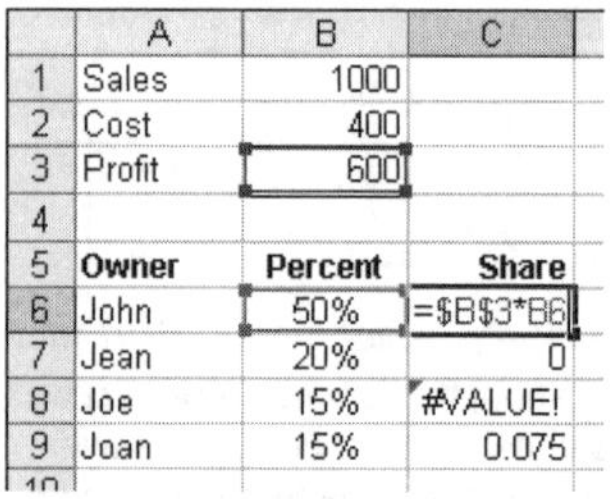

Figure 51 Rewrite the original formula so it includes an absolute reference to cell *B3*, which all of the formulas must reference.

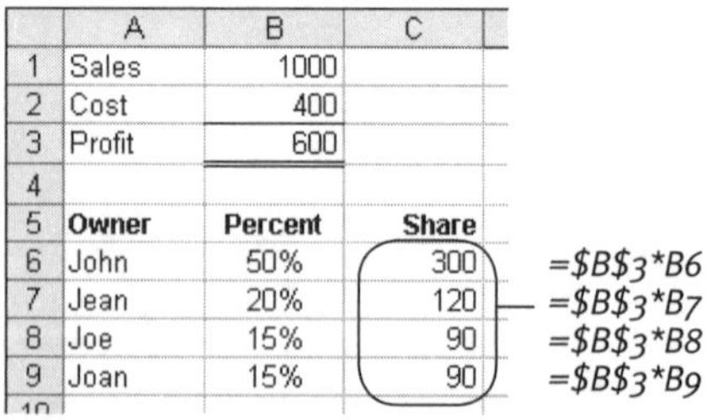

Figure 52 When the formula is copied for the other partners, only the relative reference (to the percentages) changes. The results are correct.

Figure 53 Type in the dollar signs as needed when you enter an absolute cell reference.

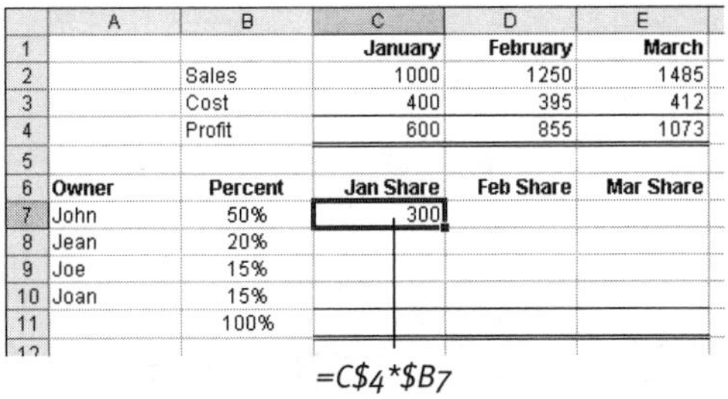

	A	B	C	D	E
1			January	February	March
2		Sales	1000	1250	1485
3		Cost	400	395	412
4		Profit	600	855	1073
5					
6	Owner	Percent	Jan Share	Feb Share	Mar Share
7	John	50%	300		
8	Jean	20%			
9	Joe	15%			
10	Joan	15%			
11		100%			
12					

$$=C\$4*\$B7$$

Figure 54 The formula in cell *C7* includes two different kinds of mixed references. It can be copied to cells *C8* through *C10* and *C7* through *E10* for correct results in all cells. Try it and see for yourself!

To include an absolute cell reference in a formula

1. Enter the formula by typing or clicking as discussed in **Chapter 2**.

2. Insert a dollar sign before the column and row references for the cell reference you want to make absolute (**Figure 53**).

3. Complete the entry by pressing Enter or clicking the Enter button ☑ on the formula bar.

✔ Tips

■ You can edit an existing formula to include absolute references by inserting dollar signs where needed. I tell you how to edit cell contents earlier in this chapter.

■ Do not use a dollar sign in a formula to indicate currency formatting. I tell you how to apply formatting to cell contents, including currency format, in **Chapter 6**.

Mixed References

Once you've mastered the concept of relative vs. absolute cell references, consider another type of reference: a *mixed cell reference*.

In a mixed cell reference, either the column or row reference is absolute while the other reference remains relative. Thus, you can use cell references like *A$1* or *$A1*. Use this when a column reference must remain constant but a row reference changes or vice versa. **Figure 54** shows a good example.

Moving Cells

Excel offers two ways to move the contents of one cell to another: the Cut and Paste commands and dragging the border of a selection. Either way, Excel moves the contents of the cell.

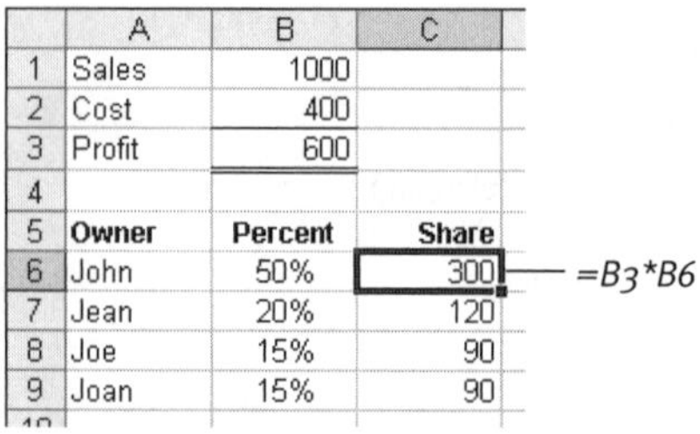

✔ Tip

- When you move a cell, Excel searches the worksheet for any cells that contain references to it and changes the references to reflect the cell's new location (**Figures 55** and **56**).

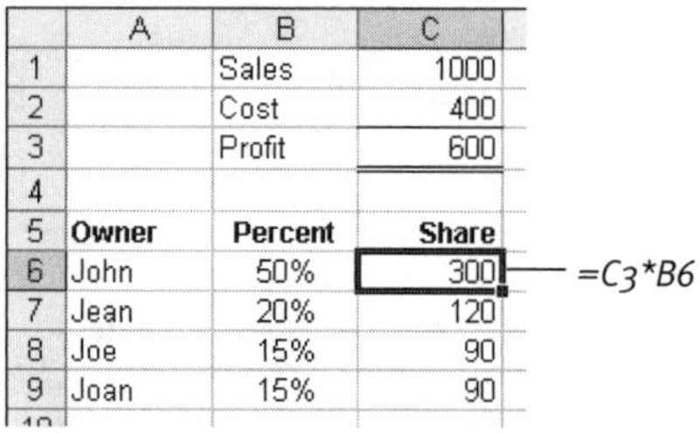

To move with Cut & Paste

1. Select the cell(s) you want to move (**Figure 57**).

2. Choose Edit > Cut (**Figure 14**), press Ctrl X, or click the Cut button ✂ on the Standard toolbar. An animated marquee appears around the selection (**Figure 58**).

3. Select the cell(s) to which you want to paste the selection (**Figure 59**).

4. Choose Edit > Paste (**Figure 14**), press Ctrl V or Enter, or click the Paste button 🗐 on the Standard toolbar. The cell contents are moved to the new location (**Figure 60**).

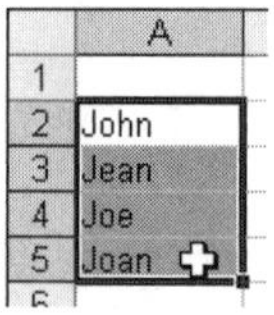

✔ Tip

- Consult the tips beneath the section titled "To copy with Copy & Paste" for Paste command warnings and tips.

	A	B	C
1	Sales	1000	
2	Cost	400	
3	Profit	600	
4			
5	**Owner**	**Percent**	**Share**
6	John	50%	300
7	Jean	20%	120
8	Joe	15%	90
9	Joan	15%	90

=B3*B6

Figure 55 Note the formula in cell *C6*.

	A	B	C
1		Sales	1000
2		Cost	400
3		Profit	600
4			
5	**Owner**	**Percent**	**Share**
6	John	50%	300
7	Jean	20%	120
8	Joe	15%	90
9	Joan	15%	90

=C3*B6

Figure 56 See how it changes when one of the cells it references moves?

Figure 57 Select the cell(s).

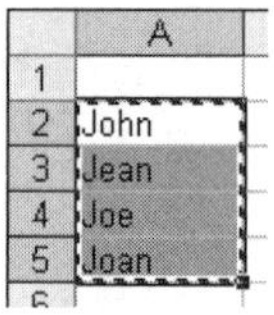

Figure 58 When you use the Cut command, a marquee appears around the selection but the selected cells do not disappear.

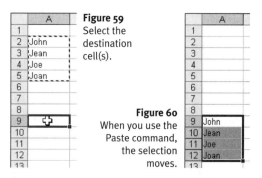

Figure 59 Select the destination cell(s).

Figure 60 When you use the Paste command, the selection moves.

MOVING WITH CUT & PASTE

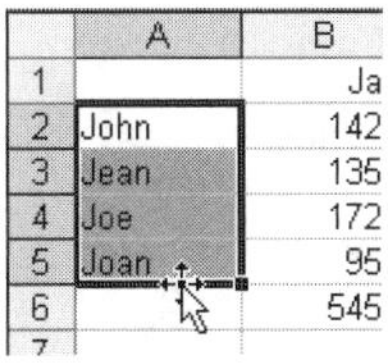

Figure 61
When you move the mouse pointer onto the border of a selection, a four-headed arrow appears beneath it.

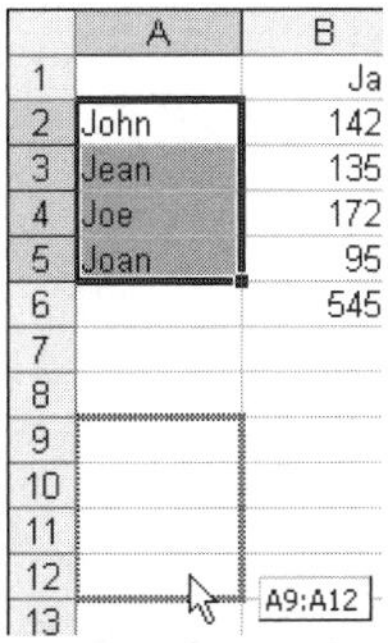

	A	B
1		Ja
2	John	142
3	Jean	135
4	Joe	172
5	Joan	95
6		545
7		

Figure 62
As you drag, a gray border moves along with the mouse pointer.

	A	B
1		Ja
2	John	142
3	Jean	135
4	Joe	172
5	Joan	95
6		545
7		
8		
9		
10		
11		
12		A9:A12
13		

Microsoft Office Excel

⚠ Do you want to replace the contents of the destination cells?

[OK] [Cancel]

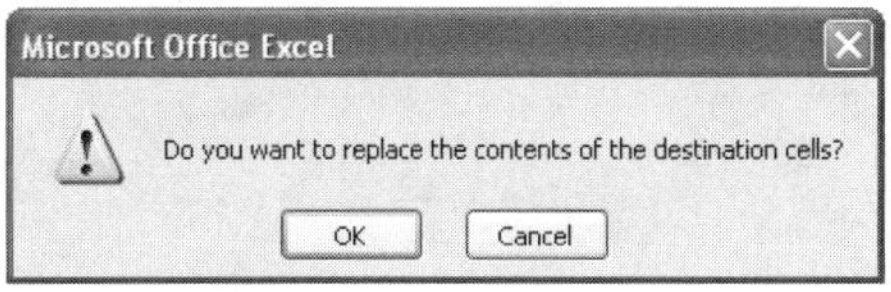

Figure 63 Excel warns you when you will overwrite cells with a selection you drag.

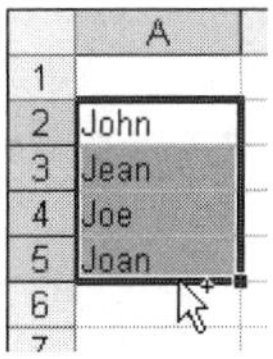

Figure 64
Hold down [Ctrl] to copy a selection by dragging it. A plus sign appears beside the mouse pointer.

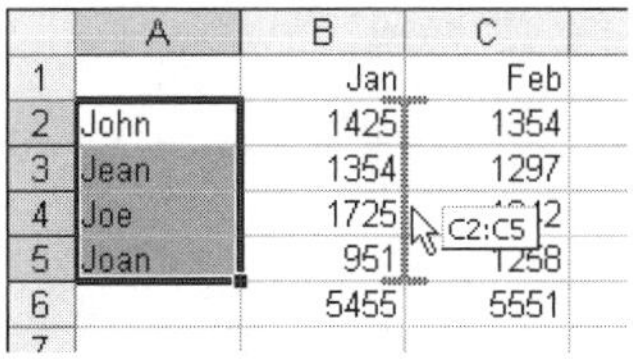

	A
1	
2	John
3	Jean
4	Joe
5	Joan
6	
7	

	A	B	C
1		Jan	Feb
2	John	1425	1354
3	Jean	1354	1297
4	Joe	1725	C2:C5 |2
5	Joan	951	1258
6		5455	5551
7			

Figure 65 Hold down [Shift] to insert a selection between other cells. A bar indicates where the cells will be inserted.

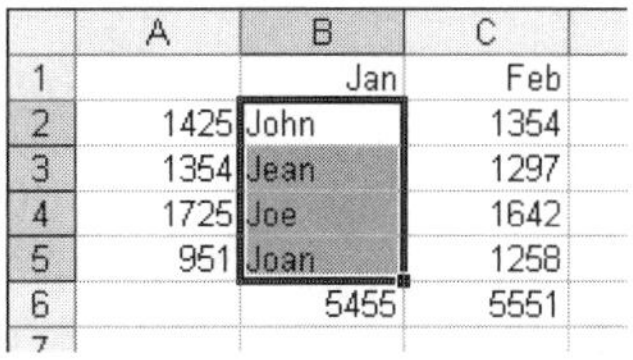

Figure 66
This makes it possible to rearrange the cells in a worksheet.

	A	B	C
1		Jan	Feb
2	1425	John	1354
3	1354	Jean	1297
4	1725	Joe	1642
5	951	Joan	1258
6		5455	5551
7			

To move with drag & drop

1. Select the cell(s) you want to move (**Figure 57**).

2. Position the mouse pointer on the border of the selection. A four-headed arrow appears beneath the mouse pointer (**Figure 61**).

3. Press the mouse button down and drag toward the new location. As you move the mouse, a gray border the same shape as the selection moves along with it and a box indicates the range where the cells will move (**Figure 62**).

4. Release the mouse button. The selection moves to its new location (**Figure 60**).

✔ Tips

■ If you try to drag a selection to cells already containing information, Excel warns you with a dialog like the one in **Figure 63**. If you click OK to complete the move, the destination cells will be over-written with the contents of the cells you are moving.

■ To copy using drag and drop, hold down [Ctrl] as you press the mouse button down. The mouse pointer turns into an arrow with a tiny plus sign (+) beside it (**Figure 64**). When you release the mouse button, the selection is copied.

■ To insert cells using drag and drop, hold down [Shift] as you press the mouse button down. As you drag, a gray bar moves along with the mouse pointer and a yellow box indicates where the cells will be inserted (**Figure 65**). When you release the mouse button, the cells are inserted (**Figure 66**).

MOVING WITH DRAG & DROP

The Office Clipboard

The Office Clipboard enables you to "collect and paste" multiple items. You simply display the Office Clipboard task pane, then copy text or objects as usual. But instead of the Clipboard contents being replaced each time you use the Copy or Cut command, all items are stored on the Office Clipboard (**Figure 67**). You can then paste any of the items on the Office Clipboard into your Excel document.

✔ Tips

- The Office Clipboard works with all Microsoft Office applications—not just Excel—so you can store items from different types of Office documents.

- This feature was referred to as *Collect and Paste* in previous versions of Microsoft Office for Windows.

To display the Office Clipboard

Choose Edit > Office Clipboard (**Figure 14**). The Office Clipboard appears as a task pane beside the document window (**Figure 68**).

✔ Tip

- The Office Clipboard automatically appears when you copy two items in a row.

To add an item to the Office Clipboard

1. If necessary, display the Office Clipboard (**Figure 68**).

2. Select the cells or object you want to copy (**Figure 57**).

3. Choose Edit > Copy (**Figure 14**), press Ctrl C, or click the Copy button on the Standard toolbar. The selection appears on the Office Clipboard (**Figure 69**).

Figure 67
The Clipboard task pane with four items: some text from Word, a graphic from Word, an Excel chart, and some Excel worksheet cells.

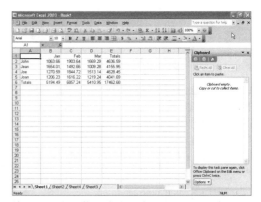

Figure 68 The Office Clipboard appears as a task pane.

Figure 69
The cells you selected are added to the Clipboard.

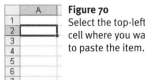

Figure 70
Select the top-left cell where you want to paste the item.

Figure 71
When you point to or click an item, a border appears around it.

Figure 72
The item you pasted appears in the document.

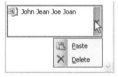

Figure 73
You can access a pop-up menu like this one for each item on the Office Clipboard.

Figure 74
Choosing Delete for an item removes it from the Office Clipboard.

To use Office Clipboard items

1. If necessary, display the Office Clipboard.

2. In the document window, select the top-left cell where you want to paste the Office Clipboard item (**Figure 70**).

3. In the Office Clipboard task pane, click on the item you want to paste into the document (**Figure 71**).

Or

1. If necessary, display the Office Clipboard.

2. Drag the item you want to use from the Office Clipboard into the document window.

The item you pasted or dragged appears in the document window (**Figure 72**).

✔ Tip

■ Not all items can be pasted into worksheet cells. Graphics, for example, are pasted on top of the worksheet layer. Graphics objects are covered in **Chapter 7**.

To remove Office Clipboard items

1. In the Office Clipboard window, point to the item you want to remove (**Figure 71**). A blue border appears around it and a pop-up menu button appears beside it.

2. Click the pop-up menu button to display a menu of two options (**Figure 73**).

3. Choose Delete. The item is removed from the Office Clipboard (**Figure 74**).

Or

Click the Clear All button at the top of the Office Clipboard (**Figure 74**) to remove all items.

Undoing, Redoing, & Repeating Actions

Excel's Edit menu offers a trio of commands that enable you to undo, redo, or repeat the last thing you did.

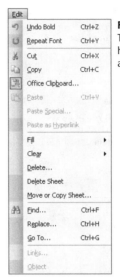

◆ **Undo** (**Figures 14** and **75**) reverses your last action. Excel supports multiple levels of undo, enabling you to reverse more than just the very last action.

◆ **Redo** (**Figure 14**) reverses the Undo command. This command is only available if the last thing you did was use the Undo command.

◆ **Repeat** (**Figure 75**) performs your last action again. This command is only available when you used any action other than the Undo or Redo command.

Figure 75
The Edit menu shown here includes Undo and repeat commands.

✔ Tips

■ The exact wording of these commands on the Edit menu (**Figures 14** and **75**) varies depending on the last action performed. The Undo command is always the first command under the Edit menu; the Redo or Repeat command (whichever appears on the menu) is always the second command under the Edit menu.

■ The Redo and Repeat commands are never available at the same time.

■ Think of the Undo command as the Oops command—anytime you say "Oops," you'll probably want to use it.

Figure 76
Use the Undo button's menu to select multiple actions to undo.

Figure 77
You can also use the Redo button's menu to select multiple actions to redo.

To undo the last action

Choose Edit > Undo (**Figures 14** or **75**) or press Ctrl Z.

Or

Click the Undo button ⟲ ▾ on the Standard toolbar.

To undo multiple actions

Choose Edit > Undo (**Figures 14** or **75**) or press Ctrl Z repeatedly.

Or

Click the triangle beside the Undo button on the Standard toolbar to display a drop-down list of recent actions. Drag down to select all the actions that you want to undo (**Figure 76**). Release the mouse button to undo all selected actions.

To reverse the last undo

Choose Edit > Redo (**Figure 14**) or press Ctrl Y.

Or

Click the Redo button ↻ ▾ on the Standard toolbar.

To reverse multiple undos

Choose Edit > Redo (**Figure 14**) or press Ctrl Y repeatedly.

Or

Click the triangle beside the Redo button on the Standard toolbar to display a drop-down list of recently undone actions. Drag down to select all the actions that you want to redo (**Figure 77**). Release the mouse button to reverse all selected undos.

To repeat the last action

Choose Edit > Repeat (**Figure 75**) or press Ctrl Y.

UNDOING, REDOING, & REPEATING ACTIONS

Working with Files

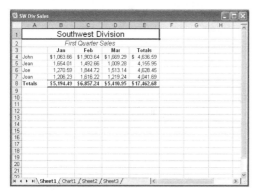

Figure 1 Here's a worksheet.

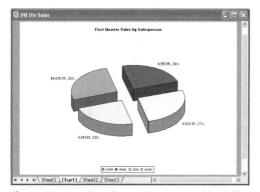

Figure 2 Here's a chart sheet in the same workbook file.

Excel Files

Microsoft Excel document files are called *workbooks*.

◆ Each workbook file includes multiple sheets.

◆ Workbook files appear in document windows.

◆ Workbook files can be saved on disk and reopened for editing and printing.

This chapter, explains how to perform a variety of tasks with workbook sheets, windows, and files.

Workbook Sheets

Excel workbook files can include up to 255 individual *sheets*, which are like pages in the workbook. Each workbook, by default, includes three sheets named *Sheet1* through *Sheet3*.

There are two kinds of sheets:

◆ A *worksheet* (**Figure 1**) is for entering information and performing calculations. You can also embed charts in a worksheet.

◆ A *chart sheet* (**Figure 2**) is for creating charts that aren't embedded in a worksheet.

✔ Tips

■ Use the multiple sheet capabilities of workbook files to keep sheets for the same project together. This is an excellent way to organize related work.

■ I tell you about worksheets throughout this book and about charts and chart sheets in **Chapter 8**.

To switch from one sheet to another

Click the sheet tab at the bottom of the workbook window (**Figure 3**) for the sheet you want.

Or

Press Ctrl Page Up or Ctrl Page Down to scroll through all of the sheets in a workbook, one at a time.

✔ Tips

- If the sheet tab for the sheet you want is not displayed, use the tab scrolling buttons (**Figure 4**) to scroll through the sheet tabs.

- To display more or fewer sheet tabs, drag the tab split box (**Figure 5**) to increase or decrease the size of the sheet tab area. As you change the size of the sheet tab area, you'll also change the size of the horizontal scroll bar at the bottom of the workbook window.

To select multiple sheets

1. Click the sheet tab for the first sheet you want to select.

2. Hold down Ctrl and click the sheet tab(s) for the other sheet(s) you want to select. The sheet tabs for each sheet you include in the selection turn white (**Figure 6**).

✔ Tips

- To select multiple adjacent sheets, click the sheet tab for the first sheet, then hold down Shift and click on the sheet tab for the last sheet you want to select. All sheet tabs in between also become selected.

- Selecting multiple sheets makes it quick and easy to print, delete, edit, format, or perform other tasks with more than one sheet at a time.

\Sheet1 / Sheet2 / Sheet3 /

Figure 3 Use sheet tabs to move from sheet to sheet in a workbook.

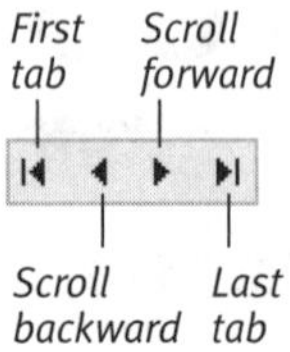

First tab *Scroll forward*

Scroll backward *Last tab*

Figure 4
Use the sheet tab scrolling buttons to view sheet tabs that are not displayed.

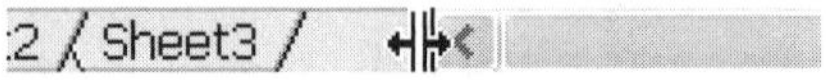

2 / Sheet3 /

Figure 5 Drag the tab split box to change the size of the sheet tab area and display more or fewer sheet tabs.

\Sheet1 / Sheet2 / Sheet3 /

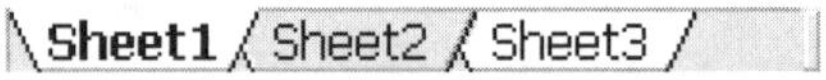

Figure 6 To select multiple sheets, hold down Ctrl while clicking each sheet tab.

`\ Sheet1 / Sheet2 \ Sheet3 /`

Figure 7 Begin by selecting the sheet you want the new sheet to be inserted before.

Figure 8
The Insert menu.

`\ Sheet1 / Sheet2 \ Sheet4 / Sheet3 /`

Figure 9 An inserted worksheet.

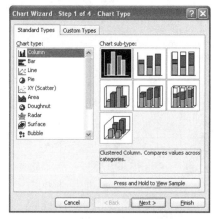

Figure 10 The first step of the Chart Wizard.

Figure 11 The last step of the Chart Wizard lets you insert the chart as a new sheet.

`\ Sheet1 / Sheet2 \ Chart1 / Sheet3 /`

Figure 12 An inserted chart sheet.

To insert a worksheet

1. Click the tab for the sheet you want to insert a new sheet before (**Figure 7**).

2. Choose Insert > Worksheet (**Figure 8**).

   A new worksheet is inserted before the one you originally selected (**Figure 9**).

✔ Tip

- By default, the new worksheet is named with the word *Sheet* followed by a number. I tell you how to rename sheets on the next page.

To insert a chart sheet

1. Click the tab for the sheet you want to insert a new sheet before (**Figure 7**).

2. Choose Insert > Chart (**Figure 8**).

3. The Chart Wizard - Step 1 of 4 dialog appears (**Figure 10**). Follow the steps in the Chart Wizard (as discussed in **Chapter 8**) to create a chart.

4. In the Chart Wizard - Step 4 of 4 dialog (**Figure 11**), select the As new sheet option button and enter a name for the sheet beside it. Then click Finish.

   A new chart sheet is inserted before the worksheet you originally selected (**Figure 12**).

INSERTING SHEETS

61

To delete a sheet

1. Click the sheet tab for the sheet you want to delete to select it.

2. Choose Edit > Delete Sheet (**Figure 13**).

3. A warning dialog (**Figure 14**) appears. Click Delete to confirm that you want to delete the sheet.

✔ Tips

■ The appearance of the Edit menu (**Figure 13**) varies depending on the type of sheet.

■ As the dialog in **Figure 14** warns, sheets are permanently deleted. That means even the Undo command won't get a deleted sheet back.

■ If another cell in the workbook contains a reference to a cell on the sheet you've deleted, that cell will display a #REF! error message. The formula in that cell will need to be rewritten.

To rename a sheet

1. Click the sheet tab for the sheet you want to rename to select it.

2. Choose Format > Sheet > Rename (**Figure 15**) or double-click the sheet tab.

3. The sheet tab becomes highlighted (**Figure 16**). Enter a new name for the sheet (**Figure 17**) and press [Enter] to save it.

The sheet tab displays the new name (**Figure 18**).

✔ Tip

■ The appearance of the Format menu (**Figure 15**) varies depending on the type of sheet.

Figure 13
The Edit menu.

Figure 14 When you delete a sheet, Excel warns you that the sheet may contain data.

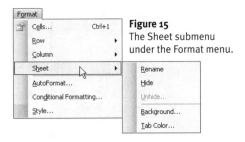

Figure 15
The Sheet submenu under the Format menu.

Sheet1

Figure 16 Double-click the sheet tab to select its name.

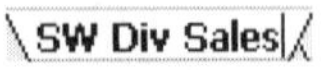

SW Div Sales

Figure 17 Enter a new name for the sheet.

Figure 18 Press [Enter] to save the new name.

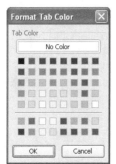

Figure 19
Use the Format Tab Color dialog to specify a color for a sheet tab.

\ **SW Div Sales** / Sheet2 / Chart1 / Sheet3 /

Figure 20 When the tab is selected, its name is underlined in the color you specified.

\ SW Div Sales \ **Sheet2** / Chart1 / Sheet3 /

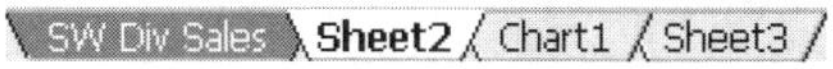

Figure 21 When a tab is not selected, its name appears in the color you specified.

To change a tab's color

1. Click the sheet tab you want to change the color of.

2. Choose Format > Sheet > Tab Color (**Figure 15**).

3. In the Format Tab Color dialog that appears (**Figure 19**), select the desired color.

4. Click OK.

   The tab color changes as follows:

   ▲ When the tab is selected, it is white but underlined with the tab color you specified (**Figure 20**).

   ▲ When the tab is not selected, it appears in the color you specified (**Figure 21**).

✔ Tips

- You can use this feature to "color code" workbook sheets. This can make sheets easier to find.

- You can change the color of more than one tab at a time. Simply follow the instructions earlier in this chapter to select all the tabs you want to change, then follow steps 2 through 4 above.

- To remove a color from a tab sheet, follow the instructions above, but select No Color in step 3.

CHANGING TAB COLORS

To hide a sheet

1. Select the sheet(s) you want to hide (**Figure 18**).

2. Choose Format > Sheet > Hide (**Figure 15**).

   The sheet and its sheet tab disappear (**Figure 22**), just as if it had been deleted. But don't worry, the sheet still exists in the workbook file.

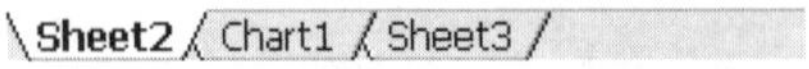

✔ Tips

- You cannot hide a sheet if it is the only sheet in a workbook.

- Don't confuse this command with the Hide command under the Window menu. These commands do two different things! I tell you about the Window menu's Hide command later in this chapter.

To unhide a sheet

1. Choose Format > Sheet > Unhide (**Figure 23**).

2. In the Unhide dialog that appears (**Figure 24**), select the sheet you want to unhide.

3. Click OK. The sheet and its sheet tab reappear.

✔ Tips

- You can only unhide one sheet at a time.

- If the Unhide command is gray (**Figure 15**), no sheets are hidden.

- Don't confuse this command with the Unhide command under the Window menu. I tell you about the Window menu's Unhide command later in this chapter.

\Sheet2 / Chart1 / Sheet3 /

Figure 22 When you hide a sheet, its tab disappears.

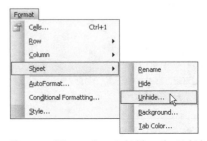

Figure 23 When a sheet is hidden, the Unhide command is available on the Sheet submenu.

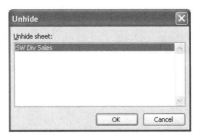

Figure 24 The Unhide dialog lists all hidden sheets.

Figure 25
Use the Move or Copy dialog to pick a destination for the selected sheet(s) and tell Excel to copy them rather than move them.

Figure 26
The To book drop-down list includes all of the currently open workbook files.

Figure 27 You can also drag a sheet tab to move it ...

Figure 28 ... or hold down Ctrl while dragging a sheet tab to copy it.

To move or copy a sheet

1. Select the tab(s) for the sheet(s) you want to move or copy.

2. Choose Edit > Move or Copy Sheet (**Figure 13**). The Move or Copy dialog appears (**Figure 25**).

3. Use the To book drop-down list (**Figure 26**) to choose the workbook you want to move or copy the sheet(s) to.

4. Use the Before sheet list to choose the sheet you want the sheet(s) to be copied before.

5. If you want to copy or duplicate the sheet rather than move it, turn on the Create a copy check box.

6. Click OK.

✔ Tips

- To move or copy sheets to another workbook, make sure that workbook is open (but not active) before you choose the Move or Copy Sheet command. Otherwise, it will not be listed in the To book drop-down list (**Figure 26**).

- If you choose (new book) from the To book drop-down list (**Figure 26**), Excel creates an empty workbook file and places the selected sheet(s) into it.

- You can use the Move or Copy Sheet command to change the order of sheets in a workbook. Just make sure the current workbook is selected in the To book drop-down list (**Figure 26**). Then select the appropriate sheet from the Before sheet scrolling list or select (move to end).

- You can also move or copy a sheet by dragging. To move the sheet, drag the sheet tab to the new position (**Figure 27**). To copy the sheet, hold down Ctrl while dragging the sheet tab (**Figure 28**).

Workbook Windows

Like most Windows programs, Excel allows you to have more than one document window open at a time. You can manipulate Excel's workbook windows a number of ways:

♦ Activate a window so you can work with its contents.

♦ Create a new window for a workbook so you can see two sheets from the same workbook at once.

♦ Arrange windows so you can see and work with more than one at a time.

♦ Close and hide windows to get them out of the way.

♦ Change a window's magnification so you can see more of its contents or see its contents more clearly.

♦ Split a window so you can see and work with two or more parts of a sheet at a time.

✔ Tip

■ I explain how to create a new workbook in **Chapter 2** and how to open an existing workbook later in this chapter.

Figure 29
The Window menu offers commands for working with—you guessed it—windows.

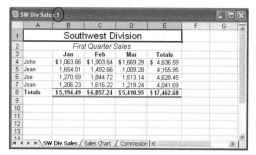

Figure 30 When you open more than one window for a workbook file, the window number appears in the title bar ...

Figure 31
... and both windows are listed on the Window menu.

To create a new window

1. Activate the workbook for which you want to create another window.

2. Choose Window > New Window (**Figure 29**).

   A new window for that workbook appears (**Figure 30**) and the new window's name appears at the bottom of the Window menu (**Figure 31**).

✔ Tip

■ If more than one window is open for a workbook and you close one of them, the workbook does not close—just that window. I tell you about closing windows later in this section.

To activate another window

Choose the name of the window you want to make active from the list of open windows at the bottom of the Window menu (**Figure 29** or **31**).

To arrange windows

1. Choose Window > Arrange (**Figure 29**).

2. In the Arrange Windows dialog that appears (**Figure 32**), select an Arrange option. **Figures 33** through **36** illustrate all of them.

3. To arrange only the windows of the active workbook, turn on the Windows of active workbook check box.

4. Click OK.

✔ Tips

- To work with one of the arranged windows, click in it to make it active.

- The window with the dark title bar is the active window.

- To make one of the arranged windows full size again, click on it to make it active and then click the window's Maximize button. The window fills the screen while the other windows remain arranged behind it. Click the Restore window button to shrink it back down to its arranged size.

Figure 32
The Arrange Windows dialog.

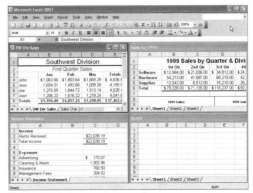

Figure 33 Tiled windows.

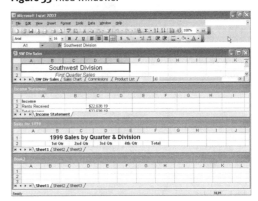

Figure 34 Horizontally arranged windows.

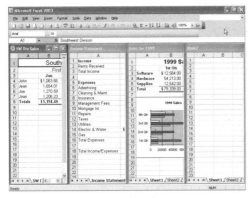

Figure 35 Vertically arranged windows.

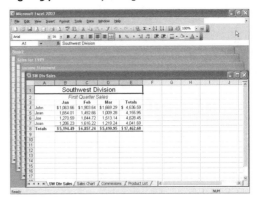

Figure 36 Cascading windows.

Figure 37
The File menu.

Figure 38 When you close a document with unsaved changes, Excel gives you a chance to save it.

Figure 39 Hold down (Shift) to display the Close All command.

Figure 40 When a window is hidden, the Unhide command is available on the Window menu.

Figure 41
Use the Unhide dialog to select the window you want to unhide.

To close a window

Click the window's close button or choose File > Close (**Figure 37**).

✔ Tips

- If the file you are closing has unsaved changes, Excel warns you (**Figure 38**). Click Yes to save changes. I tell you about saving files later in this chapter.

- To close all open windows, hold down (Shift) and choose File > Close All (**Figure 39**).

To hide a window

1. Activate the window you want to hide.

2. Choose Window > Hide (**Figure 29**). The window disappears from your screen and from the Window menu (**Figure 40**).

✔ Tips

- Hiding a window is not the same as closing it. A hidden window remains open, even though it is not listed at the bottom of the Window menu.

- Hiding a window is not the same as hiding a sheet in a workbook. I tell you about hiding sheets earlier in this chapter.

To unhide a window

1. Choose Window > Unhide (**Figure 40**).

2. In the Unhide dialog that appears (**Figure 41**), choose the window you want to unhide.

3. Click OK. The window appears.

✔ Tip

- If the Unhide command is gray (**Figures 29** and **31**), no windows are hidden.

To change a window's magnification

1. Choose View > Zoom (**Figure 42**).

2. In the Zoom dialog that appears (**Figure 43**), select the option button for the magnification you want.

3. Click OK.

Or

1. Click the arrow beside the Zoom box on the Standard toolbar to display a drop-down list of magnifications (**Figure 44**).

2. Choose the magnification you want from the menu.

✔ Tips

■ To zoom selected cells so they fill the window, select the Fit selection option button in the Zoom dialog (**Figure 43**) or choose the Selection command on the Zoom drop-down list (**Figure 44**).

■ You can enter a custom magnification in the Zoom dialog (**Figure 43**) by selecting the Custom option button and entering a value of your choice.

■ You can enter a custom magnification in the Zoom text box on the Standard toolbar by clicking the value in the box to select it, typing in a new value (**Figure 45**), and pressing Enter.

■ Zooming the window using techniques discussed here does not affect the way a worksheet will print.

■ A "zoomed" window's sheet works just like any other worksheet.

■ When you save a workbook, the magnification settings of its sheets are saved. When you reopen the workbook, the sheets appear with the last used zoom magnification.

Figure 42
The View menu.

Figure 43
Use the Zoom dialog to set the window's magnification.

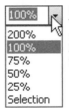

Figure 44
You can also choose a magnification from the Zoom drop-down list on the Standard toolbar.

Figure 45 You can enter a custom zoom percentage in the Zoom box on the Standard toolbar.

CHANGING WINDOW MAGNIFICATION

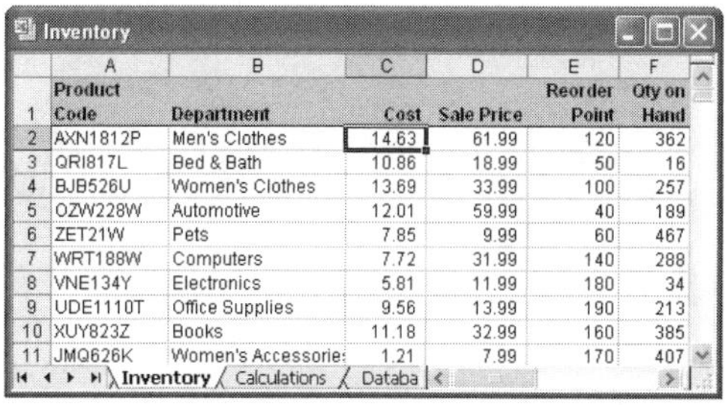

Figure 46 Position the cell pointer below and to the right of where you want the split to occur.

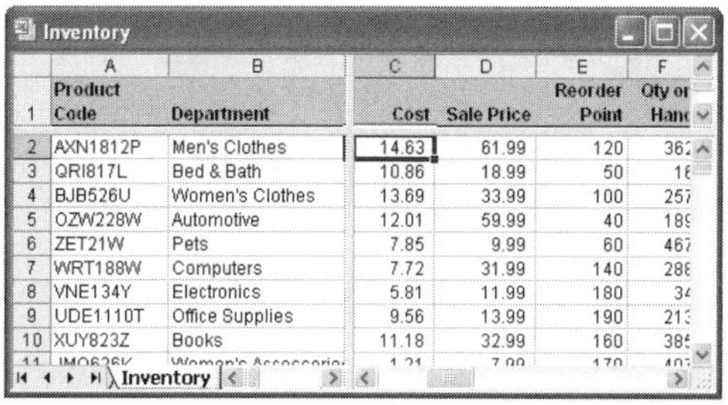

Figure 47 When you choose the Split command, the window splits.

Figure 48
Position the mouse pointer on the split bar at the end of the scroll bar.

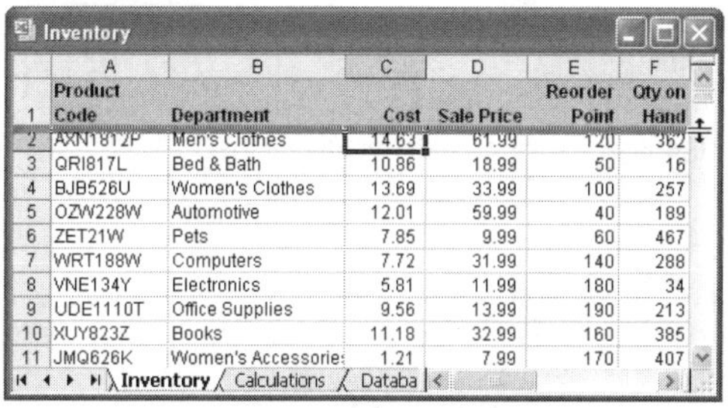

Figure 49 Drag the split bar into the window.

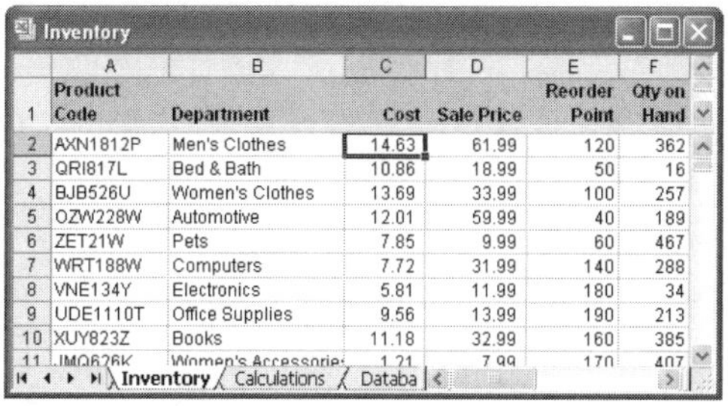

Figure 50 When you release the mouse button, the window splits.

To split a window

1. Position the cell pointer in the cell immediately below and to the right of where you want the split(s) to occur (**Figure 46**).

2. Choose Window > Split (**Figure 29**). The window splits at the location you specified (**Figure 47**).

Or

1. Position the mouse pointer on the split bar at the top of the vertical scroll bar or right end of the horizontal scroll bar. The mouse pointer turns into a double line with arrows coming out of it (**Figure 48**).

2. Press the mouse button down and drag. A split bar moves along with the mouse pointer (**Figure 49**).

3. Release the mouse button. The window splits at the bar (**Figure 50**).

To adjust the size of panes

1. Position the mouse pointer on a split bar.

2. Press the mouse button down and drag until the split bar is in the desired position.

3. Release the mouse button. The window split moves.

To remove a window split

Choose Window > Remove Split (**Figure 51**) or double-click a split bar.

Figure 51
You can use the Remove Split command to remove a window split.

Saving Files

As you work with a file, everything you do is stored in only one place: *random access memory* or *RAM*. The contents of RAM are a lot like the light in a lightbulb—as soon as you turn it off or pull the plug, it's gone. Your hard disk, a floppy disk, or a networked disk provide a much more permanent type of storage area.

You use the Save command to copy the workbook file in RAM to disk. This part of the chapter explains how.

✔ Tip

■ It's a very good idea to save documents frequently as you work to prevent data loss in the event of a computer problem.

To save a workbook file for the first time

1. Choose File > Save or File > Save As (**Figure 37**), press Ctrl S, or click the Save button 🖫 on the Standard toolbar.

2. Use the Save As dialog that appears (**Figure 52**) to navigate to the folder (and disk, if necessary) in which you want to save the file:

   ▲ Use the Save in drop-down list near the top of the dialog (**Figure 53**) to go to another location.

   ▲ Double-click a folder to open it.

   ▲ Click the Create New Folder button on the command bar to create a new folder within the current folder. Enter the name for the folder in the New Folder dialog (**Figure 54**) and click OK.

3. Enter a name for the file in the Name box.

4. Click Save. The file is saved to disk. Its name appears in the window's title bar (**Figure 55**).

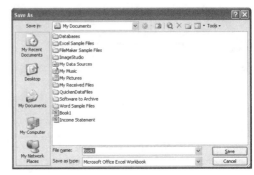

Figure 52 The Save As dialog.

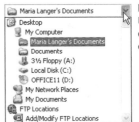

Figure 53
Use the Save in drop-down list to choose a different location.

Figure 54 The New Folder dialog.

Figure 55 The file's name appears in the title bar, along with a tiny Excel workbook file icon.

SAVING FILES

Figure 56 Use the Save as type drop-down list to save the document as a template or another type of file.

Figure 57 Excel checks to make sure you want to over-write a file with the same name.

✔ Tips

- You can use the Save as type drop-down list at the bottom of the Save As dialog (**Figure 56**) to specify a format for the file or active sheet. This enables you to save the document as a template or in a format that can be opened and read by other versions of Excel or other programs.

- If you save a file with the same name and same disk location as another file, a dialog appears, asking if you want to replace the file (**Figure 57**).

  ▲ Click Yes to replace the file already on disk with the file you are saving.

  ▲ Click No to return to the Save As dialog where you can enter a new name or specify a new disk location.

To save changes to a file

Choose File > Save (**Figure 37**), press Ctrl S, or click the Save button 🖫 on the Standard toolbar.

The file is saved with the same name in the same location on disk.

To save a file with a different name or in a different location

1. Choose File > Save As (**Figure 34**).

2. Follow steps 2 and/or 3 on the previous page to select a new disk location and/or enter a different name for the file.

3. Click Save.

SAVING FILES

Opening Existing Files

Once a file has been saved on disk, you can reopen it to read it, modify it, or print it.

To open an existing file

1. Choose File > Open (**Figure 37**) press [Ctrl][O], or click the Open button 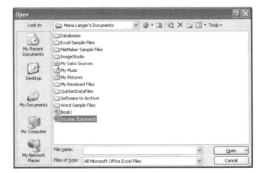 on the Standard toolbar.

Figure 58 The Open dialog.

2. Use the Open dialog that appears (**Figure 58**) to locate the file that you want to open:

   ▲ Use the Look in drop-down list near the top of the dialog (**Figure 59**) to go to another location.

   ▲ Double-click a folder to open it.

Figure 59
Use the Look in drop-down list to go to another location.

3. Select the file that you want to open and click the Open button.

   or

   Double-click the file that you want to open.

✔ Tips

■ To view only specific types of files in the Open dialog, select a format from the Files of type drop-down list at the bottom of the dialog (**Figure 60**).

Figure 60 You can narrow down or expand the list of files shown by choosing an option from the Files of type drop-down list.

■ If you select All Files from the Files of type drop-down list (**Figure 60**), you can open just about any kind of file. Be aware, however, that a file in an incompatible format may not appear the way you expect when opened.

■ You can open a recent file by selecting it from the list of recently opened files at the bottom of the File menu (**Figure 37**).

Using Functions in Formulas

	A	B	C
1	Product Inventory		
2			
3	Item Name	Item No.	Qty
4	Self	S-439	159
5	Finding Meano	F-571	341
6	Kill Phil: Take 1	K-845	415
7	Lost in Transmission	L-482	167
8	Closed Cell	C-058	684
9	Toothpick Men	T-473	218
10	Runaway Judge	R-400	189
11	Overworld	O-108	581
12	Total		
13			

Figure 1 Using the SUM function makes it easier to add up a column of numbers.

Function name *Arguments*

SUM(number1,number2,...)

Figure 2 The parts of a function. Bold components are required.

✔ Tips

- If a function comes at the beginning of a formula, it must begin with an equal sign (=).

- Some arguments are optional. In the SUM function, for example, you can have only one argument, such as a reference to a single range of cells.

Functions

A function is a predefined formula for making a specific kind of calculation. Functions make it quicker and easier to write formulas.

For example, say you need to add up a column of numbers like the one in **Figure 1**. It's perfectly acceptable to write a formula using cell references separated by the addition operator (+) like this:

$$=C_4+C_5+C_6+C_7+C_8+C_9+C_{10}+C_{11}$$

But rather than enter a lengthy formula, you can use the SUM function to add up the same numbers like this:

$$=SUM(C_4:C_{11})$$

The SUM function is only one of over 200 functions built into Excel. I list all functions in **Appendix B**.

Anatomy of a Function

As shown in **Figure 2**, each function has two main parts.

- ◆ The *function name* determines what the function does.

- ◆ The *arguments* determine what values or cell references the function should use in its calculation. Arguments are enclosed in parentheses and, if there's more than one, separated by commas.

Arguments

The argument component of a function can consist of any of the following:

◆ **Numbers** (**Figure 3**). Like any other formula, the result of a function that uses values for arguments will not change unless the formula is changed.

◆ **Text** (**Figure 4**). Excel includes a number of functions just for text. I tell you about them later in this chapter.

◆ **Cell references** (**Figures 4** through **8**). This is a practical way to write functions, since when you change cell contents, the results of functions that reference them change automatically.

◆ **Formulas** (**Figures 6** and **7**). This lets you create complex formulas that perform a series of calculations at once.

◆ **Functions** (**Figures 7** and **8**). When a function includes another function as one of its arguments, it's called *nesting functions*.

◆ **Error values** (**Figure 8**). You may find this useful to "flag" errors or missing information in a worksheet.

◆ **Logical values**. Some function arguments require TRUE or FALSE values.

=DATE(2002,6,30)

Figure 3 This example uses numbers as arguments for the DATE function.

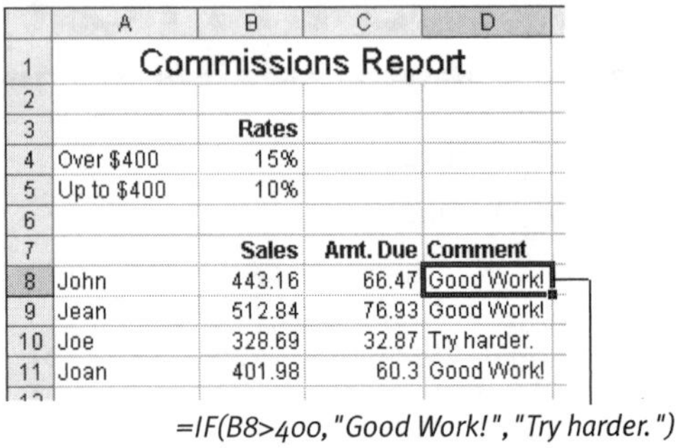

	A	B	C	D
1	Commissions Report			
2				
3		Rates		
4	Over $400	15%		
5	Up to $400	10%		
6				
7		Sales	Amt. Due	Comment
8	John	443.16	66.47	Good Work!
9	Jean	512.84	76.93	Good Work!
10	Joe	328.69	32.87	Try harder.
11	Joan	401.98	60.3	Good Work!

=IF(B8>400,"Good Work!","Try harder.")

Figure 4 This example uses cell references, numbers, and text as arguments for the IF function.

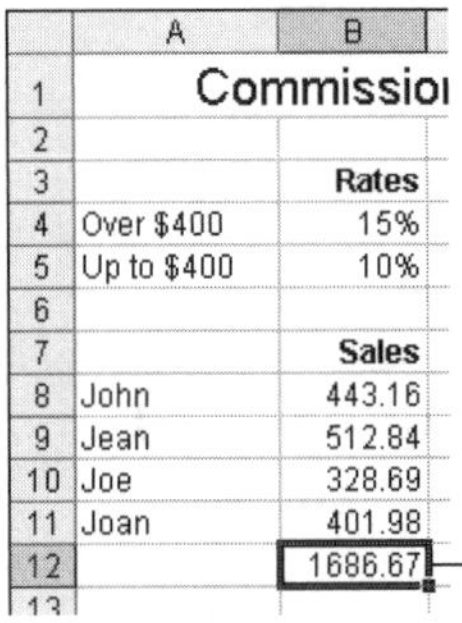

	A	B
1	Commissio	
2		
3		Rates
4	Over $400	15%
5	Up to $400	10%
6		
7		Sales
8	John	443.16
9	Jean	512.84
10	Joe	328.69
11	Joan	401.98
12		1686.67

Figure 5 This example shows two different ways to use cell references as arguments for the SUM function.

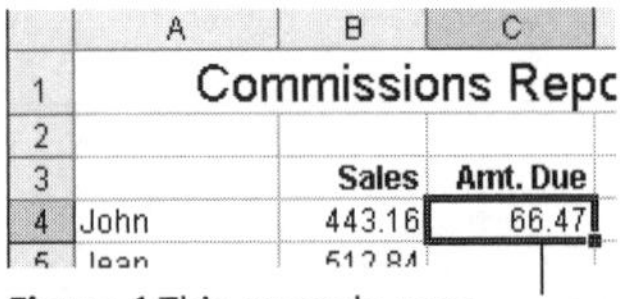

=SUM(B8:B11) or
=SUM(B8,B9,B10,B11)

	A	B	C
1	Commissions Repc		
2			
3		Sales	Amt. Due
4	John	443.16	66.47
5	Jean	512.84	

Figure 6 This example uses a formula as an argument for the ROUND function.

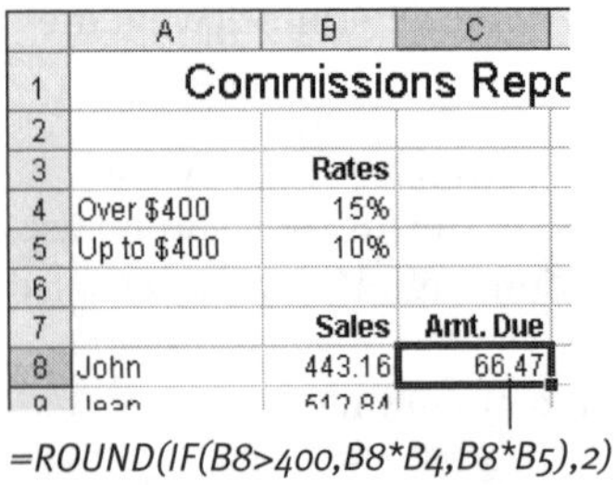

=ROUND(B4*.15,2)

	A	B	C
1	Commissions Repc		
2			
3		Rates	
4	Over $400	15%	
5	Up to $400	10%	
6			
7		Sales	Amt. Due
8	John	443.16	66.47
9	Jean	512.84	

=ROUND(IF(B8>400,B8*B4,B8*B5),2)

Figure 7 This example uses the ROUND and IF functions to calculate commissions based on a rate that changes according to sales.

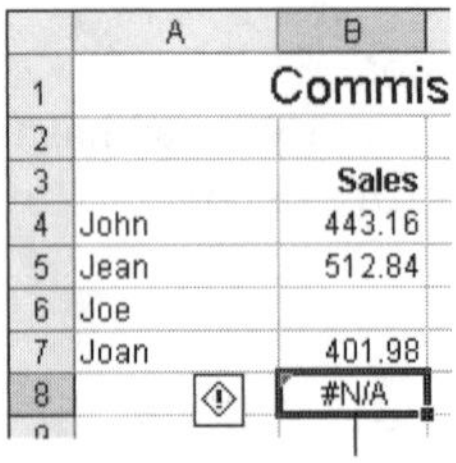

	A	B
1	Commis	
2		
3		Sales
4	John	443.16
5	Jean	512.84
6	Joe	
7	Joan	401.98
8		#N/A

Figure 8 This example uses three functions (IF, COUNTBLANK, and SUM), cell references, and error values to either indicate missing information or add a column of numbers.

=IF(COUNTBLANK(B4:B7)>0,#N/A,SUM(B4:B7))

ARGUMENTS

Figure 9 If you don't enter parentheses correctly, Excel can get confused.

Figure 10 The Formula AutoCorrect feature can fix common formula errors for you.

Entering Functions

Excel offers several ways to enter a function:

◆ By typing

◆ By typing and clicking

◆ By using the Insert Function and Function Arguments dialogs

There is no "best" way—use the methods that you like most.

✔ Tips

■ Function names are not case sensitive. *Sum* or *sum* is the same as *SUM*. Excel converts all function names to uppercase characters.

■ Do not include spaces when writing formulas.

■ When writing formulas with nested functions, it's important to properly match parentheses. If parentheses don't match, Excel either displays an error message (**Figure 9**) or offers to correct the error for you (**Figure 10**). Sometimes Excel will fix the error without displaying a message.

■ Excel's Function Argument Tooltips feature (**Figures 11** and **12** on the next page) helps you enter functions correctly by providing information about arguments as you enter a formula.

ENTERING FUNCTIONS

To enter a function by typing

1. Begin the formula by typing an equal sign (=).

2. Type in the function name.

3. Type an open parenthesis character (**Figure 11**).

4. Type in the value or cell reference for the first argument (**Figure 12**).

5. If entering more than one argument, type each of them in with commas between them.

6. Type a closed parenthesis character.

7. Press ⎡Enter⎤ or click the Enter button ☑ on the formula bar. The result of the function is displayed in the cell (**Figure 13**).

	A	B	C	D
1		Southwest Division		
2		First Quarter Sales		
3		Jan	Feb	Ma
4	John	1254	1256	243!
5	Jean	1865	1736	190!
6	Joan	1614	1284	250!
7	Joe	1987	1908	289(
8	Totals	=sum(		
9		SUM(**number1**, [number2], ...)		

Figure 11 When you begin to enter the formula, Function Argument ToolTips appear to guide you.

	A	B	C	D
1		Southwest Division		
2		First Quarter Sales		
3		Jan	Feb	Ma
4	John	1254	1256	243!
5	Jean	1865	1736	190!
6	Joan	1614	1284	250!
7	Joe	1987	1908	289(
8	Totals	=sum(B4:B7		
9		SUM(**number1**, [number2], ...)		

Figure 12 Continue typing to enter the formula.

	A	B
1		Southv
2		First (
3		Jan
4	John	1254
5	Jean	1865
6	Joan	1614
7	Joe	1987
8	Totals	6720

Figure 13 When you complete the entry, the cell containing the function displays the result of the formula.

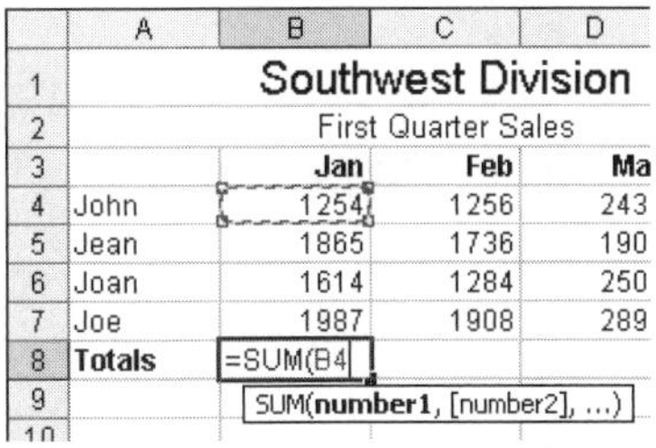

Figure 14 After typing the beginning of the function, you can click on cell references for arguments.

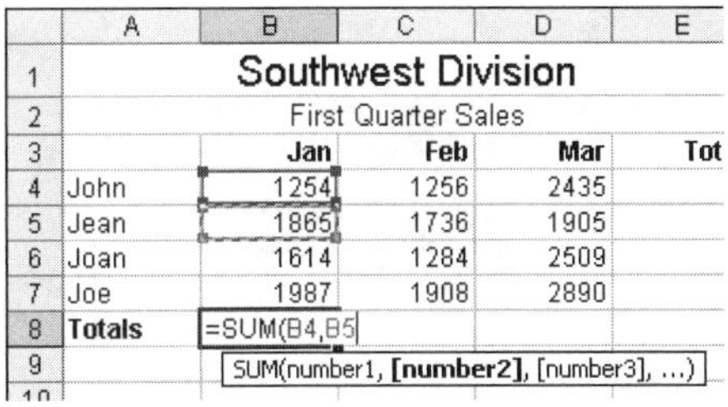

Figure 15 Type a comma before clicking to enter additional cell references for arguments.

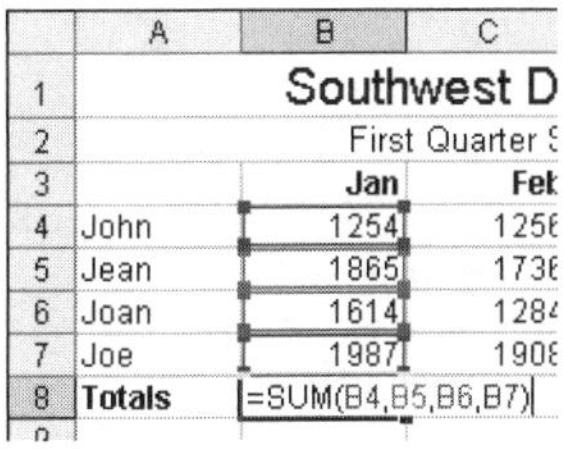

Figure 16 Be sure to type a closed parenthesis character at the end of a function.

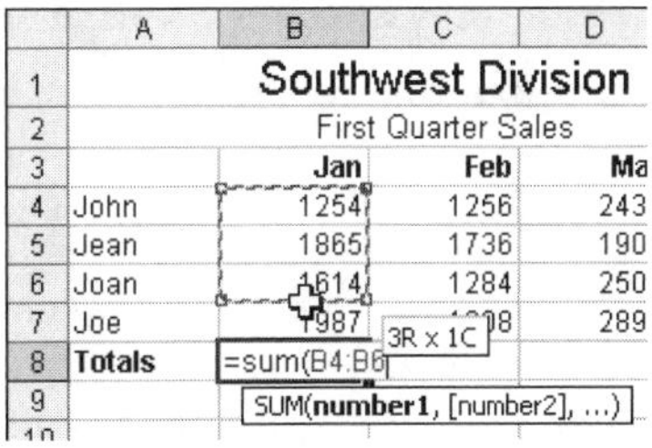

Figure 17 You can always enter a range in a formula by dragging, even when the range is an argument for a function.

To enter a function by typing & clicking

1. Begin the formula by typing an equal sign (=).

2. Type in the function name.

3. Type an open parenthesis character.

4. Type in a value or click on the cell whose reference you want to include as the first argument (**Figure 14**).

5. If entering more than one argument, type a comma, then type in a value or click on the cell for the next reference (**Figure 15**). Repeat this step for each argument in the function.

6. Type a closed parenthesis character (**Figure 16**).

7. Press ⟨Enter⟩ or click the Enter button ☑ on the formula bar.

   The result of the function is displayed in the cell (**Figure 13**).

✔ Tips

- To include a range by clicking, in step 4 or 5 above, drag the mouse pointer over the cells you want to include (**Figure 17**).

- Be careful where you click or drag when entering a function or any formula—each click or drag may add references to the formula! If you click on a cell by mistake, you can press ⟨Backspace⟩ to delete each character of the incorrectly added reference or click the Cancel button ☒ on the formula bar to start over.

ENTERING FUNCTIONS BY TYPING & CLICKING

To enter a function with dialogs

Figure 18
Choosing Function
from the Insert menu.

1. Choose Insert > Function (**Figure 18**) or click the Insert Function button fx on the formula bar to display the Insert Function dialog (**Figure 19**).

2. Choose a category from the drop-down list (**Figure 20**).

3. Click to select a function in the list box. You may have to use the scroll bar to locate the function you want.

4. Click OK.

    The Function Arguments dialog appears (**Figure 21**). It provides information about the function you selected and may include one or more entries for the argument(s).

5. Enter a value or cell reference in the appropriate text box for each required argument.

6. When you are finished entering function arguments, click OK.

    The Function Arguments dialog closes and the result of the function is displayed in the cell (**Figure 13**).

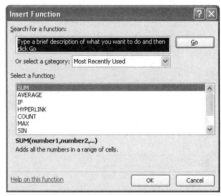

Figure 19 The Insert Function dialog.

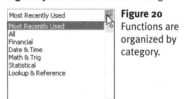

Figure 20
Functions are
organized by
category.

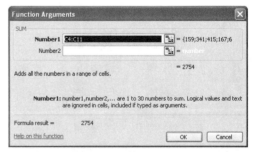

Figure 21 Use the Function Arguments dialog to enter arguments for the function.

ENTERING FUNCTIONS WITH DIALOGS

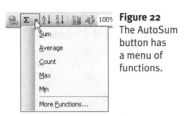

Figure 22
The AutoSum button has a menu of functions.

Figure 23 The Insert Function dialog can recommend functions based on what you tell it you want to do.

Figure 24
The Functions drop-down list at the far-left end of the formula bar.

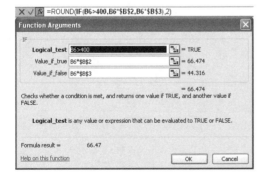

Figure 25 Only one function's options appear in the Function Arguments dialog at a time, but you can view and edit the entire formula in the formula bar.

✔ Tips

■ Another way to open the Insert Function dialog is to choose More Functions from the AutoSum menu on the Standard toolbar (**Figure 22**). Then follow steps 2 through 6 to complete the formula.

■ If you don't know which function you want, you can search for the correct function. Enter a description of what you want to do in the large text box near the top of the Insert Function dialog and click Go. A list of possible functions appears in the list (**Figure 23**).

■ In step 2, if you're not sure which category a function is in, select All. The Select a function list displays all of the functions Excel has to offer.

■ In step 5, you can click or drag in the worksheet window to enter a cell reference or range. To see obstructed worksheet cells, you can drag the Function Arguments dialog aside.

■ In step 5, you can enter a function as an argument by clicking in the argument's text box and choosing a specific function or More Functions from the Functions drop-down list at the far-left end of the formula bar (**Figure 24**). Although the Formula Palette only shows function options for one function at a time, you can view and edit the entire formula in the formula bar (**Figure 25**).

■ As you enter arguments in the Function Arguments dialog, the calculated value of your entries appears at the bottom of the dialog (**Figures 21** and **25**).

Math & Trig Functions

Excel's math and trig functions perform standard mathematical and trigonometric calculations. The next few pages discuss the most commonly used ones, starting with one so popular it even has its own toolbar button: SUM.

The SUM function

The SUM function (**Figure 5**) adds up numbers. It uses the following syntax:

SUM(number1,number2,...)

Although the SUM function can accept up to 30 arguments separated by commas, only one is required.

To use the AutoSum button

1. Select the cell below the column or to the right of the row of numbers you want to add.

2. Click the AutoSum button $\boxed{\Sigma}\boxed{\cdot}$ on the Standard toolbar once.

   Excel examines the worksheet and makes a "guess" about which cells you want to add. It writes the corresponding formula and puts a marquee around the range of cells it used (**Figure 26**).

3. If the range in the formula is incorrect, type or select the correct range. Since the reference for the range of cells is selected in the formula, anything you type or select will automatically replace it.

4. When the formula is correct, press (Enter), click the Enter button $\boxed{\checkmark}$ on the formula bar, or click the AutoSum button $\boxed{\Sigma}\boxed{\cdot}$ on the Standard toolbar a second time.

   The formula is entered and its results appear in the cell.

	A	B	C	D
1		Southwest Division		
2		First Quarter Sales		
3		Jan	Feb	Ma
4	John	1254	1256	243
5	Jean	1865	1736	190
6	Joan	1614	1284	250
7	Joe	1987	1908	289
8	Totals	=SUM(B4:B7)		
9		SUM(**number1**, [number2], ...)		
10				

Figure 26 When you click the AutoSum button, Excel writes a formula, guessing which cells you want to add.

	A	B	C	D
1	Southwest Division			
2	First Quarter Sales			
3		Jan	Feb	Mar
4	John	1254	1256	2435
5	Jean	1865	1736	1905
6	Joan	1614	1284	2509
7	Joe	1987	1908	2890
8	Totals			
9				

Figure 27 Select the cells adjacent to the columns (or rows) of cells that you want to add.

	A	B	C	D
1	Southwest Division			
2	First Quarter Sales			
3		Jan	Feb	Mar
4	John	1254	1256	2435
5	Jean	1865	1736	1905
6	Joan	1614	1284	2509
7	Joe	1987	1908	2890
8	Totals	6720	6184	9739
9				

Figure 28 When you click the AutoSum button, Excel enters the appropriate formulas in the cells.

	A	B	C	D
1	Southwest Division			
2	First Quarter Sales			
3		Jan	Feb	Mar
4	John	1254	1256	2435
5	Jean	1865	1736	1905
6	Joan	1614	1284	2509
7	Joe	1987	1908	2890
8	Totals			
9				

Figure 29 Select the cells containing the columns that you want to add.

	A	B	C	D
1	Southwest Division			
2	First Quarter Sales			
3		Jan	Feb	Mar
4	John	1254	1256	2435
5	Jean	1865	1736	1905
6	Joan	1614	1284	2509
7	Joe	1987	1908	2890
8	Totals	6720	6184	9739
9				

Figure 30 When you click the AutoSum button, Excel enters the appropriate formulas in the cells beneath the selected cells.

	A	B	C	D	E
1	Southwest Division				
2	First Quarter Sales				
3		Jan	Feb	Mar	Total
4	John	1254	1256	2435	
5	Jean	1865	1736	1905	
6	Joan	1614	1284	2509	
7	Joe	1987	1908	2890	
8	Totals				
9					

Figure 31 Select the cells you want to add, along with the cells in which you want the totals to appear.

To use the AutoSum button on multiple cells

1. Select a range of cells adjacent to the columns or rows you want to add (**Figure 27**).

2. Click the AutoSum button Σ ▾ once. Excel writes the formulas in the cells you selected (**Figure 28**).

Or

1. Select the cells containing the columns you want to add (**Figure 29**).

2. Click the AutoSum button Σ ▾ once. Excel writes all the formulas in the row of cells immediately below the ones you selected (**Figure 30**).

Or

1. Select the cells containing the columns and rows you want to add, along with the empty row beneath them and the empty column to the right of them (**Figure 31**).

2. Click the AutoSum button Σ ▾ once. Excel writes formulas in the bottom and rightmost cells (**Figure 32**).

✔ Tip

■ Be sure to check the formulas Excel writes when you use the AutoSum button. Excel is smart, but it's no mind-reader. The cells it includes may not be the ones you had in mind!

	A	B	C	D	E
1	Southwest Division				
2	First Quarter Sales				
3		Jan	Feb	Mar	Total
4	John	1254	1256	2435	4945
5	Jean	1865	1736	1905	5506
6	Joan	1614	1284	2509	5407
7	Joe	1987	1908	2890	6785
8	Totals	6720	6184	9739	22643
9					

Figure 32 When you click the AutoSum button, Excel enters the appropriate formulas in the empty cells of the selection.

The PRODUCT function

The PRODUCT function (**Figure 33**) multiplies its arguments much like the SUM function adds them. It uses the following syntax:

PRODUCT(number1,number2,...)

Although the PRODUCT function can accept up to 30 arguments separated by commas, only one is required.

The ROUND function

The ROUND function (**Figure 34**) rounds a number to the number of decimal places you specify. It uses the following syntax:

ROUND(number,num_digits)

Both arguments are required. The num_digits argument specifies how many decimal places the number should be rounded to. If 0, the number is rounded to a whole number. If less than 0, the number is rounded on the left side of the decimal point (**Figure 35**).

✔ Tips

- Rather than make a calculation in one cell and round it in another as shown in **Figures 34** and **35**, combine the two formulas in one cell (**Figure 36**).

- The ROUNDUP function works like the ROUND function, but it always rounds up to the next higher number. The num_digits argument is not required; if omitted, the number is rounded to the next highest whole number.

- The ROUNDDOWN function works just like the ROUNDUP function, but it always rounds down.

	A	B	C	D	E	F
1	Item	Cost	Markup	Qty	Value	
2	Product A	1.54	115%	152	269.192	=PRODUCT(B2:D2)
3	Product B	3.58	250%	142	1270.9	=PRODUCT(B3,C3,D3)

Figure 33 Two ways to use the PRODUCT function. The formulas in column *E* are shown in column *F*.

	A	B	C	D	E	F
1		Sales	Rate	Amount Due	Rounded	
2	John	14528.16	15%	2179.224	2179.22	=ROUND(D2,2)
3	Jean	45284.48	20%	9056.896	9056.9	=ROUND(D3,2)
4	Joe	36547.19	15%	5482.0785	5482.08	=ROUND(D4,2)
5	Joan	27582.43	15%	4137.3645	4137.36	=ROUND(D5,2)

Figure 34 Use the ROUND function to round numbers to the number of decimal places you specify. The formulas in column *E* are shown in column *F*.

	A	E	F	G
1		Total	Rounded	
2	Sales	154258.65	154300	=ROUND(E2,-2)
3	Cost	58842.87		

Figure 35 You can also use the ROUND function to round numbers to the left of the decimal point. The formula in cell *F2* is shown in cell *G2*.

	A	B	C	D	E
1		Sales	Rate	Amount Due	
2	John	14528.16	15%	2179.22	=ROUND(B2*C2,2)
3	Jean	45284.48	20%	9056.9	=ROUND(B3*C3,2)
4	Joe	36547.19	15%	5482.08	=ROUND(B4*C4,2)
5	Joan	27582.43	15%	4137.36	=ROUND(B5*C5,2)

Figure 36 You can also use the ROUND function to round the results of another formula or function. The formulas in column *D* are shown in column *E*.

	A	B	C	D	E
1	**Number**	**Even**		**Odd**	
2	159.487	160	=EVEN(A2)	161	=ODD(A2)
3	1647.1	1648	=EVEN(A3)	1649	=ODD(A3)
4	-14.48	-16	=EVEN(A4)	-15	=ODD(A4)

Figure 37 Use the EVEN and ODD functions to round a number up to the next even or odd number. The formulas in columns *B* and *D* are shown in columns *C* and *E*.

	A	B	C
1	**Number**	**Integer**	
2	159.487	159	=INT(A2)
3	1647.1	1647	=INT(A3)
4	-14.48	-15	=INT(A4)

Figure 38 Use the INT function to round a number down to the next whole number. The formulas in column *B* are shown in column *C*.

	A	B	C
1	**Number**	**Absolute Value**	
2	159.487	159.487	=ABS(A2)
3	1647.1	1647.1	=ABS(A3)
4	-14.48	14.48	=ABS(A4)

Figure 39 Use the ABS function to get the absolute value of a number. The formulas in column *B* are shown in column *C*.

The EVEN & ODD functions

The EVEN function (**Figure 37**) rounds a number up to the next even number. It uses the following syntax:

EVEN(number)

The number argument, which is required, is the number you want to round.

The ODD function works exactly the same way, but rounds a number up to the next odd number.

The INT function

The INT function (**Figure 38**) rounds a number down to the nearest whole number or integer. It uses the following syntax:

INT(number)

The number argument, which is required, is the number you want to convert to an integer.

The ABS function

The ABS function (**Figure 39**) returns the absolute value of a number—it leaves positive numbers alone but turns negative numbers into positive numbers. (Is that high school math coming back to you yet?) It uses the following syntax:

ABS(number)

The number argument, which is required, is the number you want to convert to an absolute value.

EVEN, ODD, INT, & ABS FUNCTIONS

The SQRT function

The SQRT function (**Figure 40**) calculates the square root of a number. It uses the following syntax:

SQRT(number)

The number argument, which is required, is the number you want to find the square root of.

✔ Tip

- You'll get a #NUM! error message if you try to use the SQRT function to calculate the square root of a negative number (**Figure 40**). Prevent the error by using the ABS function in the formula (**Figure 41**).

The PI function

The PI function (**Figure 42**) returns the value of pi, accurate up to 14 decimal places. It uses the following syntax:

PI( )

The RAND function

The RAND (**Figure 43**) function generates a random number greater than or equal to 0 and less than 1 each time the worksheet is calculated. It uses the following syntax:

RAND( )

✔ Tips

- Although neither the PI nor RAND function have arguments, if you fail to include the parentheses, you'll get a #NAME? error.

- The results of a formula using the RAND function changes each time the worksheet is recalculated.

	A	B	C
1	Number	Square Root	
2	36	6	=SQRT(A2)
3	22	4.69041576	=SQRT(A3)
4	-10	#NUM!	=SQRT(A4)
5			

Figure 40 Use the SQRT function to find the square root of a number.

	A	B	C
1	Number	Square Root	
2	36	6	=SQRT(ABS(A2))
3	22	4.69041576	=SQRT(ABS(A3))
4	-10	3.16227766	=SQRT(ABS(A4))
5			

Figure 41 By combining the SQRT and ABS functions, you can prevent #NUM! errors when calculating the square root of a negative number. The formulas in column *B* are shown in column *C*.

Figure 42 The PI function calculates pi to 14 decimal places, although only 9 decimal places appear by default.

	A	B	C	D
1	Low	High	Random	
2	0	1	0.39660999	=RAND()
3	0	1000	269.047871	=RAND()*(B3-A3)+A3
4	36	42	41.7868966	=RAND()*(B4-A4)+A4
5	3458	4835	4188.45821	=RAND()*(B5-A5)+A5
6				

Figure 43 The RAND function can be used alone or as part of a formula to generate a random number within a range. The formulas in column *C* are shown in column *D*.

- To generate a random number between two numbers (low and high), write a formula like this:

  =RAND()*(high–low)+low

  See **Figure 43** for some examples.

	A	B	C	D	E
1		Radians		Degrees	
2	Entry	1		45	
3					
4	Convert to Radians			0.78539816	=RADIANS(D2)
5	Convert to Degrees	57.2957795	=DEGREES(B2)		
6					
7	Sine	0.84147098	=SIN(D2)	0.70710678	=SIN(RADIANS(D2))
8	Arcsine	1.57079633	=ASIN(D2)	0.90333911	=ASIN(RADIANS(D2))
9	Cosine	0.54030231	=COS(D2)	0.70710678	=COS(RADIANS(D2))
10	Arccosine	0	=ACOS(D2)	0.66745722	=ACOS(RADIANS(D2))
11	Tangent	1.55740772	=TAN(D2)	1	=TAN(RADIANS(D2))
12	Arctangent	0.78539816	=ATAN(D2)	0.66577375	=ATAN(RADIANS(D2))
13					

Figure 44 This example shows several trig functions in action. The formulas for columns *B* and *D* are shown in columns *C* and *E*.

The RADIANS & DEGREES functions

The RADIANS function converts degrees to radians. The DEGREES function converts radians to degrees. They use the following syntax:

RADIANS(angle)

DEGREES(angle)

The angle argument, which is required, is the angle you want converted. Use degrees in the RADIANS function and radians in the DEGREES function. Both are illustrated in **Figure 44**.

The SIN function

The SIN function (**Figure 44**) calculates the sine of an angle. It uses the following syntax:

SIN(number)

The number argument, which is required, is the angle, in radians, for which you want the sine calculated.

The COS function

The COS function (**Figure 44**) calculates the cosine of an angle. It uses the following syntax:

COS(number)

The number argument, which is required, is the angle, in radians, for which you want the cosine calculated.

The TAN function

The TAN function (**Figure 44**) calculates the tangent of an angle. It uses the following syntax:

TAN(number)

The number argument, which is required, is the angle, in radians, for which you want the tangent calculated.

✔ Tip

■ To calculate the arcsine, arccosine, or arctangent of an angle, use the ASIN, ACOS, or ATAN function (**Figure 44**). Each works the same as its counterpart.

Statistical Functions

Excel's statistical functions make it easy to perform complex statistical analyses. Here's a handful of the functions I think you'll use most.

✔ Tips

- Excel's AVERAGE function does not include empty cells when calculating the average for a range of cells.

- Although the AVERAGE, MEDIAN, MODE, MIN, and MAX functions can each accept up to 30 arguments separated by commas, only one argument is required.

- You can use the AutoSum button's menu on the Standard toolbar (**Figure 22**) to enter a function using the AVERAGE, COUNT, MAX, and MIN functions.

The AVERAGE function

The AVERAGE function (**Figure 45**) calculates the average or mean of its arguments. It uses the following syntax:

  AVERAGE(number1,number2,**...)**

The MEDIAN function

The MEDIAN function (**Figure 45**) calculates the median of its arguments. The median is the "halfway point" of the numbers—half the numbers have higher values and half have lower values. The MEDIAN function uses the following syntax:

  MEDIAN(number1,number2,**...)**

	A	B	C
1	*Product Inventory*		
2			
3	**Item Name**	**Price**	
4	Dogzilla	14.99	
5	Oceanic	15.99	
6	Delayed Impact	8.99	
7	Mask of Zero	24.99	
8	Genus II	19.99	
9	Eisenhower	19.99	
10	Men in White	22.99	
11	Loaded Weapon I	13.99	
12			
13	**Average**	17.74	=AVERAGE(B4:B11)
14	**Median**	17.99	=MEDIAN(B4:B11)
15	**Mode**	19.99	=MODE(B4:B11)
16	**Minimum**	8.99	=MAX(B4:B11)
17	**Maximum**	24.99	=MIN(B4:B11)

Figure 45 This example shows a few of Excel's statistical functions at work. The formulas for column *B* are shown in column *C*.

	A	B	C
1			
2		6/30/1999	
3		154.69	
4		chocolate	
5			
6		-475.69852	
7		45	
8		ice cream	
9		$ 75.00	
10			
11	Blank Cells	5	=COUNT(B2:B9)
12	Values	7	=COUNTA(B2:B9)

Figure 46 This example of the COUNT and COUNTA functions illustrates that while the COUNT function counts only cells containing numbers (including dates and times), the COUNTA function counts *all* non-blank cells. The formulas in column *B* are shown in column *C*.

The MODE function

The MODE function (**Figure 45**) returns the mode of its arguments. The mode is the most common value. The MODE function uses the following syntax:

MODE(number1,number2,...)

If there are no repeated values, Excel returns a #NUM! error.

The MIN & MAX functions

The MIN function (**Figure 45**) returns the minimum value of its arguments while the MAX function returns the maximum value of its arguments. They use the following syntax:

MIN(number1,number2,...)

MAX(number1,number2,...)

The COUNT & COUNTA functions

The COUNT function counts how many numbers are referenced by its arguments. The COUNTA function counts how many values are referenced by its arguments. Although this may sound like the same thing, it isn't—COUNT includes only numbers or formulas resulting in numbers while COUNTA includes any non-blank cell. **Figure 46** shows an example that clarifies the difference.

The COUNT and COUNTA functions use the following syntax:

COUNT(number1,number2,...)

COUNTA(number1,number2,...)

Although either function can accept up to 30 arguments separated by commas, only one is required.

MODE, MIN, MAX, COUNT, & COUNTA FUNCTIONS

The STDEV & STDEVP functions

Standard deviation is a statistical measurement of how much values vary from the average or mean for the group. The STDEV function calculates the standard deviation based on a random sample of the entire population. The STDEVP function calculates the standard deviation based on the entire population. **Figure 47** shows an example of each.

The STDEV and STDEVP functions use the following syntax:

STDEV(number1,number2,...)

STDEVP(number1,number2,...)

Although either function can accept up to 30 arguments separated by commas, only one is required.

✔ Tip

■ To get accurate results from the STDEVP function, the arguments must include data for the entire population.

	A	B	C
1	*Product Inventory*		
2			
3	**Item Name**	**Price**	
4	Self	14.99	
5	Finding Meano	15.99	
6	Kill Phil: Take 1	8.99	
7	Lost in Transmission	24.99	
8	Closed Cell	19.99	
9	Toothpick Men	19.99	
10	Runaway Judge	22.99	
11	Overworld	13.99	
12			
13	**Average**	17.74	=AVERAGE(B4:B11)
14	**STDEV**	5.230406	=STDEV(B4:B11)
15	**STDVP**	4.892596	=STDEVP(B4:B11)
16			

Figure 47 In this example, the STDEV function assumes that the range is a random sample from a larger population of information. The STDEVP function assumes that the same data is the entire population. That's why the results differ. The formulas in column *B* are shown in column *C*.

STDEV & STDEVP FUNCTIONS

	A	B	C
1	*Depreciation Comparison*		
2			
3	Cost	$ 5,000.00	
4	Salvage Value	$ 250.00	
5	Life (in years)	5	
6			
7	Year	1	
8	Straight Line	$950.00	=SLN(B3,B4,B5)
9	Declining Balance	$2,255.00	=DB(B3,B4,B5,B7)
10	Double Declining Balan	$2,000.00	=DDB(B3,B4,B5,B7)
11	Sum of the Year's Digits	$1,583.33	=SYD(B3,B4,B5,B7)

Figure 48 A simple worksheet lets you compare different methods of depreciation using the SLN, DB, DDB, and SYD functions. The formulas in column *B* are shown in column *C*.

Financial Functions

Excel's financial functions enable you to calculate depreciation, evaluate investment opportunities, or calculate the payments on a loan. On the next few pages, I tell you about a few of the functions I think you'll find useful.

The SLN function

The SLN function (**Figure 48**) calculates straight line depreciation for an asset. It uses the following syntax:

SLN(cost,salvage,life)

Cost is the acquisition cost of the asset, salvage is the salvage or scrap value, and life is the useful life expressed in years or months. All three arguments are required.

The DB function

The DB function (**Figure 48**) calculates declining balance depreciation for an asset. It uses the following syntax:

DB(cost,salvage,life,period,month)

The cost, salvage, and life arguments are the same as for the SLN function. Period, which must be expressed in the same units as life, is the period for which you want to calculate depreciation. These first four arguments are required. Month is the number of months in the first year of the asset's life. If omitted, 12 is assumed.

The SYD function

The SYD function (**Figure 48**) calculates the sum-of-years' digits depreciation for an asset. It uses the following syntax:

SYD(cost,salvage,life,period)

The cost, salvage, life, and period arguments are the same as for the DB and DDB functions. All arguments are required.

The DDB function

The DDB function (**Figure 48**) calculates the double-declining balance depreciation for an asset. It uses the following syntax:

DDB(cost,salvage,life,period,factor)

The cost, salvage, life, and period arguments are the same as for the DB function and are required. Factor is the rate at which the balance declines. If omitted, 2 is assumed.

SLN, DB, SYD, & DDB FUNCTIONS

The PMT function

The PMT function calculates the periodic payment for an annuity based on constant payments and interest rate. This function is commonly used for two purposes: to calculate the monthly payments on a loan and to calculate the monthly contribution necessary to reach a specific savings goal.

The PMT function uses the following syntax:

PMT(rate,nper,pv,fv,type**)**

Rate is the interest rate per period, nper is the total number of periods, and pv is the present value or current worth of the total payments. These three arguments are required. The fv argument is the future value or balance desired at the end of the payments. If omitted, 0 is assumed. Type indicates when payments are due: use 0 for payments at the end of the period and 1 for payments at the beginning of the period. If omitted, 0 is assumed.

	A	B
1	Loan Amount	20000
2	Annual Interest Rate	11.50%
3	Loan Term (in Months)	48
4		
5	Monthly Payment	

Figure 49 A basic structure for a worksheet that calculates loan payments.

	A	B
1	Loan Amount	20000
2	Annual Interest Rate	11.50%
3	Loan Term (in Months)	48
4		
5	Monthly Payment	($521.78)

Figure 50 The loan payment worksheet after entering a formula with the PMT function.

	A	B
1	Loan Amount	25000
2	Annual Interest Rate	11.50%
3	Loan Term (in Months)	48
4		
5	Monthly Payment	($652.23)

Figure 51 Playing "what-if." In this example, I increased the loan amount to see how much more the monthly payment would be.

To calculate loan payments

1. Enter the text and number values shown in **Figure 49** in a worksheet. If desired, use your own amounts.

2. Enter the following formula in cell *B5*: =PMT(B2/12,B3,B1)

   This formula uses only the first three arguments of the PMT function. The rate argument is divided by 12 to arrive at a monthly interest rate since the number of periods is expressed in months and payments will be made monthly (all time units must match).

3. Press Enter or click the Enter button ✓ on the formula bar.

   The result of the formula appears in the cell as a negative number (**Figure 50**) because it is an outgoing cash flow. (A minus sign or parentheses indicates a negative number.)

✔ Tips

- If you prefer, you can use the Insert Function and Function Arguments dialogs to write the formula in step 2. Be sure to include the formula *B2/12* in the rate text box. Leave the fv and type text boxes blank.

- You can calculate loan payments without creating a whole worksheet—simply enter values rather than cell references as arguments for the PMT function. But using cell references makes it easy to play "what-if"—see how payments change when the loan amount, rate, and number of periods change. **Figure 51** shows an example.

CALCULATING LOAN PAYMENTS

To create an amortization table

1. Create a loan payment worksheet following the steps on the previous page.

2. Enter text and number values for headings as shown in **Figure 52**. Make sure there is a row with a payment number for each month of the loan term in cell *B3*.

3. In cell *B8*, enter =*B1*.

4. In cell *C8*, enter the following formula:
   =*ROUND(B8*$B$2/12,2)*

   This formula calculates the interest for the period and rounds it to two decimal places.

5. In cell *D8*, enter the following formula:
   =–*$B$5–C8*

   This formula calculates the amount of principal paid for the current month.

6. In cell *B9*, enter the following formula:
   =*ROUND(B8–D8,2)*

   This formula calculates the current month's beginning balance, rounded to two decimal places.

   At this point, your worksheet should look like the one in **Figure 53**.

7. Use the fill handle to copy the formula in cell *B9* down the column for each month.

8. Use the fill handle to copy the formulas in cells *C8* and *D8* down the columns for each month.

   Your amortization table is complete. It should look like the one in **Figure 54**.

✔ Tips

■ If desired, you can add column totals at the bottom of columns *C* and *D* to total interest (you may be shocked) and principal (which should match cell *B1*).

	A	B	C	D
1	Loan Amount	20000		
2	Annual Interest Rate	11.50%		
3	Loan Term (in Months)	48		
4				
5	Monthly Payment	($521.78)		
6				
7	Payment Number	Beg Balance	Interest	Principal
8	1			
9	2			
10	3			
11	4			
12	5			
13	6			
14	7			

Figure 52 To create an amortization table, start with this simple worksheet.

	A	B	C	D
1	Loan Amount	20000		
2	Annual Interest Rate	11.50%		
3	Loan Term (in Months)	48		
4				
5	Monthly Payment	($521.78)		
6				
7	Payment Number	Beg Balance	Interest	Principal
8	1	20000	191.67	$330.11
9	2	$19,669.89		
10	3			
11	4			
12	5			
13	6			
14	7			

Figure 53 Add formulas to calculate interest, principal, and beginning balance.

	A	B	C	D
1	Loan Amount	20000		
2	Annual Interest Rate	11.50%		
3	Loan Term (in Months)	48		
4				
5	Monthly Payment	($521.78)		
6				
7	Payment Number	Beg Balance	Interest	Principal
8	1	20000	191.67	$330.11
9	2	$19,669.89	188.5	$333.28
10	3	$19,336.61	185.31	$336.47
11	4	$19,000.14	182.08	$339.70
12	5	$18,660.44	178.83	$342.95
13	6	$18,317.49	175.54	$346.24
14	7	$17,971.25	172.22	$349.56
15	8	$17,621.69	168.87	$352.91
16	9	$17,268.78	165.49	$356.29
17	10	$16,912.49	162.08	$359.70
18	11	$16,552.79	158.63	$363.15
19	12	$16,189.64	155.15	$366.63
20	13	$15,823.01	151.64	$370.14

Figure 54 Then copy the formulas down each column for all months of the loan term.

■ I tell you more about using the fill handle in **Chapter 3**.

	A	B
1	Desired Amount	30000
2	Annual Interest Rate	8.25%
3	Months	120
4		
5	Monthly Contribution	
6		

Figure 55 A basic structure for a worksheet to calculate contributions to reach a savings goal.

	A	B
1	Desired Amount	30000
2	Annual Interest Rate	8.25%
3	Months	120
4		
5	Monthly Contribution	($161.71)
6		

Figure 56 The PMT function calculates the monthly contribution.

	A	B
1	Desired Amount	50000
2	Annual Interest Rate	8.25%
3	Months	120
4		
5	Monthly Contribution	($269.51)
6		

Figure 57 Change one value and the result of the formula changes.

To calculate contributions to reach a savings goal

1. Enter the text and number values shown in **Figure 55** in a worksheet. If desired, use your own amounts.

2. Enter the following formula in cell *B5*:
   =PMT(B2/12,B3,,B1)

   This formula uses the first four arguments of the PMT function, although the pv argument is left blank—that's why there are two commas after *B3*. The rate argument is divided by 12 to arrive at a monthly interest rate.

3. Press ⟨Enter⟩ or click the Enter button ☑ on the formula bar.

   The result of the formula is expressed as a negative number (**Figure 56**) because it is an outgoing cash flow. (A minus sign or parentheses indicates a negative number.)

✔ Tips

- If you prefer, you can use the Insert Function and Function Arguments dialogs to write the formula in step 2. Be sure to include the formula *B2/12* in the rate text box. Leave the pv and type text boxes blank.

- You can calculate the amount of a monthly contribution to reach a savings goal without creating a whole worksheet—simply enter values rather than cell references as arguments for the PMT function. But using cell references makes it easy to play "what-if"—see how contributions change when the desired amount, rate, and number of periods change. **Figure 57** shows an example.

- To force an outgoing cash flow to be expressed as a positive number, simply include a minus sign (-) right after the equals sign (=) at the beginning of the formula.

CALCULATING SAVINGS GOAL CONTRIBUTIONS

The FV function

The FV function (**Figure 58**) calculates the future value of an investment with constant cash flows and a constant interest rate. It uses the following syntax:

FV(rate,nper,pmt,pv,type**)**

Rate is the interest rate per period, nper is the total number of periods, and pmt is the amount of the periodic payments. These three arguments are required. The pv argument is the present value of the payments. Type indicates when payments are due: use 0 for payments at the end of the period and 1 for payments at the beginning of the period. If either optional argument is omitted, 0 is assumed.

The PV function

The PV function (**Figure 59**) calculates the total amount that a series of payments in the future is worth now. It uses the following syntax:

PV(rate,nper,pmt,fv,type**)**

The rate, nper, pmt, and type arguments are the same as in the FV function. Only the first three are required. The fv argument is the amount left after the payments have been made. If omitted, 0 is assumed.

The IRR function

The IRR function (**Figure 60**) calculates the internal rate of return for a series of periodic cash flows. It uses the following syntax:

IRR(values,guess**)**

The values argument, which is required, is a range of cells containing the cash flows. The guess argument, which is optional, is for your guess of what the result could be. Although seldom necessary, guess could help Excel come up with an answer when performing complex calculations.

	A	B
1	Monthly Payment	150
2	Annual Interest Rate	8.50%
3	Number of Months	12
4		
5	Future Value	($1,871.81)
6		=FV(B@/12,B3,B1)
7		

Figure 58 Use the FV function to calculate the future value of constant cash flows, like those of periodic payroll savings deductions. The formula in cell *B5* is shown in cell *B6*.

	A	B
1	Initial Investment	-25000
2		
3	Monthly Cash In	200
4	Annual Interest Rate	9%
5	Number of Months	360
6		
7	Present Value	($24,856.37)
8		=PV(B4/12,B5,B3)

Figure 59 This example uses the PV function to determine whether an investment is a good one. (It isn't because the present value is less than the initial investment.) The formula in cell *B7* is shown in cell *B8*.

	A	B
1	Year 1	-500
2	Year 2	150
3	Year 3	100
4	Year 4	125
5	Year 5	135
6	Year 6	200
7		
8	Internal Rate of Return:	12%
9		=IRR(B1:B6)
10		

Figure 60 This worksheet calculates the internal rate of return of an initial $500 investment that pays out cash over the next few years. The formula in cell *B8* is shown in cell *B9*.

	A	B	C
1	Commissions Repo		
2			
3		**Rates**	
4	Over $400	15%	
5	Up to $400	10%	
6			
7		**Sales**	**Amt. Due**
8	John	443.16	
9	Jean	512.84	
10	Joe	328.69	
11	Joan	401.98	
12		1686.67	

Figure 61 To try the IF function for yourself, start with a basic worksheet like this.

	A	B	C
1	Commissions Repo		
2			
3		**Rates**	
4	Over $400	15%	
5	Up to $400	10%	
6			
7		**Sales**	**Amt. Due**
8	John	443.16	66.47
9	Jean	512.84	
10	Joe	328.69	
11	Joan	401.98	
12		1686.67	

Figure 62 Enter the formula with the IF function in cell C8.

	A	B	C
1	Commissions Repo		
2			
3		**Rates**	
4	Over $400	15%	
5	Up to $400	10%	
6			
7		**Sales**	**Amt. Due**
8	John	443.16	66.47
9	Jean	512.84	76.93
10	Joe	328.69	32.87
11	Joan	401.98	60.3
12		1686.67	

Figure 63 Then use the fill handle to copy the formula to the other cells.

Logical Functions

You can use Excel's logical functions to evaluate conditions and act accordingly. Here's the most useful one: IF.

The IF function

The IF function evaluates a condition and returns one of two different values depending on whether the condition is met (true) or not met (false). It uses the following syntax:

IF(logical_test,value_if_true,value_if_false**)**

The logical_test argument is the condition you want to meet. This argument is required. The value_if_true and value_if_false arguments are the values to return if the condition is met or not met. If value_if_false is omitted and the result is false, 0 (zero) is returned.

The following example uses the IF function to calculate commissions based on two different commission rates.

To use the IF function

1. Create a worksheet with text and number values as shown in **Figure 61**.
2. In cell *C8*, enter the following formula: *=IF(B8>400,$B$4*B8,$B$5*B8)*

   This formula begins by evaluating the sales amount to see if it's over $400. If it is, it moves to the value_if_true argument and multiplies the higher commission rate by the sales amount. If it isn't, it moves on to the value_if_false argument and multiplies the lower commission rate by the sales amount.
3. Press Enter or click the Enter button ☑ on the formula bar to complete the formula (**Figure 62**).
4. Use the fill handle to copy the formula down the column for the rest of the salespeople (**Figure 63**).

Lookup and Reference Functions

Excel's lookup and reference functions return values based on information stored elsewhere in the workbook or in a linked worksheet.

The VLOOKUP & HLOOKUP functions

The VLOOKUP (**Figures 64** and **65**) and HLOOKUP functions return information based on data stored in a lookup table. The function attempts to match a value in one of its arguments to values in the first column (VLOOKUP) or first row (HLOOKUP) of the lookup table. If it finds a match, it returns the associated value.

The VLOOKUP and HLOOKUP functions use the following syntax:

**VLOOKUP(lookup_value,table_array,
col_index_num,range_lookup)**

**HLOOKUP(lookup_value,table_array,
row_index_num,range_lookup)**

Lookup_value is the value you want to match in the table. Table_array is the cell reference for the lookup table. Col_index_num or row_index_num is the number of the column or row, relative to the table, that contains the values you want returned. These three arguments are required. Range_lookup, which is not required, tells Excel what it should do if it can't match the lookup_value. There are two options for this argument: TRUE tells Excel to return the value associated with the next lowest value; FALSE tells Excel to return the #N/A error value. If omitted, TRUE is assumed.

✔ Tip

- The first column or row of the lookup table must be sorted in ascending order for the VLOOKUP or HLOOKUP function to work properly.

	A	B	C	D
1	Item Number:	L-482		
2	Price:	19.99	=VLOOKUP(B1,A5:D12,4,FALSE)	
3				
4	**Item Number**	**Qty**	**Item Name**	**Price**
5	C-058	684	Closed Cell	13.99
6	F-571	341	Finding Meano	8.99
7	K-845	415	Kill Phil: Take 1	19.99
8	L-482	167	Lost in Transmission	19.99
9	O-108	581	Overworld	15.99
10	R-400	189	Runaway Judge	24.99
11	S-439	159	Self	14.99
12	T-473	218	Toothpick Men	22.99

Figure 64 This example illustrates the VLOOKUP function. When you enter an item number in cell *B1*, the formula in *B2* attempts to match it to a value in the first column of the lookup table below it *(A5: D12)*. If it finds a match, it returns the value in the fourth column of the same row as the match. The formula in cell *B2* is shown in cell *C2*.

	A	B	C	D
1	Item Number:	M-234		
2	Price:	#N/A	=VLOOKUP(B1,A5:D12,4,FALSE)	
3				
4	**Item Number**	**Qty**	**Item Name**	**Price**
5	C-058	684	Closed Cell	13.99
6	F-571	341	Finding Meano	8.99
7	K-845	415	Kill Phil: Take 1	19.99
8	L-482	167	Lost in Transmission	19.99
9	O-108	581	Overworld	15.99
10	R-400	189	Runaway Judge	24.99
11	S-439	159	Self	14.99
12	T-473	218	Toothpick Men	22.99

Figure 65 If the formula in *B2* doesn't find a match, it returns the *#N/A* error value, since the optional range_lookup argument is set to *FALSE*.

	A	B	C	D	E
		Values			
1	Test	673.24	anchovy		#N/A
2	Blank Cell	FALSE	FALSE	TRUE	FALSE
3	Error other than #N/A	FALSE	FALSE	FALSE	FALSE
4	Any Error	FALSE	FALSE	FALSE	TRUE
5	Logical Value	FALSE	FALSE	FALSE	FALSE
6	#N/A Error	FALSE	FALSE	FALSE	TRUE
7	Not Text	TRUE	FALSE	TRUE	TRUE
8	Number	TRUE	FALSE	FALSE	FALSE
9	Cell Reference	TRUE	TRUE	TRUE	TRUE
10	Text	FALSE	TRUE	FALSE	FALSE

Figure 66 In this example, the IS functions were used (in the order shown to the right) to evaluate the contents of the cells in row *1* of the worksheet. The results of each function appear below the value.

	A	B
1	**Enter Your Name:**	
2		
3	**Message:**	You did not enter your name.

	A	B
1	**Enter Your Name:**	Maria
2		
3	**Message:**	Hello Maria

Figures 67 & 68 In this silly example, the formula in cell *B3*, *=IF(ISTEXT(B1), "Hello "&B1, "You did not enter your name. ")*, scolds the user for not entering a name (top), then greets her by name when she does enter it (bottom).

Information Functions

Excel's information functions return information about other cells.

The IS functions

Excel's IS functions (**Figure 66**) use the following syntax:

ISBLANK(value)

ISERR(value)

ISERROR(value)

ISLOGICAL(value)

ISNA(value)

ISNONTEXT(value)

ISNUMBER(value)

ISREF(value)

ISTEXT(value)

In each case, Excel tests for a different thing. The value argument is the value or cell reference to be tested.

✔ Tip

■ Use an IS function in conjunction with the IF function to return a value based on the condition of a cell (**Figures 67** and **68**).

Date and Time Functions

Excel's date and time functions are designed specifically to work with dates and times. I tell you about the most useful ones here.

✔ Tips

- Excel treats dates and times as serial numbers. This means that although you may enter information as a date or time—like 10/14/02 or 2:45 PM—Excel converts what you type into a number for its own internal use (see **Table 1**). A date is the number of days since January 1, 1900. A time is the portion of a day since midnight. Excel's formatting makes the number look like a date or time. I tell you about cell formatting in **Chapter 6**.

- You can change Excel's date system from the Windows 1900 system to the Macintosh 1904 system. Choose Tools > Options, click the Calculation tab, and turn on the 1904 date system check box (**Figure 69**). This will change the serial numbers for dates for all worksheets in the current workbook. I tell you more about the Options dialog in **Chapter 15**.

- If you enter a date early in the 21st century, such as *5/15/04*, Excel assumes the year is 2004, not 1904.

The DATE function

The DATE function (**Figure 3**) returns the serial number for a date. It uses the following syntax:

=DATE(year,month,day)

The year argument is the year number, the month argument is the month number, and the day argument is the day number. All arguments are required.

Table 1

Examples of How Excel Interprets Dates and Times	
You Enter	**Excel "Sees"**
10/14/2002	37543
6/29/1957	21000
2:45 PM	0.61458333
10:02:56 AM	0.4187037
1/1/1900	0
12:00 AM	0

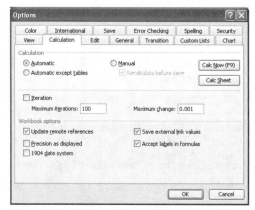

Figure 69 The Options dialog enables you to switch between the standard Windows 1900 date system and the Macintosh 1904 date system.

	A	B
1	First Date	5/7/1995
2	Second Date	10/14/1996
3	Days Between	526
4		=B2-B1

Figure 70 Calculating the number of days between two dates is as simple as subtracting the contents of one cell from another. The formula in cell *B3* is shown in cell *B4*.

	A	B
1	6/9/2001 6:35	=NOW()
2	6/9/2001	=TODAY()

Figure 71 The NOW function returns the current date and time while the TODAY function returns just the current date.

	A	B	C
1		6/29/1997	
2	Day	29	=DAY(B1)
3	Weekday	1	=WEEKDAY(B1)
4	Month	6	=MONTH(B1)
5	Year	1997	=YEAR(B1)

Figure 72 The DAY, WEEKDAY, MONTH, and YEAR functions extract portions of a date. The formulas in column *B* are shown in column *C*.

To calculate the number of days between two dates

Enter the two dates into separate cells of a worksheet, then write a formula using the subtraction operator (-) to subtract the earlier date from the later date (**Figure 70**).

Or

In a worksheet cell, write a formula using the date function, like this:
=DATE(01,10,15)-DATE(01,5,8)

The NOW & TODAY functions

The NOW and TODAY functions (**Figure 71**) return the serial number for the current date and time (NOW) or current date (TODAY). Results are automatically formatted and will change each time the worksheet is recalculated or opened. They use the following syntax:

NOW( )

TODAY( )

Although there are no arguments, the parentheses characters must be included.

The DAY, WEEKDAY, MONTH, & YEAR functions

The DAY, WEEKDAY, MONTH, and YEAR functions (**Figure 72**) return the day of the month, the day of the week, the month number, or the year number for a serial number. They use the following syntax:

DAY(serial_number)

WEEKDAY(serial_number)

MONTH(serial_number)

YEAR(serial_number)

The serial_number argument can be a cell reference, number, or date written as text, like *10/14/02* or *15-Apr-04*.

DATE & TIME FUNCTIONS

Text Functions

Excel's text functions enable you to extract, convert, concatenate, and get information about text. I tell you about a few of the more commonly used ones here.

The LOWER, UPPER, & PROPER functions

The LOWER, UPPER, and PROPER functions (**Figure 73**) convert text to lowercase, uppercase, and title case. They use the following syntax:

LOWER(text)

UPPER(text)

PROPER(text)

The text argument, which is required, is the text you want converted.

The LEFT, RIGHT, & MID functions

The LEFT, RIGHT, and MID functions (**Figure 74**) return the leftmost, rightmost, or middle characters of a text string. They use the following syntax:

LEFT(text,num_chars)

RIGHT(text,num_chars)

MID(text,start_num,num_chars)

The text argument, which is required, is the text from which characters should be extracted. The num_chars argument is the number of characters you want extracted. If omitted from the LEFT or RIGHT function, 1 is assumed. The MID function has an additional argument, start_num, which is the number of the first character from which you want to extract text. The MID function requires all arguments.

	A	B	C
1	Original Text	This IS an eXample.	
2	Lowercase	this is an example.	=LOWER(B1)
3	Uppercase	THIS IS AN EXAMPLE.	=UPPER(B1)
4	Title Case	This Is An Example.	=PROPER(B1)

Figure 73 Use the LOWER, UPPER, and PROPER functions to change the case of text. The formulas in column B are shown in column C.

	A	B	C
1	Original Text	Mississippi	
2	First 4 characters	Miss	=LEFT(B1,4)
3	Last 4 characters	ippi	=RIGHT(B1,4)
4	4 characters starting with 3rd character	ssis	=MID(B1,3,4)

Figure 74 Use the LEFT, RIGHT, and MID functions to extract characters from text. The formulas in column B are shown in column C.

	A	B	C
1	Last Name	First Name	Full Name
2	Twain	Mark	Twain Mark
3			=CONCATENATE(A2," ",B2)

Figure 75 Use the CONCATENATE function to join strings of text. The formula in cell *C2* is shown in cell *C3*.

	A	B	C	D
1	Amount Due	124.95		
2	Date Due	8/15/1994		
3				
4	The total amount due is $124.95. Please pay by 08/15/94.			

Figure 76 The formula in cell A4, = *"The total amount due is "&DOLLAR(B1)&". Please pay by "&TEXT(B2,"mm/dd/yy")&". "*, writes a sentence using the contents of two cells, the concatenate operator, and two text functions.

The CONCATENATE Function

The CONCATENATE function (**Figure 75**) joins or concatenates two or more strings of text. It uses the following syntax:

CONCATENATE(text1,text2,...)

Each text argument can include single cell references, text, or numbers you want to join. The CONCATENATE function can accept up to 30 arguments, but only two are required.

✔ Tips

- Excel recognizes the ampersand character (&) as a concatenation operator in formulas. You can concatenate text by including an ampersand between cells or text strings in a formula, like this: *=B2&" "&A2*

- If you want spaces between the strings, be sure to include the space character, between double quote characters, as an argument (**Figure 75**).

- Creative use of the CONCATENATE function or operator makes it possible to give documents a personal touch. **Figure 76** shows an example.

CONCATENATING TEXT

Formatting Cells

Southwest Division				
First Quarter Sales				
	Jan	Feb	Mar	Total
John	1425	1354	1674	4453
Jean	1354	1297	1152	3803
Joe	1725	1642	1657	5024
Joan	951	1258	1499	3708
Totals	5455	5551	5982	16988

Figure 1 While content should be more important than appearance, you can bet that this worksheet won't get as much attention ...

Southwest Division			
First Quarter Sales			
	Jan	Feb	Mar	Total
John	$ 1,425.00	$ 1,354.00	$ 1,674.00	$ 4,453.00
Jean	1,354.00	1,297.00	1,152.00	3,803.00
Joe	1,725.00	1,642.00	1,657.00	5,024.00
Joan	951.00	1,258.00	1,499.00	3,708.00
Totals	$ 5,455.00	$ 5,551.00	$ 5,982.00	$ 16,988.00

Figure 2 ... as this one.

✔ Tips

- Excel may automatically apply formatting to cells, depending on what you enter. For example, if you use a date function, Excel formats the results of the function as a date. You can change Excel's formatting at any time to best meet your needs.

- Most formatting is applied to cells, not cell contents. If you use the Clear Contents command to clear a cell, the formatting remains and will be applied to whatever data is next entered into it.

Formatting Basics

To paraphrase an old Excel mentor of mine, formatting a worksheet is like putting on its makeup. The worksheet's contents may be perfectly correct, but by applying formatting, you can make a better impression on the people who see it (**Figures 1** and **2**).

Excel offers a wide range of formatting options you can use to beautify your worksheets:

- ◆ **Number formatting** lets you change the appearance of numbers, dates, and times.

- ◆ **Alignment** lets you change the way cell contents are aligned within the cell.

- ◆ **Font formatting** lets you change the appearance of text and number characters.

- ◆ **Borders** let you add lines around cells.

- ◆ **Patterns** let you add color, shading, and patterns to cells.

- ◆ **Column and row formatting** let you change column width and row height.

You can apply formatting to cells using a variety of techniques: with Formatting toolbar buttons, shortcut keys, menu commands, or the Conditional Formatting or AutoFormat features.

Number Formatting

By default, Excel applies the General number format to worksheet cells. This format displays numbers just as they're entered (**Figure 3**).

Excel offers a wide variety of predefined number formatting options for different purposes:

- **Number** formats are used for general number display.

- **Currency** formats are used for monetary values.

- **Accounting** formats are used to line up columns of monetary values.

- **Date** formats are used to display dates.

- **Time** formats are used to display times.

- **Percentage** formats are used to display percentages.

- **Fraction** formats are used to display decimal values as fractions.

- **Scientific** format is used to display values in scientific notation.

- **Text** format is used to display cell contents as text, the way it was entered.

- **Special** formats include a variety of special purpose formatting options.

- **Custom** lets you create your own number format using formatting codes.

You can change number formatting of selected cells with options on the Formatting toolbar (**Figure 5**) or in the Number tab of the Format Cells dialog (**Figures 9** through **12**).

1548.36	
12458	
14.2	
-354.85	
116.028	
0.2	
1.25459E+14	

Figure 3 General formatting displays the numbers just as they're typed in and uses scientific notation when they're very big.

Number 1	1.5049	$	1.50
Number 2	3.504	$	3.50
	5.0089	$	5.01

Figure 4 The two columns contain identical values, but the column on the right is formatted with the Currency style. Because Excel performs calculations with the numbers underlying any formatting, the total on the right appears incorrect!

✔ Tips

- If the integer part of a number is longer than the width of the cell or 11 digits, General number format displays it in scientific notation (**Figure 3**).

- Number formatting changes only the appearance of a number. Although formatting may remove decimal places from displayed numbers, it does not round numbers. **Figure 4** illustrates this. Use the ROUND function, which I discuss in **Chapter 5**, to round numbers in formulas.

- If you include characters such as dollar signs or percent symbols with a number you enter, Excel automatically assigns an appropriate built-in format to the cell.

To apply number formatting with the Formatting toolbar

To apply one of the predefined number formats on the Formatting toolbar (**Figure 5**), click its button:

Figure 5 The Formatting toolbar offers all kinds of options for formatting worksheet cells.

General		0.15	1163.2	-
Currency Style	$	0.15	$1,163.20	$ ı
Percent Style		15%	116320%	-¹
Comma Style		0.15	1,163.20	ı

Figure 6 Three different numbers, each with one of the Formatting toolbar's number formats applied.

- ◆ **Currency Style** $ displays the number as currency, with a dollar sign, commas, and two decimal places.

- ◆ **Percent Style** % displays the number as a percentage with a percent symbol and two decimal places.

- ◆ **Comma Style** , displays the number with a comma and two decimal places.

Figure 6 shows examples of these formats.

To change the number of decimal places

Click one of the Decimal buttons in the Formatting toolbar (**Figure 5**):

- ◆ **Increase Decimal** displays an additional decimal digit.

- ◆ **Decrease Decimal** displays one less decimal digit.

APPLYING NUMBER FORMATTING

To apply number formatting with the Format Cells dialog

1. Choose Format > Cells (**Figure 7**) or press Ctrl 1.

2. In the Format Cells dialog that appears, click the Number tab to display its options (**Figure 8**).

3. Choose a number format category from the Category scrolling list.

4. Set options in the dialog. The options vary for each category; **Figures 9** through **12** show examples. Check the Sample area to see the number in the active cell with the formatting options you selected applied.

5. Click OK to apply the formatting.

Figure 7
The Format menu offers access to most of the formatting commands discussed in this chapter.

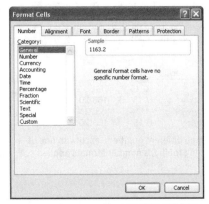

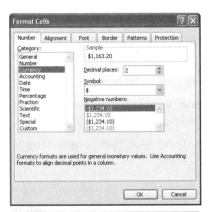

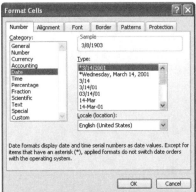

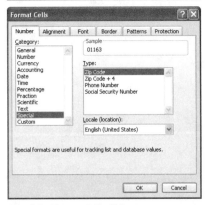

Figures 8, 9, 10, 11, & 12 Examples of options in the Number tab of the Format Cells dialog.

APPLYING NUMBER FORMATTING

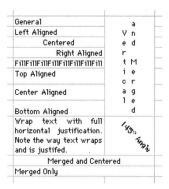

Figure 13 Examples of cells with different alignment options applied.

Jan	Feb
1,254	1,256
1,865	1,736
1,614	1,284
1,987	1,908
6,720	6,184

Figure 14 Headings sometimes look better when they're right aligned (right) rather than centered (left) over columns of numbers.

Alignment

Excel offers a wide variety of options to set the way characters are positioned within a cell (**Figure 13**):

◆ **Text Alignment** options position the text within the cell.

◆ **Orientation** options control the angle at which text appears within the cell.

◆ **Text Control** options control how text appears within the cell.

◆ **Right-to-left** options control the reading order of cell contents. This option is useful for languages that read characters from right-to-left rather than left-to-right.

You can change alignment settings for selected cells with the Formatting toolbar (**Figure 5**) or the Alignment tab of the Format Cells dialog (**Figure 15**).

✔ Tips

■ By default, within each cell, Excel left aligns text and right aligns numbers. This is called General alignment.

■ Although it's common to center headings over columns containing numbers, the work-sheet may actually look better with headings right aligned. **Figure 14** shows an example.

To set text alignment with the Formatting toolbar

Click the Formatting toolbar button for the type of alignment you want to apply:

◆ **Align Left** ▤ aligns cell contents against the left side of the cell.

◆ **Center** ▤ centers cell contents between the left and right sides of the cell.

◆ **Align Right** ▤ aligns cell contents against the right side of the cell.

To set alignment with the Format Cells dialog

1. Choose Format > Cells (**Figure 7**) or press Ctrl 1.

2. The Format Cells dialog appears. If necessary, click the Alignment tab to display its options (**Figure 15**).

3. Choose an option from the Horizontal drop-down list (**Figure 16**):

   ▲ **General** applies default alignment.

   ▲ **Left (Indent)** aligns cell contents against the left side of the cell. It also allows you to indent cell contents.

   ▲ **Center** centers cell contents between the left and right sides of the cell.

   ▲ **Right (Indent)** aligns cell contents against the right side of the cell.

   ▲ **Fill** repeats the cell contents to fill the cell.

   ▲ **Justify** stretches multiple lines of text across the cell so all lines except the last fill the cell from left to right.

   ▲ **Center Across Selection** centers the active cell's contents across the selected cells.

   ▲ **Distributed (Indent)** distributes the cell's contents horizontally within the cell.

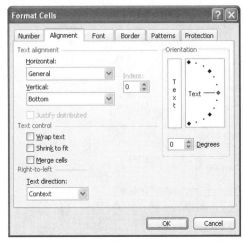

Figure 15 The Alignment tab of the Format cells dialog.

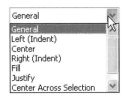

Figure 16
Options on the Horizontal drop-down list.

Figure 17
Options on the Vertical drop-down list.

Figure 18 This cell's contents were indented by clicking the Increase Indent button twice.

Figure 19 To indent text, set Text alignment options like this.

4. Choose an option from the Vertical drop-down list (**Figure 17**):

▲ **Top** aligns cell contents against the top of the cell.

▲ **Center** centers cell contents between the top and bottom of the cell.

▲ **Bottom** aligns cell contents against the bottom of the cell.

▲ **Justify** stretches multiple lines of text from the top to the bottom of the cell.

▲ **Distributed** distributes the cell's contents vertically within the cell.

5. Click OK.

To indent cell contents with the Formatting toolbar

Click the Formatting toolbar button for the indentation change you want:

◆ **Decrease Indent** ⊞ decreases the amount of indentation.

◆ **Increase Indent** ⊞ increases the amount of indentation (**Figure 18**).

To indent cell contents with the Format Cells dialog

1. Choose Format > Cells (**Figure 7**) or press Ctrl 1.

2. In the Format Cells dialog that appears, click the Alignment tab to display its options (**Figure 15**).

3. Choose Left (Indent) from the Horizontal drop-down list (**Figure 16**).

4. In the Indent text box, enter the number of characters by which you want to indent cell contents (**Figure 19**).

5. Click OK.

To set text control options with the Format Cells dialog

1. Choose Format > Cells (**Figure 7**) or press Ctrl 1.

2. In the Format Cells dialog that appears, click the Alignment tab to display its options (**Figure 15**).

3. Turn on any valid combination of the check boxes in the Text control area.

4. Click OK.

✔ Tip

■ As shown in **Figures** 20 through 22, the Wrap text and Shrink to fit options can be used to fit cell contents within a cell.

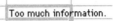

Figure 20 Select a cell with too much information.

Figure 21 Here's the cell from **Figure 20** with Wrap text applied.

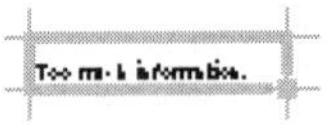

Figure 22 Here's the cell from **Figure 20** with Shrink to fit applied.

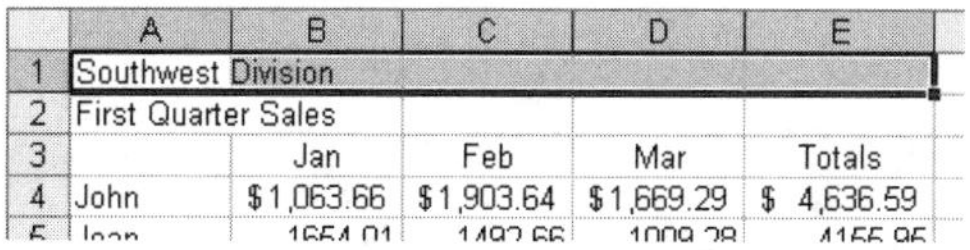

Figure 23 Select the cells you want to merge and center.

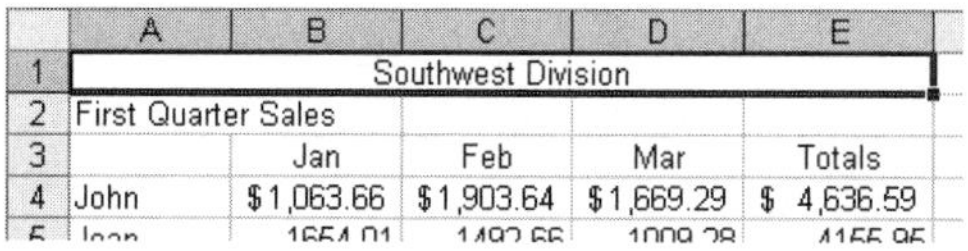

Figure 24 The cells are merged together and the cell contents are centered in the merged cell.

To merge & center cells with the Formatting toolbar

1. Select the cell(s) whose contents you want to center, along with the cells of the columns to the right that you want to center across (**Figure 23**).

2. Click the Merge and Center button 📊 on the Formatting toolbar. The cell contents shift so they're centered between the left and right sides of the selected area (**Figure 24**).

To merge & center cells with the Format Cells dialog

1. Select the cell(s) whose contents you want to center, along with the cells of the columns to the right that you want to center across (**Figure 23**).

2. Choose Format > Cells (**Figure 7**) or press Ctrl 1.

3. In the Format Cells dialog that appears, click the Alignment tab to display its options (**Figure 15**).

4. Choose Center from the Horizontal drop-down list (**Figure 16**).

5. Turn on the Merge cells check box.

6. Click OK. The cell contents shift so they're centered between the left and right sides of the selected area (**Figure 24**).

✔ Tips

■ This technique is handy for centering worksheet titles over the cells in use.

■ You can get similar results by choosing Center Across Selection from the Horizontal drop-down list (**Figure 16**) in step 4 and skipping step 5. The cells, however, are not merged, so an entry into one of the adjacent cells could obscure the centered contents.

MERGING & CENTERING CELLS

To change cell orientation with the Format Cells dialog

1. Choose Format > Cells (**Figure 7**) or press ⌃Ctrl 1.

2. In the Format Cells dialog that appears, click the Alignment tab (**Figure 15**).

3. Set options in the Orientation area (**Figure 25**) using one of these methods:

   ▲ To display text characters one above the other, click the Vertical Orientation button.

   ▲ To display text characters at an angle, drag the red diamond in the rotation area to match the angle you want.

   ▲ To display text characters at an angle, enter an angle value in the Degrees box.

4. Click OK.

✔ Tips

■ You cannot set orientation options if Center Across Selection is chosen from the Horizontal drop-down list (**Figure 16**). Choose another option before you set orientation.

■ You can enter either a positive or negative value in the Degrees box (**Figure 25**).

■ Rotated text appears better when printed than it does on screen (**Figure 25**).

■ Changing the orientation of a cell's contents can change the height of the cell's row (**Figure 26**).

■ Rotating the text in column headings often enables you to decrease column width, thus enabling you to fit more information on screen or on paper. I tell you how to change column width later in this chapter.

Vertical orientation button

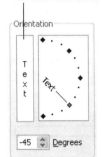

Figure 25
Set options using the orientation area of the Format Cells dialog.

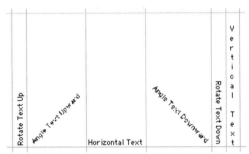

Figure 26 You can achieve a variety of orientation effects by setting options in the Alignment tab of the Format Cells dialog.

CHANGING CELL ORIENTATION

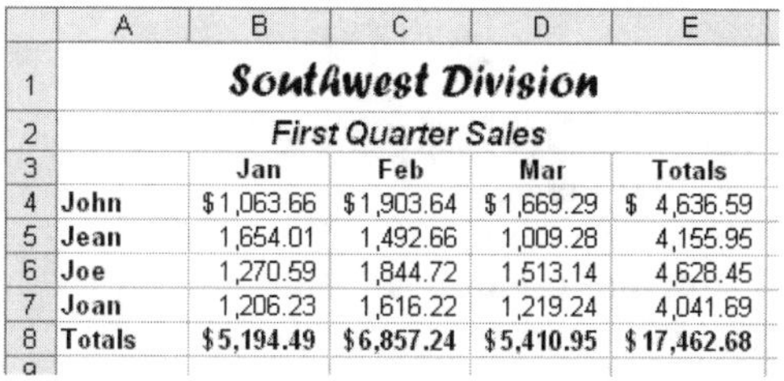

	A	B	C	D	E
1	*Southwest Division*				
2	*First Quarter Sales*				
3		Jan	Feb	Mar	Totals
4	John	$1,063.66	$1,903.64	$1,669.29	$ 4,636.59
5	Jean	1,654.01	1,492.66	1,009.28	4,155.95
6	Joe	1,270.59	1,844.72	1,513.14	4,628.45
7	Joan	1,206.23	1,616.22	1,219.24	4,041.69
8	Totals	$5,194.49	$6,857.24	$5,410.95	$17,462.68

Figure 27 This example shows font, font size, and font style applied to the contents of cells.

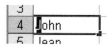

Figure 28 You can also select individual characters within a cell …

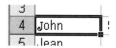

Figure 29 … and apply formatting to them.

Font Formatting

Excel uses 10 point Arial as the default font or typeface for worksheets. You can apply a variety of font formatting options to cells, some of which are shown in **Figure 27**:

- ◆ **Font** is the typeface used to display characters. This includes all fonts properly installed in your system.

- ◆ **Font style** is the weight or angle of characters. Options usually include Regular, Bold, Italic, and Bold Italic.

- ◆ **Size** is the size of characters, expressed in points.

- ◆ **Underline** is character underlining. Don't confuse this with borders, which can be applied to the bottom of a cell, regardless of its contents.

- ◆ **Color** is character color.

- ◆ **Effects** are special effects applied to characters.

You can apply font formatting with the Formatting toolbar, shortcut keys, and the Format Cells dialog.

✔ Tip

- ■ You can change the formatting of individual characters within a cell. Just double-click the cell to make it active, select the characters you want to change (**Figure 28**), and use the appropriate font formatting technique to change the characters (**Figure 29**).

To apply font formatting with the Formatting toolbar or shortcut keys

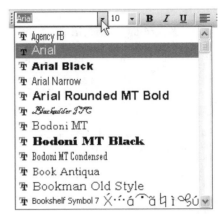

1. Select the cell(s) or character(s) you want to apply font formatting to.

2. To change the font, choose a font from the Font drop-down list (**Figure 30**).

   or

   Click on the Font box to select its contents (**Figure 31**), type in the name of the font you want to apply (**Figure 32**), and press Enter.

Figure 30 The Font drop-down list on the Formatting toolbar lists all of the fonts properly installed in your system.

Figure 31 Click the font name to select it ...

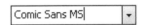

3. To change the character size, choose a size from the Font Size drop-down list (**Figure 33**).

   or

   Click on the Font Size box to select its contents, type in a size, and press Enter.

Figure 32 ... then type in the name of the font that you want to apply.

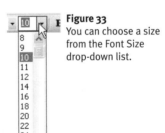

4. To change the character style, click any combination of font style buttons or press corresponding shortcut keys:

   ▲ **Bold** B or Ctrl B makes characters appear bold.

   ▲ *Italic* I or Ctrl I makes characters appear slanted.

   ▲ <u>Underline</u> U or Ctrl U applies a single underline to characters.

Figure 33 You can choose a size from the Font Size drop-down list.

5. To change the character color, choose a color from the Font Color menu (**Figure 34**).

✔ Tips

- Font size must be between 1 and 409 points in half-point increments. (In case you're wondering, 72 points equals 1 inch.)

- The Automatic color option (**Figure 34**) enables Excel to automatically apply color based on other formatting options.

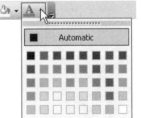

Figure 34 The Font Color menu on the Formatting toolbar enables you to apply color to characters.

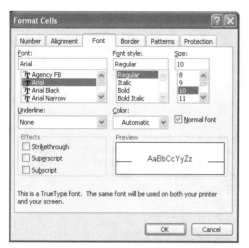

Figure 35 The Font tab of the Format Cells dialog.

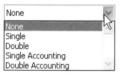

Figure 36
Excel offers several underlining options.

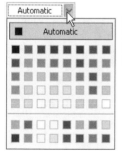

Figure 37
The Color drop-down list in the Format Cells dialog.

To apply font formatting with the Format Cells dialog

1. Select the cell(s) or character(s) whose font you want to change.

2. Choose Format > Cells (**Figure 7**) or press Ctrl 1.

3. In the Format Cells dialog that appears, click the Font tab to display its options (**Figure 35**).

4. Set options as desired:

   ▲ Select a font from the Font list or type a font name into the text box above the list.

   ▲ Select a style from the Font style list or type a style name into the text box above the list.

   ▲ Select a size from the Size list or type a size into the text box above the list.

   ▲ Choose an underline option from the Underline drop-down list (**Figure 36**).

   ▲ Choose a font color from the Color drop-down list (**Figure 37**).

   ▲ Turn on check boxes in the Effects area to apply font effects.

5. When the sample text in the Preview area looks just the way you want, click OK.

✔ Tips

■ To return a selection to the default font, turn on the Normal font check box in the Format Cells dialog (**Figure 35**).

■ The accounting underline options in the Underline drop-down list (**Figure 36**) stretch almost the entire width of the cell.

■ The Automatic color option (**Figure 37**) enables Excel to automatically apply color based on other formatting options.

Borders

Excel offers many border styles that you can apply to separate cells or a selection of cells (**Figure 38**).

Use the Formatting toolbar or the Format Cells dialog to add and format borders.

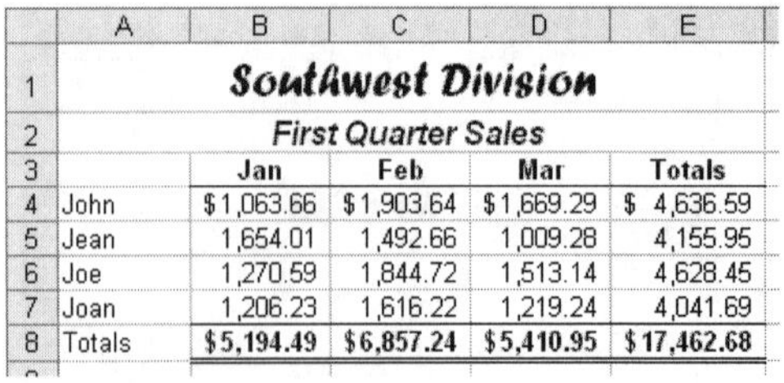

To add borders with the Formatting toolbar

1. Select the cell(s) you want to add borders to.

2. Choose the type of border you want to apply from the Borders menu (**Figure 39**).

✔ Tips

■ To remove borders from a selection, choose the top left button on the Border menu (**Figure 39**). If the border does not disappear, it may be applied to a cell adjoining the one you selected.

■ The accounting underline options on the Underline drop-down list in the Format Cells dialog (**Figure 36**) are not the same as borders. They do not stretch across the entire width of the cell and they only appear when the cell is not blank.

	A	B	C	D	E
1		*Southwest Division*			
2		*First Quarter Sales*			
3		Jan	Feb	Mar	Totals
4	John	$1,063.66	$1,903.64	$1,669.29	$ 4,636.59
5	Jean	1,654.01	1,492.66	1,009.28	4,155.95
6	Joe	1,270.59	1,844.72	1,513.14	4,628.45
7	Joan	1,206.23	1,616.22	1,219.24	4,041.69
8	Totals	$5,194.49	$6,857.24	$5,410.95	$17,462.68

Figure 38 Use borders to place lines under headings and above and below column totals. (For this illustration, gridlines have been turned off so you can clearly see the borders; I explain how to turn off gridlines in Chapter 15.)

Figure 39
The Borders menu on the Formatting toolbar.

ADDING BORDERS

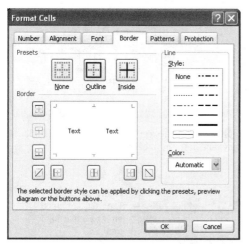

Figure 40 The Border tab of the Format Cells dialog with several cells in the same row selected.

To add borders with the Format Cells dialog

1. Select the cell(s) to which you want to add borders.

2. Choose Format > Cells (**Figure 7**) or press Ctrl 1.

3. In the Format Cells dialog that appears, click the Border tab to display its options (**Figure 40**).

4. Select a line style in the Line area.

5. If desired, select a color from the Color drop-down list, which looks just like the one in **Figure 37**.

6. Set individual borders for the selected cells using one of these methods:

   ▲ Click one of the buttons in the Presets area to apply a predefined border. (None removes all borders from the selection.)

   ▲ Click a button in the Border area to add a border to the corresponding area.

   ▲ Click between the lines in the illustration in the Border area to place corresponding borders.

7. Repeat steps 4, 5, and 6 until all the desired borders for the selection are set.

8. Click OK.

✔ Tip

■ To get the borders in your worksheet to look just the way you want, be prepared to make several selections and trips to the Border tab of the Format Cells dialog.

ADDING BORDERS

Cell Shading

Excel's shading feature lets you add color to cells (**Figure 41**), either with or without patterns. You can do this with options on the Formatting toolbar or in the Format Cells dialog.

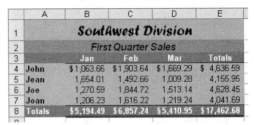

Figure 41 Use Excel's cell shading feature to add fill colors and patterns to cells.

✔ Tips

■ By combining two colors with a pattern, you can create various colors and levels of shading.

■ Be careful when adding shading to cells! If the color is too dark, cell contents may not be legible.

■ To improve the legibility of cell contents in shaded cells, try making the characters bold.

■ For a different look, use a dark color for the cell and make its characters white (**Figure 41**).

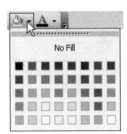

Figure 42
The Fill Color menu on the Formatting toolbar.

To apply shading with the Formatting toolbar

1. Select the cell(s) to which you want to apply shading.

2. Choose a color from the Fill Color menu (**Figure 42**).

✔ Tip

■ To remove colors from a selection, choose No Fill from the Fill Color menu (**Figure 42**).

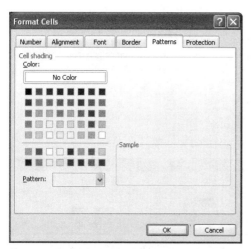

Figure 43 The Patterns tab of the Format Cells dialog.

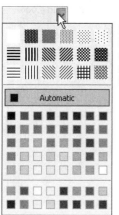

Figure 44
Use the Pattern drop-down list to choose a pattern and a foreground color.

To apply shading with the Format Cells dialog

1. Select the cell(s) to which you want to apply shading.

2. Choose Format > Cells (**Figure 7**) or press Ctrl 1.

3. In the Format Cells dialog that appears, click the Patterns tab to display its options (**Figure 43**).

4. Select a color from the Color palette in the Cell shading area of the dialog. This is the background color.

5. If desired, choose a foreground color and pattern from the Pattern drop-down list (**Figure 44**).

6. When the Sample area of the dialog looks just the way you want your selection to look, click OK.

Styles

Once you get the hang of using Excel's formatting options, check out its Style feature. This advanced feature, which is beyond the scope of this book, lets you combine formats into named styles that you can apply to any cell in the workbook. This can save time and ensure consistency.

✔ Tips

- Excel's style feature works a lot like Word's style feature.

- To access the style feature choose Format > Style (**Figure 7**).

Conditional Formatting

Excel's Conditional Formatting feature enables you to set up special formatting that is automatically applied by Excel only when cell contents meet certain criteria.

For example, say you have a worksheet containing the total sales for each member of your company's sales staff. You want to display all sales over $5,000 in bold, blue type with a light blue background and black border. You can use Conditional Formatting to automatically apply the desired formatting in cells containing values over 5,000 (**Figure 45**).

To apply Conditional Formatting

1. Select the cells to which you want to apply Conditional Formatting.

2. Choose Format > Conditional Formatting (**Figure 7**) to display the Conditional Formatting dialog (**Figure 46**).

3. Use the drop-down lists and text boxes in the Condition 1 part of the dialog to set up the criteria for applying formatting. **Figure 47** shows an example.

4. Click the Format button to display a special version of the Format Cells dialog that offers tabs for Font, Border, and Patterns only (**Figure 48**). Use the dialog to set formatting options for cells meeting the condition.

5. To add another condition for applying the formatting, click the Add button. The dialog expands to offer an additional condition set (**Figure 49**). Repeat steps 3 and 4.

6. Repeat step 5 for each condition you want to add.

7. When you're finished specifying conditions and formatting, click OK.

Figure 45 Conditional Formatting instructs Excel to format cells based on their contents.

Figure 46 The Conditional Formatting dialog.

Figure 47 This condition set applies formatting to selected cells containing values greater than 5,000.

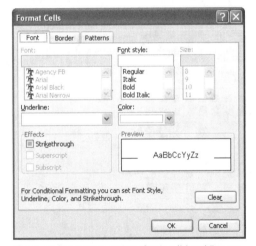

Figure 48 Formatting options for Conditional Formatting are slightly limited.

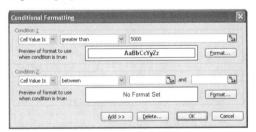

Figure 49 The Conditional Formatting dialog expands so you can add more conditions.

APPLYING CONDITIONAL FORMATTING

Figure 50 When you click the Format Painter button, a marquee appears around the original selection and the mouse pointer turns into the Format Painter pointer.

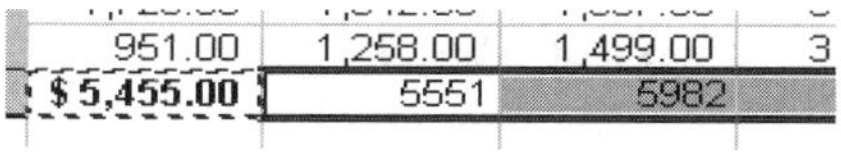

Figure 51 Drag to select the cells to which you want to copy formats.

Figure 52 When you release the mouse button, the formatting is applied.

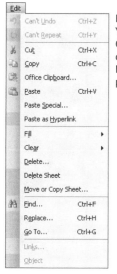

Figure 53
You can also use the Copy and Paste Special commands under the Edit menu to copy and paste formatting.

The Format Painter

The Format Painter lets you copy cell formatting and apply it to other cells. This can help you format worksheets quickly and consistently.

To use the Format Painter

1. Select a cell with the formatting you want to copy.

2. Click the Format Painter button 🖌 on the Standard toolbar. The mouse pointer turns into a little plus sign with a paintbrush beside it and a marquee appears around the original selection (**Figure 50**).

3. Use the Format Painter pointer to select the cells you want to apply the formatting to (**Figure 51**). When you release the mouse button, the formatting is applied (**Figure 52**).

✔ Tips

■ You can double-click the Format Painter button 🖌 in step 1 to keep applying a copied format throughout the worksheet. Press (Esc) or click the Format Painter button 🖌 again to stop applying the format and return the mouse pointer to normal.

■ You can also use the Copy and Paste Special commands under the Edit menu (**Figure 53**) to copy the formatting of selected cells and paste it into other cells.

USING THE FORMAT PAINTER

123

Column Width & Row Height

If the data you enter into a cell doesn't fit, you can make the column wider to accommodate all the characters. You can also make columns narrower to use worksheet space more efficiently. And although Excel automatically adjusts row height when you increase the font size of cells within the row, you can increase or decrease row height as desired.

Excel offers two ways to change column width and row height: with the mouse and with Format menu commands.

✔ Tips

- If text typed into a cell does not fit, it appears to overlap into the cell to its right (**Figure 54**). Even though the text may appear to be in more than one cell, all of the text is really in the cell in which you typed it. (You can see for yourself by clicking in the cell to the right and looking at the formula bar—it will not contain any part of the text!) If the cell to the right of the text is not blank, the text appears truncated (**Figure 55**). Don't let appearances fool you. The text is still all there. The missing part is just hidden by the contents of the cell beside it.

- If a number doesn't fit in a cell, the cell fills up with pound signs (#) (**Figure 56**). To display the number, make the column wider (**Figure 57**) or change the number formatting to omit symbols and decimal places (**Figure 58**). I tell you how to make columns wider on the next page and how to change number formatting earlier in this chapter.

- Setting column width or row height to 0 (zero) hides the column or row.

Figure 54 When text doesn't fit in a cell, it appears to overlap into the cell beside it ...

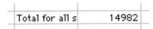

Figure 55 ... unless the cell beside it isn't blank.

Figure 56 When a number doesn't fit in a cell, the cell fills with # signs.

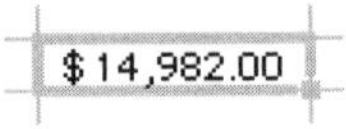

Figure 57 You can make the number fit by making the cell wider ...

Figure 58 ... or by changing the number's formatting to remove decimal places.

Figure 59 Position the mouse pointer on the right border of a column heading ...

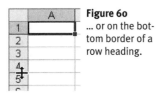

Figure 60
... or on the bottom border of a row heading.

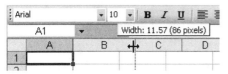

Figure 61 Drag to reposition the border, thus changing the width of the column (as shown here) or height of the row.

✔ Tips

■ When you change column width or row height, you change the width or height for the entire column or row, not just selected cells.

■ To change column width or row height for more than one column or row at a time, select multiple columns or rows and drag the border of one of them.

To change column width or row height with the mouse

1. Position the mouse pointer on the line right after the column letter(s) (**Figure 59**) or right below the row number (**Figure 60**) of the column or row you want to change. The mouse pointer turns into a line with two arrows coming out of it.

2. Press the mouse button and drag:

   ▲ To make a column narrower, drag to the left.

   ▲ To make a column wider, drag to the right.

   ▲ To make a row taller, drag down.

   ▲ To make a row shorter, drag up.

   As you drag, a dotted line moves along with the mouse pointer and the width or height of the column or row appears in a yellow box (**Figure 61**).

3. Release the mouse button. The column width or row height changes.

■ If you drag a column or row border all the way to the left or all the way up, you set the column width or row height to 0, hiding the column or row from view. I tell you more about hiding columns and rows next.

■ To quickly set the width or height of a column or row to fit its contents, double-click the column or row heading border. I tell you more about this AutoFit feature later in this chapter.

To change column width or row height with menu commands

1. Select the column(s) or row(s) whose width or height you want to change.

2. Choose Format > Column > Width (**Figure 62**) or choose Format > Row > Height (**Figure 63**).

3. In the Column Width dialog (**Figure 64**) or Row Height dialog (**Figure 65**), enter a new value. Column width is expressed in standard font characters while row height is expressed in points.

4. Click OK to change the selected columns' width or rows' height.

To hide columns or rows

1. Select the column(s) (**Figure 66**) or row(s) you want to hide.

2. Choose Format > Column > Hide (**Figure 62**) or Format > Row > Hide (**Figure 63**). The selected column(s) or row(s) disappear (**Figure 67**).

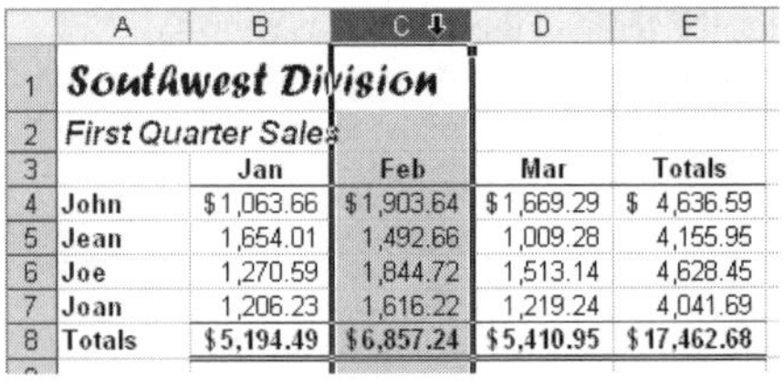

✔ Tip

■ Hiding a column or row is not the same as deleting it. Data in a hidden column or row still exists in the worksheet and can be referenced by formulas.

To unhide columns or rows

1. Select the columns or rows on both sides of the hidden column(s) or row(s) (**Figure 68**).

2. Choose Format > Column > Unhide (**Figure 62**) or Format > Row > Unhide (**Figure 63**).

   The hidden column(s) or row(s) reappear (**Figure 69**).

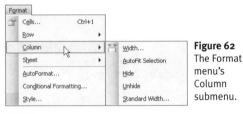

Figure 62 The Format menu's Column submenu.

Figure 63 The Format menu's Row submenu.

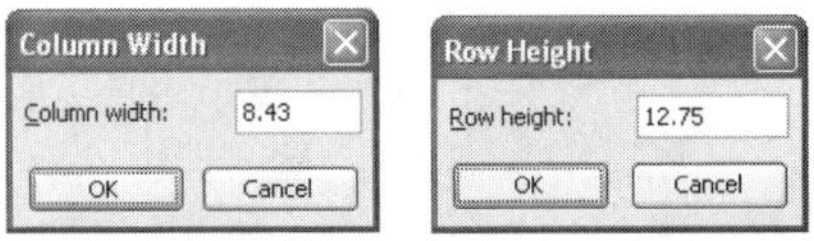

Figures 64 & 65 The Column Width (left) and Row Height (right) dialogs.

Figure 66 Select the column that you want to hide.

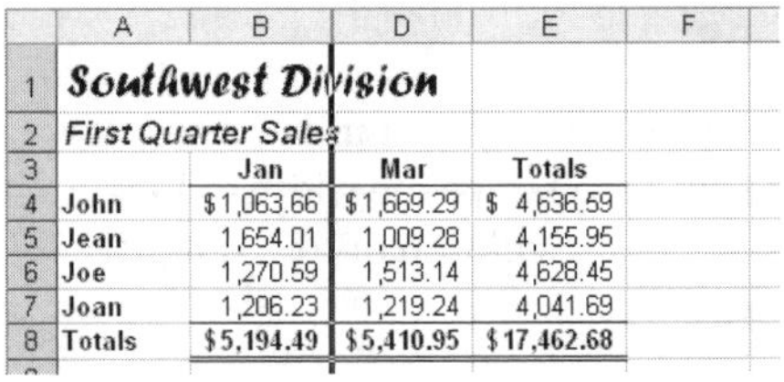

Figure 67 When you choose the Hide command, the column disappears.

Figure 68 Select the rows above and below the hidden row.

Figure 69 When you choose the Unhide command, the hidden row reappears.

CHANGING COLUMN WIDTH & ROW HEIGHT

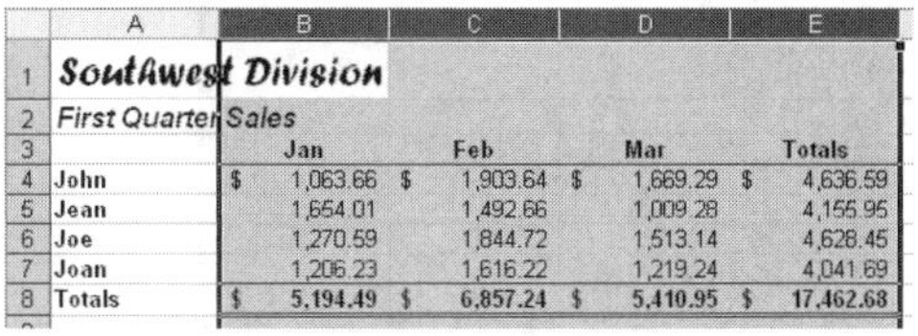

Figure 70 Select the columns for which you want to change the width.

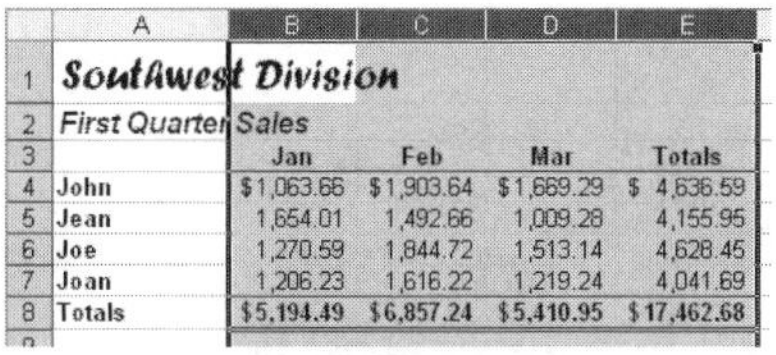

Figure 71 When you choose the AutoFit Selection command, the width of the columns changes so they're only as wide as they need to be to fit cell contents.

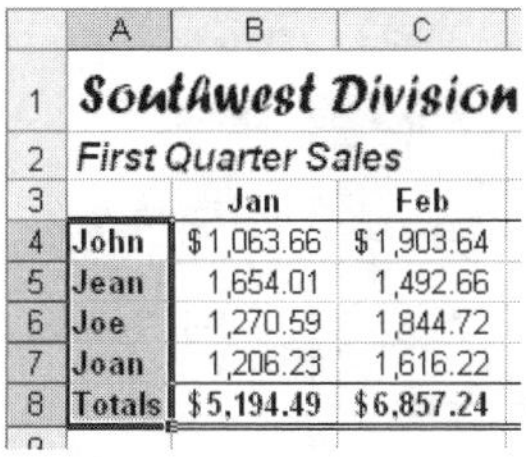

Figure 72 Select the cells that you want Excel to measure for the AutoFit feature.

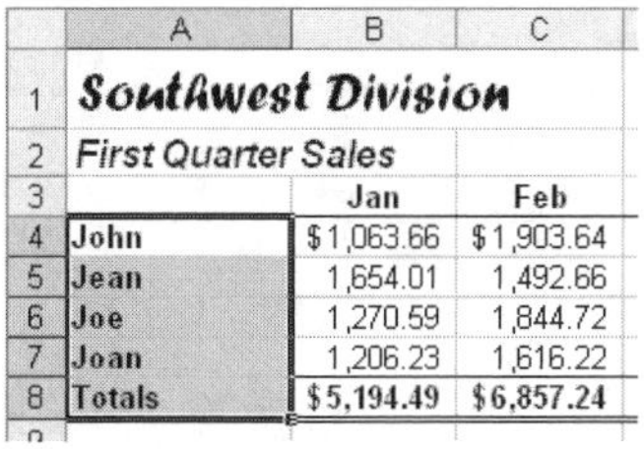

Figure 73 When you choose the AutoFit Selection command, Excel resizes the entire column based on the width of the contents in the selected cells.

AutoFit

Excel's AutoFit feature automatically adjusts a column's width or a row's height so it's only as wide or as high as it needs to be to display the information within it. This is a great way to adjust columns and rows to use worksheet space more efficiently.

To use AutoFit

1. Select the column(s) or row(s) for which you want to change the width or height (**Figure 70**).

2. Choose Format > Column > AutoFit Selection (**Figure 62**) or Format > Row > AutoFit (**Figure 63**).

   or

   Double-click on the border to the right of the column heading (**Figure 59**) or below the row heading (**Figure 60**).

   The column width or row height changes to fit cell contents (**Figure 71**).

✔ Tips

- To adjust a column's width without taking every cell into consideration—for example, to exclude a cell containing a lot of text—select only the cells for which you want to adjust the column (**Figure 72**). When you choose Format > Column > AutoFit Selection (**Figure 62**), only the cells you selected are measured for the AutoFit adjustment (**Figure 73**).

- Use the Wrap text and AutoFit features to keep your columns narrow. I tell you about Wrap text earlier in this chapter.

USING AUTOFIT

AutoFormat

Excel's AutoFormat feature offers a quick way to dress up tabular data in worksheets by applying predefined formats. If you're like me and like to leave design for designers, you'll welcome this feature.

To use AutoFormat

1. Select the portion of the worksheet you want to format (**Figure 74**).
2. Choose Format > AutoFormat (**Figure 7**) to display the AutoFormat dialog (**Figure 75**).
3. Choose a format from the Table format list. A preview of the format appears in the list so you can decide whether you like it before you apply it.
4. Click OK. Your worksheet is formatted instantly (**Figure 76**).

✔ Tip

- To pick and choose among the different kinds of formatting automatically applied, click the Options button in the AutoFormat dialog. The box expands to display check boxes for each type of formatting (**Figure 77**). To exclude a type of change from the AutoFormat process, turn off its check box.

Southwest Division				
First Quarter Sales				
	Jan	Feb	Mar	Totals
John	1063.66	1903.64	1669.29	4636.59
Jean	1654.01	1492.66	1009.28	4155.95
Joe	1270.59	1844.72	1513.14	4628.45
Joan	1206.23	1616.22	1219.24	4041.69
Totals	5194.49	6857.24	5410.95	17462.68

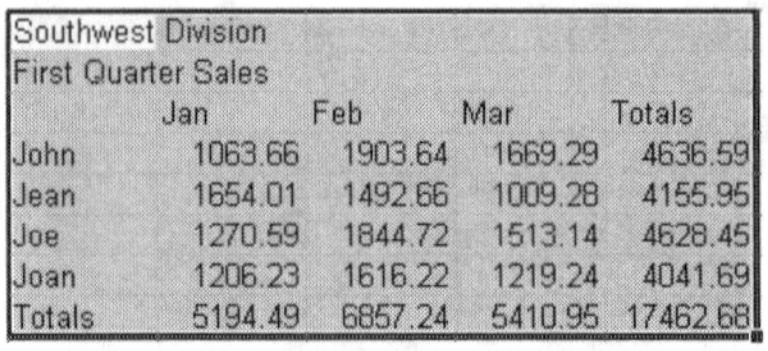

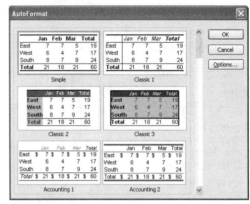

Figure 74 Select the part of the worksheet you want to format.

Figure 75 The AutoFormat dialog.

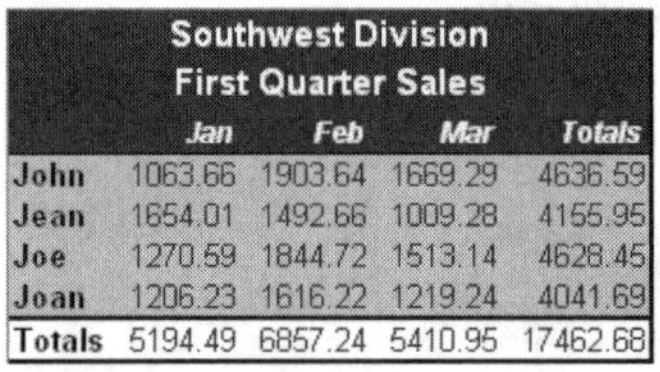

Southwest Division				
First Quarter Sales				
	Jan	Feb	Mar	Totals
John	1063.66	1903.64	1669.29	4636.59
Jean	1654.01	1492.66	1009.28	4155.95
Joe	1270.59	1844.72	1513.14	4628.45
Joan	1206.23	1616.22	1219.24	4041.69
Totals	5194.49	6857.24	5410.95	17462.68

Figure 76 The worksheet in **Figure 74** with the Classic 3 AutoFormat applied.

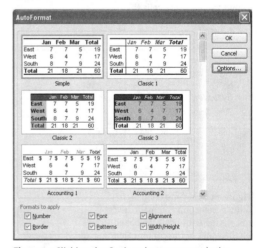

Figure 77 Clicking the Options button expands the AutoFormat dialog so you can select which parts of the format should be applied.

	A	B	C	D	E
1	*Southwest Division*				
2	*First Quarter Sales*				
3		Jan	Feb	Mar	Totals
4	John	$1,063.66	$1,903.64	$1,669.29	$ 4,636.59
5	Jean	1,654.01	1,492.66	1,009.28	4,155.95
6	Joe	1,270.59	1,844.72	1,513.14	4,628.45
7	Joan	1,206.23	1,616.22	1,219.24	4,041.69
8	Totals	$5,194.49	$6,857.24	$5,410.95	$17,462.68

Figure 78 Select the cells you want to remove formatting from.

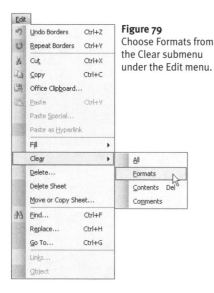

Figure 79
Choose Formats from the Clear submenu under the Edit menu.

	A	B	C	D	E
1	*Southwest Division*				
2	*First Quarter Sales*				
3		Jan	Feb	Mar	Totals
4	John	1063.66	$1,903.64	$1,669.29	$ 4,636.59
5	Jean	1654.01	1,492.66	1,009.28	4,155.95
6	Joe	1270.59	1,844.72	1,513.14	4,628.45
7	Joan	1206.23	1,616.22	1,219.24	4,041.69
8	Totals	5194.49	$6,857.24	$5,410.95	$17,462.68

Figure 80 The formatting is removed but the cell contents remain.

Removing Formatting from Cells

You can use the Formats command on the Clear submenu under the Edit menu (**Figure 79**) to remove formatting from cells, leaving cell contents—such as values and formulas—intact.

✔ Tips

- When you remove formats from a cell, you return font formatting to the normal font and number formatting to the General format. You also remove borders or shading added to the cell.

- Removing formatting does not affect column width or row height.

To remove formatting from cells

1. Select the cell(s) you want to remove formatting from (**Figure 78**).

2. Choose Edit > Clear > Formats (**Figure 79**). The formatting is removed but cell contents remain (**Figure 80**).

Working with Graphic Objects

Graphic Objects

Microsoft Excel makes it easy to add a variety of graphic objects to your worksheets and charts:

◆ **Drawn objects**, such as lines, arrows, and shapes, can draw attention to important information on a document.

◆ **AutoShapes** enable you to draw a variety of interesting and useful shapes quickly and easily.

◆ **Text boxes** offer a flexible way to add annotations to a document.

◆ **Clip art** can make a worksheet or chart more visually appealing with professionally created graphic images.

◆ **Pictures from files** on disk make it possible to add your own images, such as a company logo or product illustration.

◆ **Organization charts** can provide additional information about your company's organization.

◆ **WordArt** enables you to add highly stylized text to your documents.

◆ **Pictures from a scanner or camera** enable you to import images directly from your scanner or a digital camera into Excel documents.

This chapter explains how you can include all of these types of graphic objects in your Excel documents.

The Drawing Toolbar

Excel's Drawing toolbar (**Figure 1**) includes a wide range of tools you can use to add lines, arrows, shapes, and text boxes to your worksheets and charts. Through creative use of these tools, you can add impact and improve the appearance of all your Excel documents.

Figure 1 The Drawing toolbar.

To display the Drawing toolbar

Click the Drawing button on the Standard toolbar. A border appears around the button (**Figure 2**) when the Drawing toolbar is displayed.

Or

Choose View > Toolbars > Drawing (**Figure 3**).

✔ Tip

■ By default, the Drawing toolbar appears at the bottom of the screen. I explain how to move toolbars in **Chapter 1**.

To hide the Drawing toolbar

Click the Drawing button on the Standard toolbar.

Or

Choose View > Toolbars > Drawing (**Figure 3**).

Figure 2 When you click the Drawing button, a border appears around it.

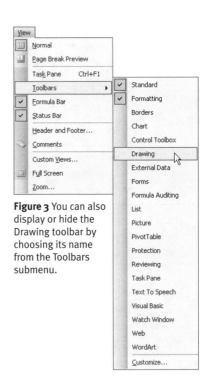

Figure 3 You can also display or hide the Drawing toolbar by choosing its name from the Toolbars submenu.

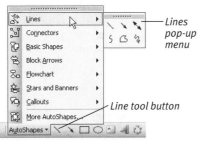

Figure 4 Although the Drawing toolbar includes a Line tool button, the Lines pop-up menu offers additional tools for drawing lines.

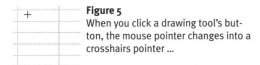

Figure 5
When you click a drawing tool's button, the mouse pointer changes into a crosshairs pointer ...

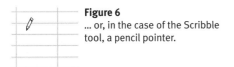

Figure 6
... or, in the case of the Scribble tool, a pencil pointer.

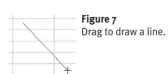

Figure 7
Drag to draw a line.

Figure 8
A freshly drawn line.

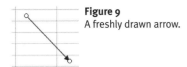

Figure 9
A freshly drawn arrow.

Drawing Objects

Many of the tools on the Drawing toolbar let you draw *objects*—lines or shapes—in worksheet or chart windows. Excel lets you draw lines, rectangles, squares, ovals, circles, shapes (including complex AutoShapes), and text boxes. Objects you draw can be selected, resized, moved, or copied at any time.

To draw a line or arrow

1. Click the appropriate button on the Drawing toolbar's Lines pop-up menu (**Figure 4**) to select it:

   ▲ **Line** ◺ draws straight lines.

   ▲ **Arrow** ◹ draws straight lines with an arrowhead on one end.

   ▲ **Double Arrow** ◹ draws straight lines with arrowheads on both ends.

   ▲ **Curve** ⌇ draws smoothly curved lines.

   ▲ **Freeform** ⌖ draws lines combining straight and freeform segments.

   ▲ **Scribble** ⌇ draws lines wherever you drag the mouse.

   When you click the tool's button the mouse pointer turns into a crosshairs pointer (**Figure 5**) or, in the case of the Scribble tool, a pencil (**Figure 6**).

2. Position the mouse pointer where you want to begin drawing.

3. To draw a line, arrow, or double arrow, press the mouse button down and drag. As you move the mouse, a line is drawn (**Figure 7**). Release the mouse button to stop drawing (**Figures 8** and **9**).

   or

Continued on next page...

Continued from previous page.

To draw a curve, move the mouse to stretch a line (**Figure 7**) and click where you want the curve to appear (**Figure 10**). Repeat this process to draw as many curves as desired. Then either click the starting point or double-click the ending point to stop drawing (**Figure 11**).

or

To draw a freeform shape, click the Freeform tool 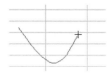, then combine clicking and dragging to draw straight lines and freeform lines: click from point to point to draw straight lines and drag (with a pencil tool that appears automatically) to draw freeform lines (**Figure 12**). Either click the starting point or double-click the ending point to stop drawing (**Figure 13**).

or

To draw a scribble, click the Scribble tool 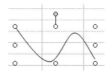, then press the mouse button down and drag the pencil pointer to get the desired line shape (**Figure 14**). Release the mouse button to stop drawing (**Figure 15**).

✔ Tips

- To draw a line or arrow that's perfectly vertical, horizontal, or at a 45° angle, hold down ⟨Shift⟩ in step 3.

- To force the line's end to snap to the worksheet grid, hold down ⟨Ctrl⟩ in step 3.

- To draw multiple lines with the same tool, double-click the tool's button to select it. The tool remains active until you either click the tool's button again, click another button, or press ⟨Esc⟩.

- The small white circles in **Figures 8**, **9**, **11**, **13**, and **15** are selection handles. I tell you more about selection handles later in this chapter.

Figure 10
Using the Curve tool, click to indicate where the curve should appear.

Figure 11
A curved line with two curves.

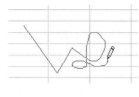

Figure 12 Using the Freeform tool, click to draw straight lines and drag to draw freeform lines.

Figure 13
Double-clicking ends the line without creating a closed-in shape.

Figure 14
To use the Scribble tool, hold the mouse button down and drag the pencil pointer.

Figure 15
Releasing the mouse button completes the scribble.

DRAWING LINES & ARROWS

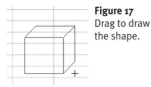

Figure 16
Choose a shape from one of the submenus on the AutoShapes pop-up menu.

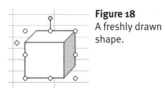

Figure 17
Drag to draw the shape.

Figure 18
A freshly drawn shape.

Figures 19 & 20
When you drag the AutoShapes menu (above) or one of its submenus (left) away from the toolbar, it turns into a floating toolbar.

To draw an AutoShape

1. Click a shape or line tool button on one of the submenus on the Drawing toolbar's AutoShapes pop-up menu (**Figure 16**). The mouse pointer turns into a crosshairs pointer (**Figure 5**).

2. Position the crosshairs where you want to begin drawing the shape or line.

3. Press the mouse button and drag. As you move the mouse, the shape or line begins to take form (**Figure 17**).

4. Release the mouse button to complete the shape (**Figure 18**).

✔ Tips

- The AutoShapes feature makes it easy to draw complex lines and shapes.

- The Connectors submenu on the Auto-Shapes menu offers options for creating lines that connect two shapes.

- The AutoShapes menu and its submenus (**Figure 16**) can be dragged off the toolbar to create separate floating toolbars (**Figures 19** and **20**).

- To draw multiple shapes with the same tool, double-click the tool's button to select it. The tool remains active until you either click the button again, click another button, or press Esc.

DRAWING AUTOSHAPES

To add a text box

1. Click the Text Box button 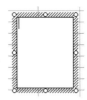 on the Drawing toolbar (**Figure 1**). The mouse pointer turns into a special crosshairs pointer (**Figure 21**).

2. Position the crosshairs where you want to begin drawing the text box.

3. Press the mouse button and drag. As you move the mouse, the text box begins to take form (**Figure 22**).

4. Release the mouse button to complete the text box. An insertion point appears within it (**Figure 23**).

5. Enter the text you want in the text box (**Figure 24**).

✔ Tips

- A text box is like a little word processing document within an Excel sheet. Once created, you can enter and format text within it.

- Text boxes offer more flexibility than worksheet cells when entering long passages of text.

- To edit text in a text box, double-click inside it to select one or more characters. Then use the arrow keys to move the insertion point. Use standard editing techniques to modify text.

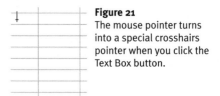

Figure 21
The mouse pointer turns into a special crosshairs pointer when you click the Text Box button.

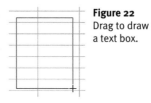

Figure 22
Drag to draw a text box.

Figure 23
When you release the mouse button, the text box appears with a blinking insertion point inside it.

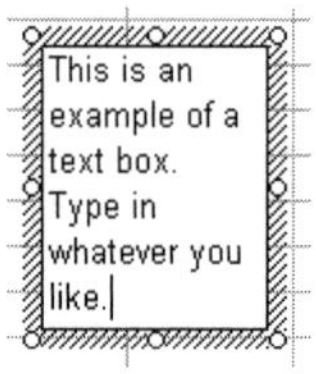

Figure 24
You can type whatever text you like in the text box.

This is an example of a text box. Type in whatever you like.

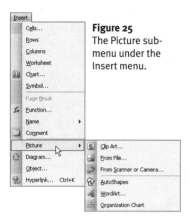

Figure 25
The Picture sub-menu under the Insert menu.

Figure 26
The Clip Art task pane.

Figures 27 & 28 The Search in (left) and Results should be (right) drop-down lists.

Inserting Pictures

In addition to drawing graphic objects, you can also insert existing pictures into your documents. This enables you to include more complex graphic elements in your Excel worksheets and charts.

Although you can use buttons on the Drawing toolbar (**Figure 1**) to insert some types of pictures, the Picture submenu on the Insert menu (**Figure 25**) offers far more options.

To insert clip art

1. Choose Insert > Picture > Clip Art (**Figure 25**) or click the Insert Clip Art button on the Drawing toolbar (**Figure 1**) to display the Clip Art task pane (**Figure 26**).

2. Enter a search word in the Search box.

3. To search only some collections of clip art, display the Search in drop-down list (**Figure 27**) and click check boxes to toggle search location options on or off. You can click the + button beside a category to display options within it.

4. To specify the type of media you want to find, display the Results should be drop-down list (**Figure 28**) and click check boxes to toggle media type options on or off. You can click the + button beside a category to display options within it.

5. Click Go.

Continued on next page...

INSERTING CLIP ART

Continued from previous page.

6. Wait while Excel searches for clip art that matches the criteria you specified. When it's done, it displays matches in the Clip Art task pane (**Figure 29**).

7. Click the thumbnail view of a clip art item to insert it in the document (**Figure 30**).

✔ Tips

■ The first time you use the Clip Art command, a dialog may appear, asking whether you want to catalog all media files. Click the Now button to perform this task so you can search through the clip art files.

■ The Picture toolbar (**Figure 30**) includes advanced tools for working with a selected picture.

To insert a picture from a file

1. Choose Insert > Picture > From File (**Figure 25**) or click the Insert Picture From File button ▨ on the Drawing toolbar (**Figure 1**) to display the Insert Picture dialog (**Figure 31**).

2. Locate and select the file you want to insert.

3. Click Insert. The picture file is inserted and the Picture toolbar appears (**Figure 32**).

✔ Tip

■ The Picture toolbar includes advanced tools for working with a selected picture.

Figure 29
Clip art that matches the criteria you specified appears in the task pane.

Figure 30
Click a thumbnail to insert its image.

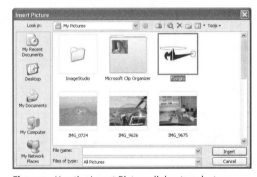

Figure 31 Use the Insert Picture dialog to select an image file on disk, like a company logo.

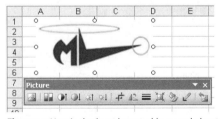

Figure 32 Here's the logo inserted in a worksheet.

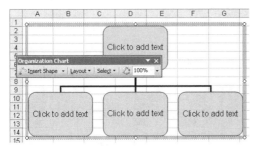

Figure 33 Excel inserts a basic organization chart, all ready for customization, along with the Organization Chart toolbar.

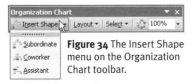

Figure 34 The Insert Shape menu on the Organization Chart toolbar.

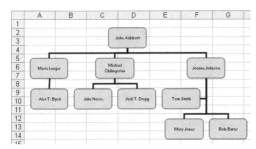

Figure 35 Here's the completed organization chart.

To insert an organization chart

1. Choose Insert > Picture > Organization Chart (**Figure 25**). A box containing a basic organization chart structure appears, along with the Organization Chart toolbar (**Figure 33**).

2. Modify the contents of the default organization chart's boxes to add names, titles, and comments. To edit the contents of a box, click it and type in the new information.

3. Modify the chart's structure as follows:

   ▲ To add a box, select the box you want to attach it to and choose an option from the Insert Shape menu on the Organization Chart toolbar (**Figure 34**).

   ▲ To remove a box, click the box to select it and press (Backspace).

   ▲ To move a box, drag it to a new position on the chart.

4. When you are finished modifying the chart, click anywhere outside it. The completed chart appears in the document and the Organization Chart toolbar disappears (**Figure 35**).

✔ Tip

■ To edit an organization chart, click it to select it. The Organization Chart toolbar reappears. Follow the instructions in step 3 to make desired changes.

INSERTING ORGANIZATION CHARTS

To insert WordArt

1. Choose Insert > Picture > WordArt (**Figure 25**) or click the Insert WordArt button on the Drawing toolbar (**Figure 1**).

2. In the WordArt Gallery dialog that appears (**Figure 36**), click to select a WordArt style.

3. Click OK.

4. In the Edit WordArt Text dialog that appears next (**Figure 37**), change the sample text to the text that you want to display. You can also select a different font and font size and turn on bold and/or italic formatting.

5. Click OK. The WordArt image is inserted in the document and the WordArt toolbar appears (**Figure 38**).

✔ Tip

■ Once you have created a WordArt image, you can use buttons on the WordArt toolbar to modify it. The toolbar only appears when the WordArt image is selected.

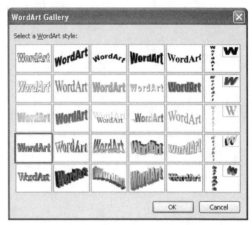

Figure 36 The WordArt Gallery dialog has many styles to choose from.

Figure 37 Enter and apply some text formatting to the text you want to appear.

Figure 38 The WordArt image appears in the document, along with the WordArt toolbar.

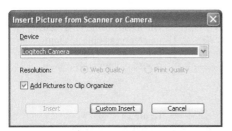

Figure 39 Use this dialog to select the scanner or camera you want to access.

Figure 40 Excel displays a dialog you can use to scan, select, or capture the image. In this example, it has opened the Logitech Camera window, to allow me to capture a still image from a QuickCam digital video camera.

Figure 41 The picture is inserted in the Excel document and the Picture toolbar appears.

To insert a picture from a scanner or digital camera

1. Make sure the scanner software is properly installed and that the scanner is connected to your computer and turned on. Then place the image you wish to scan on the scanning surface.

   or

   Make sure the digital camera software is properly installed and that the camera is connected to your computer and turned on.

2. Choose Insert > Picture > From Scanner or Camera (**Figure 25**).

3. The Insert Picture from Scanner or Camera dialog appears (**Figure 39**). If necessary, use the drop-down list to choose the device you wish to access.

4. Click Custom Insert. A dialog with options for your device appears (**Figure 40**).

5. Follow the instructions that appear onscreen to scan, select, or capture the image.

   When you are finished, the image appears in the Excel document and the Picture toolbar appears (**Figure 41**).

✔ Tips

- If the Insert Picture from Scanner or Camera dialog (**Figure 39**) does not appear after step 3, your scanner or camera is probably not installed correctly. Consult the documentation that came with the device to set it up and try again.

- The appearance of the dialog that appears in step 4 (**Figure 40**) varies depending on the device you are using. Consult the documentation that came with the device for more information.

- The Picture toolbar includes advanced tools for working with a selected picture.

Working with Graphic Objects

Once you have drawn or inserted a graphic object into your Excel document, you can select, move, resize, modify, or delete it.

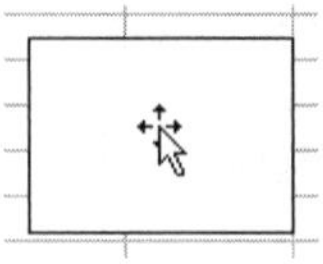

To select an object

1. Position the mouse pointer on the object. A four-headed arrow appears beneath the mouse pointer arrow (**Figure 42**).

2. Click. Selection handles appear around the object (**Figure 43**).

✔ Tips

- If a shape does not have any fill, you must click on its border to select it. I tell you about fill color later in this chapter.

- To change the mouse pointer into a selection pointer so the standard worksheet pointer (the fat plus sign) doesn't appear while you're working with drawing objects, click the Select Objects button ⬚ on the Drawing toolbar (**Figure 1**). The button turns light gray and the mouse pointer changes to an arrow. To get the regular pointer back, click the Select Objects button again, double-click any worksheet cell, or press Esc once or twice.

To deselect an object

Click on any other object or anywhere else in the window. The selection handles disappear.

Figure 42
When you position the mouse pointer on an object, a four-headed arrow appears with the mouse pointer arrow.

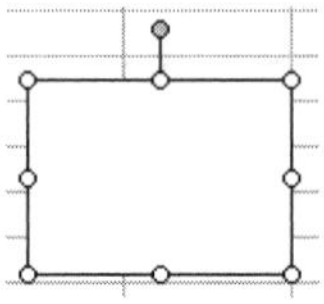

Figure 43
Selection handles appear around selected objects.

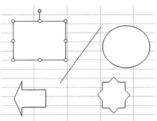

Figure 44
Select the
first object.

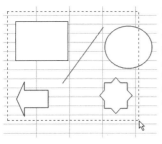

Figure 45
Then hold down
Shift and click
to select other
objects.

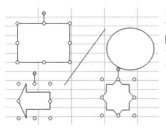

Figure 46
You can use
the selection
pointer to draw
a boundary box
that completely
surrounds the
objects you want
to select.

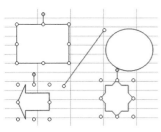

Figure 47
When you release
the mouse button,
all objects within
the boundary are
selected. Because
the circle wasn't
surrounded, it
isn't selected.

To select multiple objects

1. Follow the instructions on the previous page to select the first object (**Figure 44**).

2. Hold down Shift and continue to click objects until all have been selected (**Figure 45**).

Or

1. Click the Select Objects button on the Drawing toolbar to activate the selection pointer.

2. Use the pointer to drag a rectangle that completely surrounds all the objects you want to select (**Figure 46**).

3. Release the mouse button. Selection handles appear around each object (**Figure 47**).

✔ Tips

- To select all the objects on a worksheet, click the Select Objects button on the Drawing toolbar and press Ctrl A.

- To deselect objects from a multiple selection, hold down Shift while clicking on the objects you want to deselect.

SELECTING MULTIPLE OBJECTS

To group objects

1. Select all the objects you want to include in the group (**Figure 47**).

2. Choose Group from the Drawing toolbar's Draw menu (**Figure 48**).

   The objects are grouped together, with only one set of selection handles (**Figure 49**).

✔ Tips

- Grouping multiple objects enables you to select, move, and modify all of the objects in the group by clicking any one of them.

- In addition to grouping individual objects, you can also group groups of objects.

To ungroup objects

1. Select the grouped objects you want to ungroup (**Figure 49**).

2. Choose Ungroup from the Drawing toolbar's Draw menu (**Figure 48**).

   Separate selection handles appear for each object (**Figure 47**).

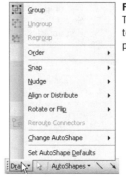

Figure 48
The Drawing toolbar's Draw pop-up menu.

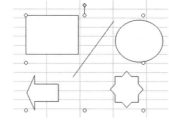

Figure 49
The objects selected in **Figure 47** after grouping them.

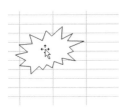

Figure 50
Position the
mouse pointer
on the object.

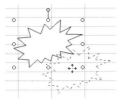

Figure 51
Drag to move
the object.

Figure 52
The Edit menu.

To move an object by dragging

1. Position the mouse pointer on the object so that the four-headed arrow appears (**Figure 50**).

2. Press the mouse button and drag. An outline of the object moves along with the mouse pointer (**Figure 51**).

3. When the object's outline is in the desired position, release the mouse button. The object moves.

✔ Tips

- To restrict an object's movement so that it moves only horizontally or vertically, hold down Shift while dragging.

- To restrict an object's movement so that it snaps to the worksheet gridlines, hold down Alt while dragging.

To move an object with the Cut & Paste commands

1. Select the object you want to move.

2. Choose Edit > Cut (**Figure 52**), press Ctrl X, or click the Cut button on the Standard toolbar. The object disappears.

3. To paste the object into a different sheet, switch to that sheet.

4. Choose Edit > Paste (**Figure 52**), press Ctrl V, or click the Paste button on the Standard toolbar. The object appears.

5. If necessary, drag the object into the desired position on the sheet.

✔ Tip

- This technique is most useful when moving an object to another sheet.

MOVING OBJECTS

To copy an object by dragging

1. Position the mouse pointer on the object so that the four-headed arrow appears (**Figure 50**).

2. While holding down Ctrl, press the mouse button and drag. An outline of the object moves along with the mouse pointer, which displays a plus sign inside it (**Figure 53**).

3. When you release the mouse button a copy of the object appears at the outline (**Figure 54**).

To copy an object with the Copy & Paste commands

1. Select the object you want to copy.

2. Choose Copy from the Edit menu (**Figure 52**), press Ctrl C, or click the Copy button on the Standard toolbar.

3. To paste the object into a different sheet, switch to that sheet.

4. Choose Paste from the Edit menu (**Figure 52**), press Ctrl V, or click the Paste button on the Standard toolbar.

To delete an object

1. Select the object(s) or group of objects you want to delete.

2. Press Backspace or Delete.

   or

   Choose Edit > Clear > All (**Figure 55**).

   The object(s) disappear.

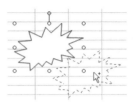

Figure 53
Hold down Ctrl while dragging ...

Figure 54
... to copy an object.

Figure 55
The Clear submenu under the Edit menu when an object is selected.

COPYING OBJECTS

Figure 56 Position the mouse pointer on a selection handle and it turns into a resizing pointer.

Figure 57 Drag to stretch (or shrink) the object.

Figure 58 When you release the mouse button, the object resizes.

To resize an object

1. Select the object you want to resize.

2. Position the mouse pointer on a selection handle. The mouse pointer turns into a double-headed arrow (**Figure 56**).

3. Press the mouse button and drag to stretch or shrink the object. The mouse pointer turns into a crosshairs and an outline of the object moves with your mouse pointer as you drag (**Figure 57**).

4. When the outline of the object reflects the size you want, release the mouse button. The object is resized (**Figure 58**).

✔ Tips

- To resize an object or group proportionally, hold down ⟨Shift⟩ while dragging a corner selection handle.

- To resize the object so that the handle you drag snaps to the worksheet gridlines, hold down ⟨Ctrl⟩ while dragging.

- To resize multiple objects at the same time, select the objects, then resize one of them. All selected objects will stretch or shrink.

RESIZING OBJECTS

To customize an AutoShape

1. Select the AutoShape you want to customize.

2. Position the mouse pointer on the yellow diamond handle. The mouse pointer turns into a hollow white arrowhead pointer.

3. Drag the yellow diamond. As you drag, the outline of the customized shape moves with the mouse pointer (**Figures 59** and **61**).

4. Release the mouse button.The shape changes (**Figures 60** and **62**).

✔ Tips

- This technique can only be used on Auto Shape lines or shapes that display a yellow diamond when selected.

- You can also customize an AutoShape by dragging its green circle to rotate it.

Drag this diamond to customize the shape.

Figures 59 & 60
Drag the yellow diamond (left) to customize the AutoShape (right).

Drag this diamond to customize the shape.

Figures 61 & 62
You can even turn a smile (left) into a frown (right).

Figure 63 The Line Style button menu.

Figure 64 The Font Color button menu.

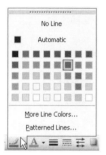

Figure 65 The Line Color button menu.

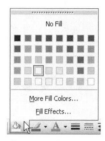

Figure 66 The Fill Color button menu.

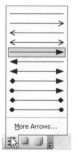

Figure 67
The Arrow Style button menu.

Figure 68 The Dash Style button menu.

To format lines & shapes with the Drawing toolbar

1. Select the line or shape you want to format.

2. Use menus and submenus on the Drawing toolbar (**Figure 1**) to format the object:

   ▲ To change the line thickness of a line or shape border, choose an option from the Line Style button ≡ menu (**Figure 63**).

   ▲ To change the color of text within an object, choose an option from the Font Color button ⒜▾ menu (**Figure 64**).

   ▲ To change the line color of a line or shape border, choose an option from the Line Color button ✐▾ menu (**Figure 65**).

   ▲ To change the fill color of a shape, choose an option from the Fill Color button ◇▾ menu (**Figure 66**).

   ▲ To add, change, or remove arrow components for a line or arrow, choose an option from the Arrow Style button ⇄ menu (**Figure 67**).

   ▲ To change the style of a dashed line or dashed shape border, choose an option from the Dash Style button ▦ menu (**Figure 68**).

Continued on next page...

FORMATTING LINES & SHAPES

Continued from previous page.

▲ To add, remove, or change the shadow of a line or shape, choose an option from the Shadow Style button  menu (**Figure 69**).

▲ To add, change, or remove three dimensional effects for a simple shape, choose an option from the 3-D Style button  menu (**Figure 70**).

✔ Tips

■ The formatting options that are available depend on the line or shape that is selected.

■ You can combine as many formatting options as you like.

To format lines & shapes with the Format AutoShape dialog

1. Select the line or shape you want to format and choose Format > AutoShape (**Figure 71**) or press Ctrl 1.

    or

    Double-click the line or shape you want to format.

2. The Format AutoShape dialog appears. Click the Colors and Lines tab to display its options (**Figures 72, 73,** and **74**).

3. Set options as desired:

    ▲ To change the fill color, choose an option from the Color menu in the Fill area of the dialog (**Figure 75**).

    ▲ To enable objects to be seen through a fill color, drag the Transparency slider to the right.

    ▲ To change the line color, choose an option from the Color menu in the Line area of the dialog (**Figure 76**).

Figure 69 The Shadow Style button menu.

Figure 70 The 3-D Style button menu.

Figure 71 With a line or shape selected, choose AutoShape from the Format menu.

Figure 72 The Format AutoShape dialog for a shape, ...

Figure 73 ... for a line or arrow, ...

FORMATTING LINES & SHAPES

Figure 74 ... and for a connector.

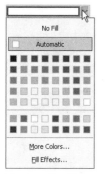

Figure 75 The Fill Color menu.

Figure 77 The Dashed menu.

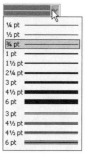

Figure 79 The Line Style menu.

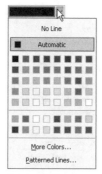

Figure 76 The Line Color menu.

Figure 78 The Connector menu.

Figure 80
The Begin style menu.
The End style menu looks the same, but the arrows point the other way.

Figure 81
The End size menu.
The Begin size menu looks the same, but the arrows point the other way.

▲ To change the dashed style, choose an option from the Dashed menu in the Line area of the dialog (**Figure 77**).

▲ To change a connector's style, choose an option from the Connector menu in the Line area of the dialog (**Figure 78**).

▲ To change the line style, choose an option from the Style menu in the Line area of the dialog (**Figure 79**).

▲ To change the line weight, enter a value in pixels in the Weight box in the Line area of the dialog.

▲ To change the style of arrowheads on a line or arrow, choose options from the Begin style and End style menus in the Arrows area of the dialog (**Figure 80**). When you choose an arrow style, you can also set the arrow size by choosing options from the Begin size and End size menus (**Figure 81**).

4. When you've finished setting options in the dialog, click OK.

✔ Tips

■ As shown in **Figures 72**, **73**, and **74**, the formatting options that are available in the dialog depend on the line or shape that is selected.

■ You can combine as many formatting options as you like to customize the appearance of lines and shapes.

FORMATTING LINES & SHAPES

Stacking Order

Each time you draw a shape, Excel puts it on a new drawing layer. When you draw a shape that overlaps another shape, the first shape may be partially obscured by the one "on top" of it (**Figure 82**).

To change stacking order

1. Select the object(s) you want to move to another layer (**Figure 83**).

2. Choose an option from the Order sub-menu on the Drawing toolbar's Draw menu (**Figure 84**):

   ▲ **Bring to Front** moves the object(s) to the top layer (**Figure 85**).

   ▲ **Send to Back** moves the object(s) to the bottom layer (**Figure 86**).

   ▲ **Bring Forward** moves the object(s) up one layer.

   ▲ **Send Backward** moves the object(s) down one layer.

✔ Tips

■ Once you've gotten objects in the order you want, consider grouping them so they stay just the way you want them to. I tell you how to group objects earlier in this chapter.

■ You cannot move graphic objects behind the worksheet layer.

Figure 82
Because each object is drawn in a separate layer, objects can be obscured by other objects "on top" of them.

Figure 83
To change an object's layer, start by selecting it.

Figure 84 The Order submenu under the Drawing toolbar's Draw menu.

Figure 85
A selected object can be brought to the top layer ...

Figure 86
... or sent to the bottom layer.

Creating Charts

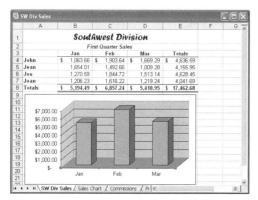

Figure 1 Here's a 3-D column chart embedded in a worksheet file.

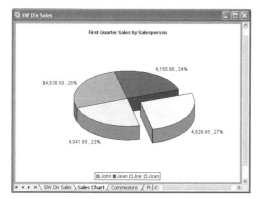

Figure 2 Here's a 3-D pie chart on a chart sheet of its own.

Charts

A chart is a graphic representation of data. A chart can be embedded in a worksheet (**Figure 1**) or can be a chart sheet of its own (**Figure 2**).

With Microsoft Excel, you can create many different types of charts. The 3-D column chart and 3-D pie chart shown here (**Figures 1** and **2**) are only two examples. Since each type of chart has at least one variation and you can customize any chart you create, there's no limit to the number of ways you can present data graphically with Excel.

✔ Tips

- Include charts with worksheets whenever you want to emphasize worksheet results. Charts can often communicate information like trends and comparative results better than numbers alone.

- A skilled chartmaker can, through choice of data, chart format, and scale, get a chart to say almost anything about the data it represents!

153

The Chart Wizard

Excel's Chart Wizard walks you through the creation of a chart. It uses illustrated dialogs to prompt you for information. In each step of the Chart Wizard, you get to see what your chart looks like. At any point, you can go back and make changes to selections. When you're finished, your chart appears. You can then use a variety of chart formatting commands and buttons to change the look of your chart.

To use the Chart Wizard

1. Select the data you want to include in the chart (**Figure 3**).

2. Choose Insert > Chart (**Figure 4**) or click the Chart Wizard button  on the Standard toolbar.

3. In the Chart Wizard – Chart Type dialog (**Figure 5**), click to select one of the chart types in the scrolling list. Then click to select one of the chart sub-types on the right side of the dialog. Click Next.

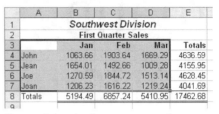

Figure 3 Select the data you want to chart.

Figure 4
Choose Chart from the Insert menu.

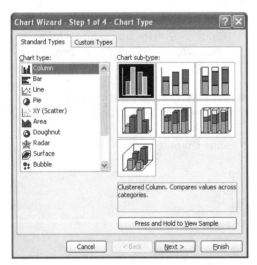

Figure 5 The first step of the Chart Wizard enables you to select a chart type.

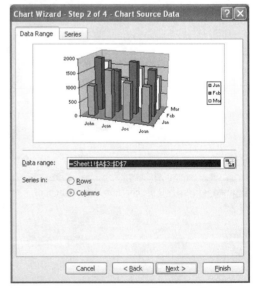

Figure 6 The second step of the Chart Wizard enables you to check and, if necessary, change the range to be charted.

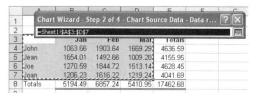

Figure 7 You can collapse the Chart Wizard dialog to see which range is selected.

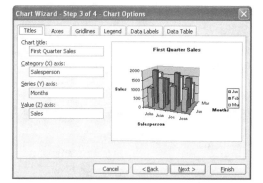

Figure 8 Chart Wizard Titles options.

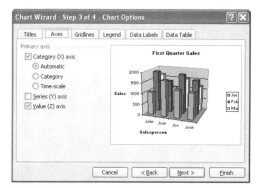

Figure 9 Chart Wizard Axes options.

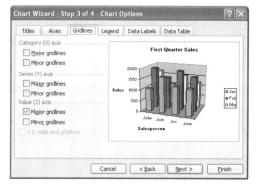

Figure 10 Chart Wizard Gridlines options.

4. In the Chart Wizard – Chart Source Data dialog (**Figure 6**), check the contents of the Data range text box to assure that it indicates the data you want to chart. You can see which data range will be charted by clicking the Collapse Dialog button ⊞ beside the Data range text box so you can see the sheet behind the dialog (**Figure 7**). If incorrect, select the correct range. If necessary, click the Expand Dialog button ⊞ to display the entire dialog again. You can also select a different Series in option button to change the way data is charted. Then click Next.

5. In the Chart Wizard – Chart Options dialog, use the tabs at the top of the dialog to set a variety of formatting options:

   ▲ **Titles** (**Figure 8**) enables you to set a chart title and axes titles.

   ▲ **Axes** (**Figure 9**) enables you to select which axes you want to display.

   ▲ **Gridlines** (**Figure 10**) enables you to select which gridlines to display.

   ▲ **Legend** (**Figure 11**) enables you to show and position or hide the legend.

Continued on next page...

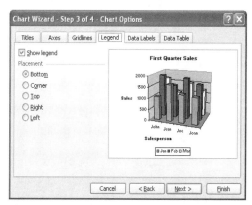

Figure 11 Chart Wizard Legend options.

USING THE CHART WIZARD

155

Continued from previous page.

▲ **Data Labels** (**Figure 12**) enables you to set the type of data labels that should be displayed.

▲ **Data Table** (**Figure 13**) enables you to include a data table with the chart.

Set options as desired. When you change a setting, the sample chart changes accordingly. When you are finished, click Next.

6. In the Chart Wizard — Chart Location dialog (**Figure 14**), select the radio button to set the location for the chart:

▲ **As new sheet** puts the chart on a new chart sheet. You can enter a name in the text box to name the new sheet when you create it.

▲ **As object in** puts the chart on another sheet in the workbook. You can use the drop-down list to select the sheet.

7. Click Finish.

Excel creates and inserts the chart with the settings and in the location you specified.

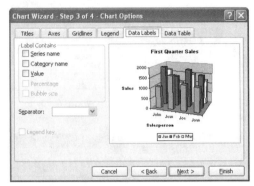

Figure 12 Chart Wizard Data Labels options.

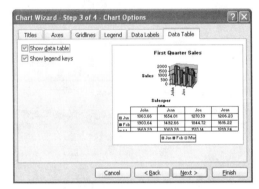

Figure 13 Chart Wizard Data Table options.

Figure 14 The final step of the Chart Wizard.

USING THE CHART WIZARD

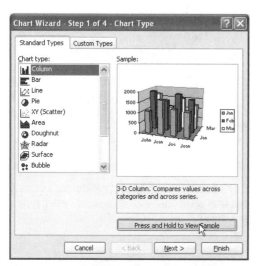

Figure 15 You can preview what your chart will look like with the chart type and subtype you selected by clicking a button in the first window of the Chart Wizard.

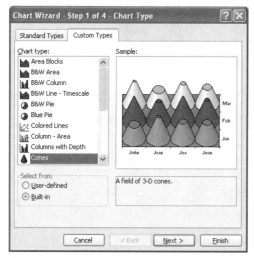

Figure 16 The Chart Wizard also allows you to select some custom chart types from the Chart Gallery.

✔ Tips

- At any time while using the Chart Wizard, you can click the Back button to move to a previous step. Any changes you make in a previous step are carried forward when you continue.

- In step 3, to see what your data would look like when charted with the chart type and sub-type you selected, click and hold down the Press and Hold to View Sample button (**Figure 15**).

- In step 3, you can select one of the custom chart types by clicking the Custom Types tab (**Figure 16**). Then follow the instructions in step 3 for that tab.

- In step 4, you can add, modify, or delete data series for the chart in the Series tab (**Figure 17**). I tell you about working with data series later in this chapter.

Continued on next page...

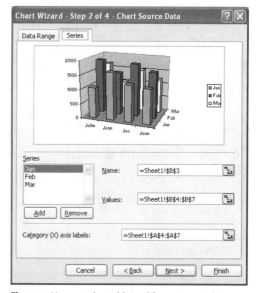

Figure 17 You can also add, modify, or remove data series from a chart within the Chart Wizard.

Continued from previous page.

- I explain all the options in step 5 throughout this chapter.

- In step 5, axes and gridlines options are only available for charts that have axes or gridlines. Pie charts, for example, have neither axes nor gridlines.

- A chart embedded in a worksheet or a chart sheet is a special kind of graphic. You can move, copy, resize, or delete it just like any other graphic object. I tell you how to work with graphics in **Chapter 7**.

- If an embedded chart is too small to properly display data (**Figure 18**), resize it. The larger the chart, the better it will display (**Figure 19**).

- You can also improve the appearance of an embedded chart by resizing or removing chart elements such as legends, axes labels, and data tables.

- You're not stuck with the formatting you select in the Chart Wizard. I tell you about chart formatting options throughout this chapter.

- Don't be afraid to experiment with the Chart Wizard. Try different options to see what effects you can achieve. You can always delete the chart and start fresh. Deleting a chart does not change data.

To reuse the Chart Wizard

1. Activate the chart by switching to its chart sheet or, if it's an embedded chart, by clicking within it.

2. Click the Chart Wizard button 📊 on the Standard toolbar.

3. Follow the steps on the previous pages to set or change Chart Wizard options for the chart.

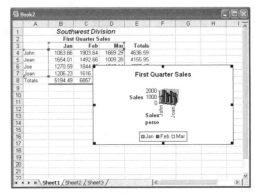

Figure 18 When you create an embedded chart, Excel just plops it in the worksheet.

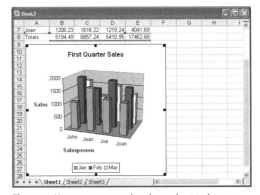

Figure 19 You can move and resize a chart to improve its appearance.

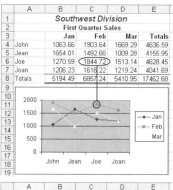

Figures 20 & 21
A linked worksheet and chart before (top) and after (bottom) a change to a cell's contents. When you change one, the other changes automatically.

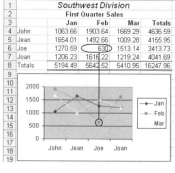

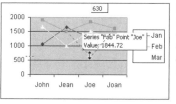

Figure 22 Dragging a data point changes the data in the linked cell.

Figure 23 This illustration shows both the Range Finder feature and the SERIES formula.

Figure 24 If you delete cells linked to a chart, you may see a dialog like this.

Worksheet & Chart Links

When you create a chart based on worksheet data, the worksheet and chart are linked. Excel knows exactly which worksheet and cells it should look at to plot the chart. If the contents of one of those cells changes, the chart changes accordingly (**Figures** 20 and 21).

✔ Tips

- The link works both ways. With some chart types, you can drag a data point to change the data in the source worksheet (**Figure** 22). This makes a good planning tool for businesses interested in maintaining trends.

- Excel's Range Finder feature places a color-coded box around ranges in a selected chart (**Figure** 23), making them easy to spot.

- You can see (and edit) the links between a chart and a worksheet by activating the chart, selecting one of the data series, and looking at the formula bar. In the formula bar, you should see a formula with a SERIES function that specifies the sheet name and absolute cell references for the range making up that series. **Figure** 23 shows an example.

- If you delete worksheet data or an entire worksheet that is linked to a chart, Excel warns you with a dialog like the one in **Figure** 24. Click OK and then, if you removed the data by mistake, choose Edit > Undo Delete, click the Undo button on the Standard toolbar, or press Ctrl Z to get the deleted data back.

WORKSHEET & CHART LINKS

Data Series & Points

A *data series* is a group of related data in a chart. A data series normally corresponds to the values in a linked range of cells in a single column or row of a single worksheet. When plotted on a chart, each data series is assigned its own color or pattern.

Each cell within a data series is called a *data point*. Data points are individually plotted on a chart.

You can change a data series included in a chart at any time using four different methods:

◆ Use Range Finder handles to modify a series in an embedded chart.

◆ Use the Source Data dialog to add, modify, or remove a series.

◆ Use the Copy and Paste commands to paste in a new series.

◆ Use drag-and-drop editing to add a new series.

I tell you about all of these techniques next.

To modify a data series with Range Finder handles

1. Click the chart to activate it. Range Finder frames with handles appear around each data series (**Figure 25**).

2. Position the mouse pointer on the handle for the series you want to change. The mouse pointer turns into a two-headed arrow.

3. Press the mouse button, and drag to stretch or shrink the series (**Figure 26**).

4. When you release the mouse button, the series (and any related series) changes, thus changing the information plotted in the chart (**Figure 27**).

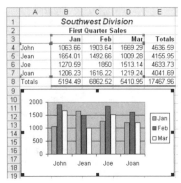

Figure 25 When you activate a chart, Range Finder frames appear around each data series.

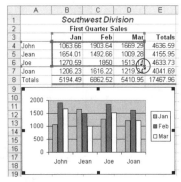

Figure 26 Drag a Range Finder handle to change the size of the series.

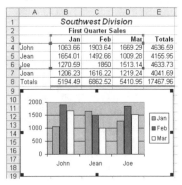

Figure 27 When you release the mouse button, the series—and the chart—changes.

✔ Tip

■ You can only use this method with an embedded chart.

USING RANGE FINDER HANDLES

Figure 28
The Chart menu appears only when a chart is active.

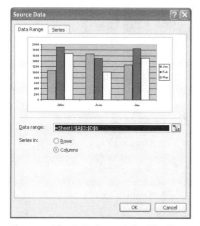

Figure 29 The Data Range tab of the Source Data dialog.

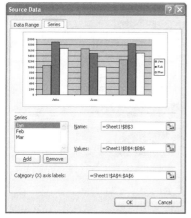

Figure 30 The Series tab of the Source Data dialog.

✔ Tips

■ The Source Data dialog looks (and works) just like the second step of the Chart Wizard (**Figures 6** and **17**). In fact, you can use the Chart Wizard to make any of the changes discussed on this page.

To modify data series with the Source Data dialog

1. Activate the chart by switching to its chart sheet or, if it's an embedded chart, by clicking within it.

2. Choose Chart > Source Data (**Figure 28**) to display the Source Data dialog (**Figures 29** and **30**).

3. Click the Data Range tab (**Figure 29**):

   ▲ To change the range of data plotted in the chart, select a new data range. As you select the range, it is automatically entered in the Data range text box.

   ▲ To switch the series from column to row or row to column, select the appropriate Series in radio button.

   or

   Click the Series tab (**Figure 30**):

   ▲ To add a data series, click the Add button, then drag in the worksheet to enter a range in the Name and Values text boxes.

   ▲ To modify a data series, select the name of the series you want to change, then drag in the worksheet to modify the range in the Name and/ or Values text boxes.

   ▲ To remove a data series, select the name of the series you want to remove and click the Remove button.

4. Consult the sample chart in the dialog to see the affect of your changes. When the chart reflects the correct ranges, click OK.

■ You can click the Collapse Dialog 🔲 or Expand Dialog 🔲 buttons to change the size of the Source Data dialog.

■ Removing a data series does not delete data from the source worksheet.

To add a data series with the Copy & Paste commands

1. In the worksheet, select the data you want to add to the chart (**Figure 31**). Be sure to include column or row headings if they should be included as labels.

2. Choose Edit > Copy (**Figure 32**), press Ctrl C, or click the Copy button on the Standard toolbar. A marquee appears around the selected cells.

3. Activate the chart to which you want to add the data by switching to its chart sheet or, if it's an embedded chart, by clicking within it.

4. Choose Edit > Paste (**Figure 32**), press Ctrl V, or click the Paste button on the Standard toolbar. The chart changes to include the additional data (**Figure 33**).

✔ Tips

- In order for this technique to work properly, the data you add must be the same kind of data originally charted. For example, if you originally plotted totals to create a pie chart, you can't successfully add a series of numbers that aren't totals to the chart.

- For additional control over how data is pasted into a chart, choose Edit > Paste Special (**Figure 32**) in step 4 above. The Paste Special dialog (**Figure 34**) will sometimes appear on its own when you paste a range into a chart.

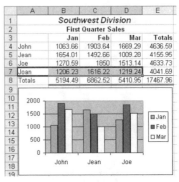

Figure 31 Select the data that you want to add to the chart.

Figure 32 The Edit menu includes the Copy, Paste, and Paste Special commands, which you can use to add data to a chart.

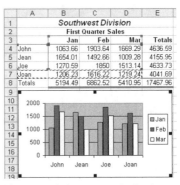

Figure 33 When you paste in the data, the chart changes accordingly.

Figure 34 The Paste Special dialog offers options for pasting data into charts.

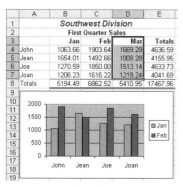

Figure 35 Select the data you want to add to the chart.

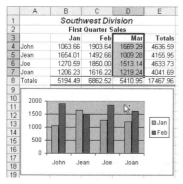

Figure 36 Drag the selection onto the chart.

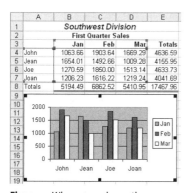

Figure 37 When you release the mouse button, the data is added to the chart.

To add a data series with drag & drop

1. In the worksheet, select the data you want to add to the chart (**Figure 35**). Be sure to include column or row headings if they should be included as labels.

2. Position the mouse pointer on the border of the selection. The mouse pointer turns into a hand.

3. Press the mouse button and drag the selection on top of the chart. The mouse pointer gets a little plus sign inside it and the chart border changes (**Figure 36**).

4. Release the mouse button. The chart changes to include the additional data (**Figure 37**).

✔ Tips

- In order for this technique to work properly, the data you add must be the same kind of data originally charted. For example, if you originally plotted totals to create a pie chart, you can't successfully add a series of numbers that aren't totals to the chart.

- This technique only works for charts that are embedded in the worksheet containing the original data.

- To add data contained in noncontiguous ranges, use one of the other methods discussed in this section.

ADDING DATA SERIES WITH DRAG & DROP

To remove a data series

1. Click to select the series you want to remove. Selection handles appear at each data point in the series (**Figure 38**).

2. Choose Edit > Clear > Series (**Figure 39**) or press ⟨Delete⟩.

   The series disappears (**Figure 40**). If the chart included a legend, it is revised to exclude the deleted data.

✔ Tips

- Removing a series from a chart does not delete data from the source worksheet.

- You can also remove a data series with the Source Data dialog (**Figure 30**). I tell you how earlier in this chapter.

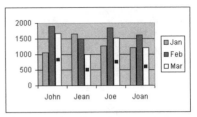

Figure 38 Select the series you want to remove.

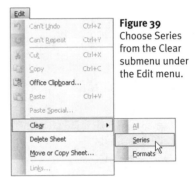

Figure 39 Choose Series from the Clear submenu under the Edit menu.

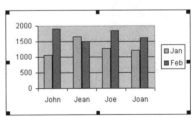

Figure 40 All trace of the series is removed from the chart.

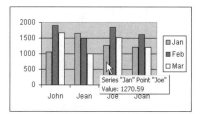

Figure 41 Chart tips identify the chart elements and values you point to.

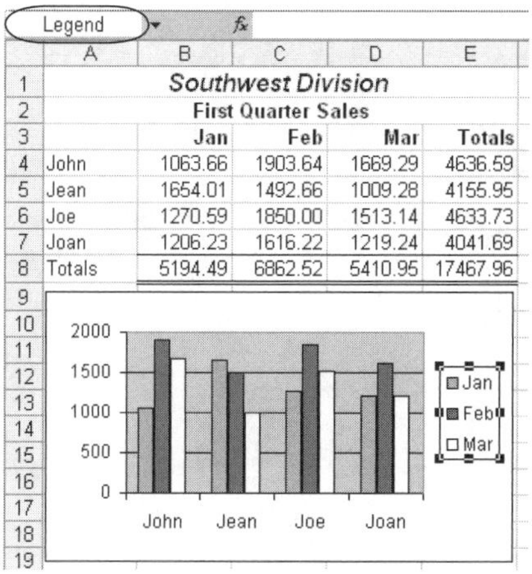

	A	B	C	D	E
1		*Southwest Division*			
2		**First Quarter Sales**			
3		Jan	Feb	Mar	Totals
4	John	1063.66	1903.64	1669.29	4636.59
5	Jean	1654.01	1492.66	1009.28	4155.95
6	Joe	1270.59	1850.00	1513.14	4633.73
7	Joan	1206.23	1616.22	1219.24	4041.69
8	Totals	5194.49	6862.52	5410.95	17467.96

Figure 42 The name of a selected element appears in the Name box on the formula bar.

Chart Elements

Each chart is made up of multiple *elements*, each of which can be selected, then modified or formatted to fine-tune the appearance of a chart.

To identify a chart element

Point to the element you want to identify. Excel displays the name (and values, if appropriate) for the element in a yellow Chart Tip box (**Figure 41**).

To select a chart element

Click the element you want to select. Selection handles or a selection box (or both) appear around it (**Figure 42**).

✔ Tips

- To select a single data point, first click to select the data series, then click the point to select it.

- Excel displays the name of a selected chart element in the Name box on the formula bar (**Figure 42**).

Chart Type

Excel includes dozens of standard and custom chart types. You select the chart type when you create a chart with the Chart Wizard, but you can change the type at any time. You can also add your formatted charts to the Chart Gallery so you can use them to create future charts.

To change the chart type

1. Activate the chart by switching to its chart sheet or, if it's an embedded chart, by clicking within it.

2. Choose Chart > Chart Type (**Figure 28**) to display the Chart Type dialog.

3. Click the Standard Types tab (**Figure 43**):

   ▲ To select a standard chart type, select a Chart type, then select a Chart sub-type.

   ▲ To apply a chart type to a selected data series, turn on the Apply to selection check box.

   ▲ To remove formatting you have applied to the chart, turn on the Default formatting check box.

   or

   Click the Custom Types tab:

   ▲ To select a built-in chart type, select the Built-in radio button (**Figure 44**), then select a Chart type.

   ▲ To select a user-defined chart type, select the User-defined radio button (**Figure 45**), then select a Chart type.

4. Click OK to apply the chart type.

✔ Tip

■ The Chart Type dialog looks just like the first step of the Chart Wizard (**Figures 5** and **15**). In fact, you can use the Chart Wizard to make any of the changes discussed on this page.

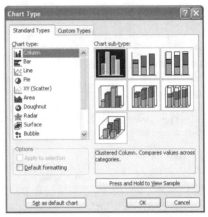

Figure 43 The Standard Types tab of the Chart Type dialog.

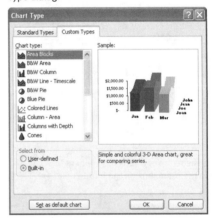

Figure 44 The Custom Types tab of the Chart Type dialog with Built-in selected.

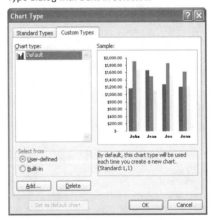

Figure 45 The Custom Types tab of the Chart Type dialog with User-defined selected.

Figure 46 Use the Add Custom Chart Type dialog to enter a name and description for a chart type.

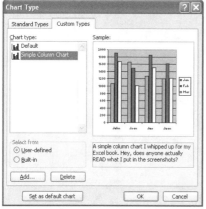

Figure 47 The chart type you added appears in the User-defined Chart type list.

To set the default chart type

1. Choose Chart > Chart Type (**Figure 28**) to display the Chart Type dialog.

2. Click the Standard Types tab (**Figure 43**).

3. Select the Chart type and sub-type you want to set as the default chart type.

4. Click the Set as default chart button.

5. Click OK.

✔ Tip

- The default chart type is the one automatically selected for creating a new chart.

To add a user-defined chart to the Chart Type dialog

1. Activate the formatted chart you want to add by switching to its chart sheet or, if it's an embedded chart, by clicking within it.

2. Choose Chart > Chart Type (**Figure 28**) to display the Chart Type dialog.

3. Click the Custom Types tab.

4. Select the User-defined radio button (**Figure 45**).

5. Click the Add button.

6. In the Add Custom Chart Type dialog that appears (**Figure 46**), enter a name and description for the chart in the appropriate text boxes.

7. Click OK. The chart appears in the User-defined Chart type list (**Figure 47**).

8. Click OK.

✔ Tip

- This feature makes it easy to create the same basic charts over and over again with different data—like you might have to do for a monthly report.

Chart Options

Chart options refer to the inclusion and basic formatting of chart elements such as titles, axes, gridlines, legend, data labels, and data tables. You set chart options with the Chart Options dialog.

To use the Chart Options dialog

1. Activate the chart by switching to its chart sheet or, if it's an embedded chart, by clicking within it.

2. Choose Chart > Chart Options (**Figure 28**) to display the Chart Options dialog (**Figures 48** through **53**).

3. Click the tab for the type of option you want to set.

4. Set options as desired.

5. Repeat steps 3 and 4 for each type of option you want to set.

6. Click OK to apply your settings.

✔ Tips

- I provide details on all options on the following pages.

- The Chart Options dialog looks just like the third step of the Chart Wizard (**Figures 8** through **13**). In fact, you can use the Chart Wizard to make any of the changes discussed on this page.

- Each time you make a change in the Chart Options dialog, the effect of your change is reflected in the chart preview within the dialog. Use this feature to check your changes before clicking OK.

- The options available in the Chart Options dialog vary based on the type of chart that is selected. If a specific option is not available, either it will not appear or it will appear in gray within the dialog.

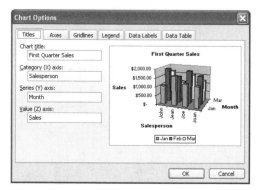

Figure 48 The Titles tab of the Chart Options dialog for a 3-D column chart. The sample illustration shows all titles set.

Titles

Titles are textual labels that appear in specific locations on the chart.

To set chart titles

1. In the Chart Options dialog, click the Titles tab to display its options (**Figure 48**).

2. Enter titles in the desired text boxes:

    ▲ **Chart title** is the chart's main title. It appears at the top of the chart.

    ▲ **Category (X) axis** is the category axis title. Available for most 2-D and 3-D chart types, it appears along the bottom (front) axis.

    ▲ **Series (Y) axis** is the series axis title. Available for most chart types, it appears down the left side of a 2-D chart and along the bottom (back) axis of a 3-D chart.

    ▲ **Value (Z) axis** is the value axis title. Available only for 3-D chart types, it appears down the left side of the chart.

To remove a chart title

1. In the Chart Options dialog, click the Titles tab to display its options (**Figure 48**).

2. Clear the text box(es) for the titles you want to remove.

Axes

Axes are the bounding lines of a chart. 2-D charts have two axes: X and Y. 3-D charts have three axes: X, Y, and Z. Pie and dough-nut charts do not have axes at all.

✔ Tip

■ In case you're wondering, *axes* (pro-nounced *ax-eez*) is the plural of *axis*. While axes are also tools for chopping wood, you can't chop wood with Excel.

To set axes options

1. In the Chart Options dialog, click the Axes tab to display its options (**Figure 49**).

2. Turn on the check boxes for the axes you want to display:

   ▲ **Category (X) axis** appears along the bottom (front) axis.

   ▲ **Series (Y) axis** appears down the left side of a 2-D chart and along the bottom (back) axis of a 3-D chart.

   ▲ **Value (Z) axis**, which is available only for 3-D chart types, appears down the left side of the chart.

3. If you turned on the Category (X) axis option in step 2, select one of the for-matting option radio buttons:

   ▲ **Automatic** instructs Excel to check the formatting of the category data to determine whether it should use time-scale or category formatting.

   ▲ **Category** instructs Excel to use the category data for the X axis.

   ▲ **Time-Scale** instructs Excel to create a time scale for the X axis.

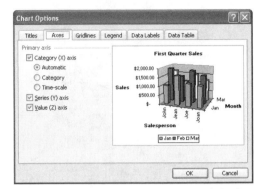

Figure 49 The Axes tab of the Chart Options dialog for a 3-D column chart. The sample illustration shows all axes displayed.

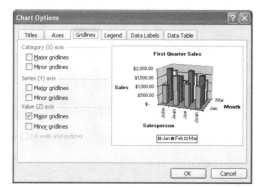

Figure 50 The Gridlines tab of the Chart Options dialog for a 3-D column chart. The sample illustration shows only the major gridlines for the Value (Z) axis turned on.

Gridlines

Gridlines are lines indicating major and minor scale points along a chart's walls. They can make it easier to follow chart points to their corresponding values on a chart axis. Pie and doughnut charts do not have gridlines.

✔ Tip

- Although gridlines can make a chart's data easier to read, too many gridlines can clutter a chart's walls, making data impossible to read.

To set gridlines

1. In the Chart Options dialog, click the Gridlines tab to display its options (**Figure 50**).

2. Turn on the check boxes for the gridlines you want to display on each axis:
   - ▲ **Major gridlines** correspond to major tickmark units for the axis scale.
   - ▲ **Minor gridlines** correspond to minor tickmark units for the axis scale.

3. To apply a 2-D appearance to 3-D chart walls and gridlines, turn on the 2-D walls and gridlines check box. This option is only available for certain types of charts.

✔ Tips

- I explain how to set the scale for an axis later in this chapter.

- I define the three axes on the previous page.

Legend

A legend is a box with color-coded labels identifying a chart's data series. You can turn a legend on or off and set its position within the chart area.

✔ Tip

- Excel creates the legend based on cells selected as part of the data source. That's why it's a good idea to include headings in the selected range when you create a chart.

To add a legend

1. In the Chart Options dialog, click the Legend tab to display its options (**Figure 51**).

2. Turn on the Show legend check box.

3. Select one of the radio buttons for a legend position:

   ▲ **Bottom** displays the legend at the bottom-center of the chart.

   ▲ **Corner** displays the legend at the top-right corner of the chart.

   ▲ **Top** displays the legend at the top-center of the chart.

   ▲ **Right** displays the legend at the right-middle of the chart.

   ▲ **Left** displays the legend at the left-middle of the chart.

✔ Tips

- You can also move a legend by dragging it to a new position within the chart.

- The legend position can affect the size of a chart's plot area.

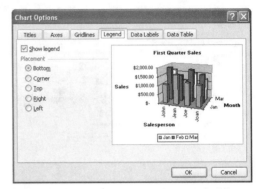

Figure 51 The Legend tab of the Chart Options dialog for a 3-D column chart. The sample illustration shows a legend placed at the bottom of the chart.

To remove the legend

1. In the Chart Options dialog, click the Legend tab to display its options (**Figure 51**).

2. Turn off the Show legend check box.

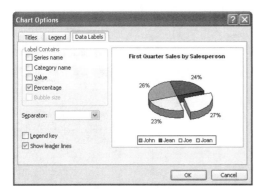

Figure 52 The Data Labels tab of the Chart Options dialog for a 3-D pie chart. The sample illustration shows percent data labels.

Data Labels

Data labels provide additional information about specific data points.

✔ Tip

■ The Chart Options dialog enables you to set data labels for all chart points. To set data labels for just a single data series or data point, select the series or point, then use the Format dialog, which I tell you about later in this chapter.

To add data labels

1. In the Chart Options dialog, click the Data Labels tab to display its options (**Figure 52**).

2. Turn on any valid combination of Label Contains check boxes:

   ▲ **Series name** displays the name of the data series.

   ▲ **Category name** displays the name of the data category.

   ▲ **Value** displays the value for each data point.

   ▲ **Percentage** displays the percentage of the whole for each data point. This option is only available for pie and doughnut charts.

   ▲ **Bubble size** displays the size of bubbles in a bubble chart.

3. To set the separator character when displaying multiple data labels, choose an option from the Separator drop-down list.

4. To show the legend color key beside a data label, turn on the Legend key check box.

5. For a pie or doughnut chart, to display a line from the data point to the data label, turn on the Show leader lines check box.

To remove data labels

1. In the Chart Options dialog, click the Data Labels tab to display its options (**Figure 52**).

2. Turn off all Label Contains check boxes.

Data Table

A data table is the data plotted on the chart, in tabular format.

✔ Tips

- Data tables are more useful on chart sheets than on embedded charts, since embedded charts can include the worksheet on which the chart is based.

- Data tables are not available for pie and doughnut charts.

To add a data table

1. In the Chart Options dialog, click the Data Table tab to display its options (**Figure 53**).

2. Turn on the Show data table check box.

3. To show the legend color key in the data table, turn on the Show legend keys check box.

To remove a data table

1. In the Chart Options dialog, click the Data Table tab to display its options (**Figure 53**).

2. Turn off the Show data table check box.

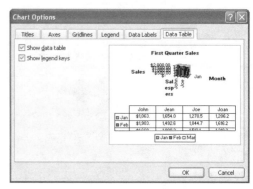

Figure 53 The Data Table tab of the Chart Options dialog for a 3-D column chart. The sample illustration shows a data table with legend keys turned on.

ADDING & REMOVING A DATA TABLE

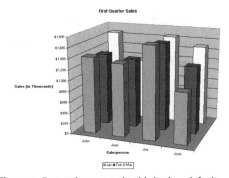

Figure 54 Formatting can make this boring, default chart ...

Figure 55 ... look interesting!

Formatting Chart Elements

You can use the Format dialog to apply a variety of formatting to chart elements:

◆ **Font** enables you to change the appearance of an element's font characters.

◆ **Number** enables you to change the number formatting of values.

◆ **Alignment** enables you to change the alignment and orientation of text.

◆ **Patterns** enables you to change an element's color and pattern. It also enables you to set axis tick mark styles.

◆ **Placement** enables you to set the position for a chart legend.

◆ **Scale** enables you to change the values that appear on an axis.

◆ **Shape** enables you to change the shape of data points.

◆ **Data Labels** enables you to set data labels for a single data series or data point. I discuss these options earlier in this chapter.

◆ **Series Order** enables you to change the order in which data series appear.

◆ **Options** enables you to set data series spacing options.

Figures 54 and **55** may give you an idea of what you can do with chart formatting.

In this section, I tell you how chart formatting works and discuss some of the formatting options available just for charts.

✔ Tip

■ I discuss pattern, font, number, and alignment formatting in **Chapter 6**. I discuss legend position and data labels earlier in this chapter.

To use the Format dialog

1. Select the chart element that you want to format and choose the first command under the Format menu (**Figures 56**, **57**, and **58**) or press Ctrl 1.

    or

    Double-click the element that you want to format.

2. In the Format dialog that appears, click the tab for the type of option you want to set.

3. Set options as desired.

4. Repeat steps 2 and 3 for each type of option you want to set.

5. Click OK to apply the formatting.

✔ Tips

■ The exact name of the menu command in step 1 varies depending on the chart element that is selected. You can see this in **Figures 56**, **57**, and **58**.

■ The exact name of the Format dialog in step 2 varies depending on the chart element that is selected. You can see this in **Figures 59** and **61**.

To set the data point shape

1. Open the Format Data Series dialog for a selected data series.

2. Click the Shape tab to display its options (**Figure 59**).

3. Click to select the desired shape.

4. Click OK. The shape is applied to the selected data series (**Figure 60**).

✔ Tip

■ This option is only available for certain 3-D charts.

Figures 56, 57, & 58 The first command under the Format menu enables you to format the selected chart element.

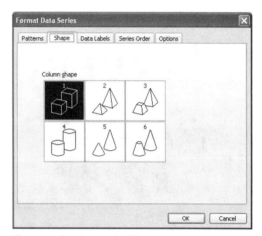

Figure 59 The Shape tab of the Format Data Series dialog enables you to select a shape to apply to the selected series in a 3-D chart.

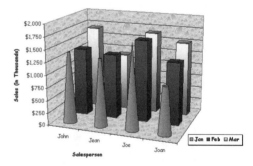

Figure 60 In this example, shape style #6 was applied to one data series.

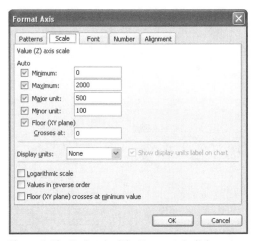

Figure 61 The Scale tab of the Format Axis dialog.

To set the scale

1. Open the Format Gridlines or Format Axis dialog for the gridline or axis for which you want to set the scale.

2. Click the Scale tab to display its options (**Figure 61**).

3. Enter the scale values you want to use in the text boxes:

   ▲ **Minimum** is the minimum value on the scale. It is normally set to 0.

   ▲ **Maximum** is the maximum value on the scale. It is normally set to a round number larger than the highest value plotted.

   ▲ **Major unit** is the unit corresponding to major gridlines and tick marks.

   ▲ **Minor unit** is the unit corresponding to minor gridlines and tick marks.

   ▲ **Floor (XY plane) Crosses at** is the value at which the X and Y axes cross each other. It is normally set to 0.

4. To set the display units, choose an option from the Display units drop-down list. Your options are None, Hundreds, Thousands, Millions, Billions, and Trillions. You can then turn on the check box beside this option to display the units label near the axis on the chart.

5. Turn on check boxes for special scale options as desired:

   ▲ **Logarithmic scale** recalculates the values in the text boxes as powers of 10.

   ▲ **Values in reverse order** reverses the order in which the scale appears, putting the largest values at the bottom or left side of the axis.

   ▲ **Floor (XY plane) crosses at minimum value** overrides the Floor (XY plane) Crosses at value and sets it to the minimum value.

6. Click OK.

✔ Tip

■ In step 3, when you enter a value in a text box, its corresponding check box should turn itself off automatically; you can turn it back on to use the default setting.

SETTING SCALE

To set tick marks

1. Open the Format Axis dialog for the axis for which you want to set the tick marks.

2. Click the Patterns tab to display its options (**Figure 62**).

3. Select the radio button for the desired Tick mark labels option:

   ▲ **None** omits tick mark labels.

   ▲ **Low** displays tick mark labels at the bottom or to the right of the plot area.

   ▲ **High** displays tick mark labels at the top or to the left of the plot area.

   ▲ **Next to axis** displays tick mark labels next to the selected axis. This is the default option.

4. Select the radio buttons for the desired Major tick mark type and Minor tick mark type:

   ▲ **None** omits tick marks.

   ▲ **Inside** displays tick marks inside the plot area.

   ▲ **Outside** displays tick marks outside the plot area.

   ▲ **Cross** displays tick marks that cross the axis line.

5. If desired, use options in the Lines area to modify the appearance of the axis line.

6. Click OK.

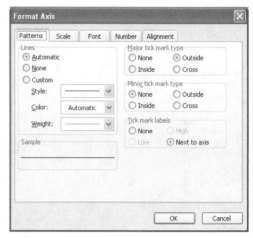

Figure 62 The Patterns tab of the Format Axis dialog.

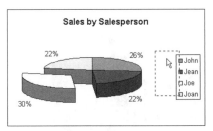

Figure 63 To move a chart element, drag it to its new position.

Figure 64 When you release the mouse button, it moves.

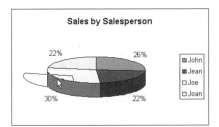

Figure 65 When you move a piece of a pie chart away from the rest of the pie ...

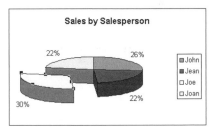

Figure 66 ... you get an "exploded" effect.

Other Formatting Options

In addition to formatting individual chart elements, you can make other modifications to a chart to change the way it appears. Here are a few additional options you may find handy.

To move a chart element

1. Click the element to select it.

2. Position the mouse pointer on the element, press the mouse button, and drag. As you drag, an outline of the element moves with the mouse pointer (**Figure 63**).

3. Release the mouse button. The element moves (**Figure 64**).

✔ Tip

■ You can use this technique with most chart elements.

To "explode" a pie chart

1. Select the data point for the pie piece you want to move.

2. Drag the pie piece away from the pie (**Figure 65**).

3. Release the mouse button. The piece moves away from the pie (**Figure 66**).

✔ Tip

■ If desired, you can drag more than one piece away from the pie.

MOVING ELEMENTS, EXPLODING PIES

To rotate a 3-D chart

1. Open or select the chart you want to rotate (**Figure 67**).

2. Choose 3-D View from the Chart menu (**Figure 28**).

3. In the 3-D View dialog (**Figure 68**), click the Elevation, Rotation, and Perspective buttons to change the view of the chart.

4. When you're finished making changes, click OK. The chart rotates (**Figure 69**).

✔ Tips

- You can click the Apply button in the 3-D View dialog (**Figure 68**) to get a first-hand look at the modified chart without closing the dialog. You may have to drag the 3-D View dialog out of the way to see your chart.

- You can click the Default button in the 3-D View dialog to return the chart to its default rotation.

- Some changes in the 3-D View dialog may change the size of the chart.

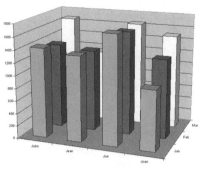

Figure 67 A chart before rotation.

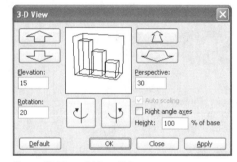

Figure 68 The 3-D View dialog.

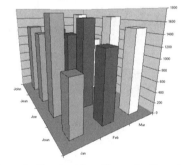

Figure 69 The chart from **Figure 67** after rotation.

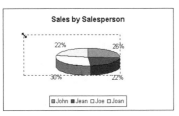

Figure 70
Drag a selection handle ...

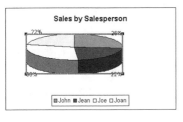

Figure 71
... to resize almost any chart element.

To resize a chart element

1. Click the element to select it.

2. Position the mouse pointer on one of the resizing handles for the element, press the mouse button, and drag. As you drag, the border of the element moves with the mouse pointer (**Figure 70**).

3. Release the mouse button. The element resizes (**Figure 71**).

✔ Tip

■ You can use this technique with most chart elements.

Printing

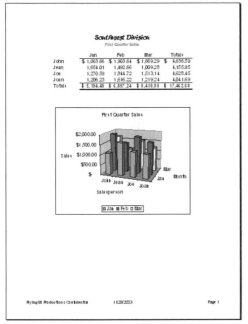

Figure 1 Print Preview lets you see reports before you commit them to paper.

✔ Tips

- When you save a document, Excel saves many Page Setup and Print options with it.

Printing

In most cases, when you create a worksheet or chart, you'll want to print it. With Microsoft Excel, you can print all or part of a sheet, multiple sheets, or an entire workbook—all at once. Excel gives you control over page size, margins, headers, footers, page breaks, orientation, scaling, page order, and content. Its Print Preview feature (**Figure 1**) shows you what your report will look like when printed, so you can avoid wasteful, time-consuming reprints.

Printing is basically a three-step process:

1. Use the Page Setup dialog to set up your report for printing. (You can skip this step if you set the report up the first time you printed it and don't need to change the setup.)

2. Use the Print Preview feature to take a look at your report before committing it to paper. You can skip this step if you already know what the report will look like.

3. Use the Print command to send the desired number of copies to the printer for printing.

In this chapter, I explain each of these steps.

- This chapter assumes that your computer is already set up for printing. If it is not, consult the documentation that came with your printer for setup information.

The Page Setup Dialog

The Page Setup dialog (**Figure 2**) enables you to set up a document for printing. Setup options are organized under the following tabs:

◆ **Page** (**Figure 2**) lets you set the orientation, scaling, first page number, paper size, and print quality.

◆ **Margins** (**Figures 6** and **7**) lets you set the page margins, the distance the header and footer should be from the edge of the paper, and the positioning of the document on the paper.

◆ **Header/Footer** (**Figure 8**) lets you select a standard header and footer or create custom ones.

◆ **Sheet** (**Figure 14**) lets you specify the print area, print titles, items to print, and page order. If a chart sheet is active when you choose Page Setup, you'll see a Chart tab (**Figure 22**) rather than a Sheet tab. Use it to specify the printed chart size and print quality.

To open the Page Setup dialog

Choose File > Page Setup (**Figure 3**).

Or

Click the Setup button in the Print Preview window (**Figure 23**).

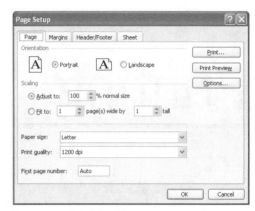

Figure 2 The Page tab of The Page Setup dialog.

Figure 3
The File menu offers a number of print-related commands.

Figure 4 The Paper Size drop-down list.

Figure 5 The Print quality drop-down list.

To set page options

1. In the Page Setup dialog, click the Page tab to display its options (**Figure 2**).

2. In the Orientation area, select the desired orientation option:

   ▲ **Portrait**, the default option for worksheets, prints vertically down the page.

   ▲ **Landscape**, the default option for chart sheets, prints horizontally across the page.

3. For a worksheet only, in the Scaling area, select the desired scaling option:

   ▲ **Adjust to** enables you to specify a percentage of the normal size for printing. Be sure to enter a value in the text box. This option is selected by default with 100 in the text box.

   ▲ **Fit to** instructs Excel to shrink the report so it fits on the number of pages you specify. Be sure to enter values in the two text boxes.

4. Choose an option from the Paper size drop-down list (**Figure 4**). These options vary depending on your printer.

5. Choose an option from the Print quality drop-down list (**Figure 5**). These options vary depending on your printer.

6. If desired, in the First page number text box, enter a value that should be used as the page number on the first page of the report. This enables you to start page numbering at a value other than 1.

7. Click OK to save your settings.

✔ Tips

■ Neither scaling option is available for chart sheets. You can change the scaling for a chart sheet on the Chart tab of the Page Setup dialog, which I discuss later in this chapter.

■ The options that appear in this dialog vary from printer to printer. To learn more about the options for your printer, consult the documentation that came with the printer.

To set margins & centering options

1. In the Page Setup dialog, click the Margins tab to display its options (**Figure 6** or 7).

2. Enter values in the Top, Left, Right, and Bottom text boxes to set the amount of space between the edge of the paper and the report content.

3. Enter values in the Header and Footer text boxes to set the amount of space between the edge of the paper and the header and footer content.

4. For a worksheet only, turn on the desired Center on page check boxes:

   ▲ **Horizontally** centers the report content between the left and right margins.

   ▲ **Vertically** centers the report content between the top and bottom margins.

5. Click OK to save your settings.

✔ Tips

■ As you make changes in this window, the preview area changes accordingly. This helps you get an idea of what the document will look like when previewed or printed.

■ You can also set margins in the Print Preview window. I explain how later in this chapter.

■ Do not set margins to smaller values than the Header and Footer values or Excel will print your report over the header or footer.

■ Some printers cannot print close to the edge of the paper. If part of your report is cut off when printed, increase the margin, header, and footer values.

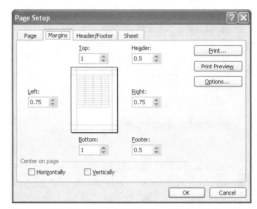

Figure 6 The Margins tab of the Page Setup dialog for a worksheet ...

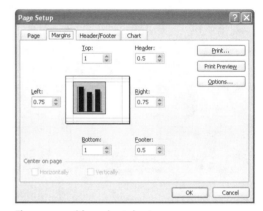

Figure 7 ... and for a chart sheet.

SETTING MARGINS & CENTERING OPTIONS

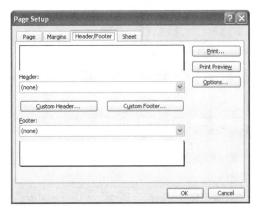

Figure 8 The Header/Footer tab of the Page Setup dialog.

Figure 9 The Header and Footer drop-down lists offer a number of predefined headers and footers.

Figure 10 The header and footer you select appear in the sample areas in the dialog.

To add built-in headers & footers

1. In the Page Setup dialog, click the Header/Footer tab to display its options (**Figure 8**).

2. Choose options from the Header and Footer drop-down lists (**Figure 9**).

   The option(s) you selected appear in the sample area(s) in the dialog (**Figure 10**).

3. Click OK to save your settings.

✔ Tips

- The drop-down list for Footer is identical to the one for Header (**Figure 9**).

- Excel gets your name and company name from entries you made when you installed Excel. To change the name, choose Tools > Options, enter a new User name in the General tab of the Options dialog, and click OK. You cannot change the company name without reinstalling Excel. I tell you more about changing Excel's options in **Chapter 15**.

- To change the formatting of text in the header or footer, you need to use the Custom Header or Custom Footer button in the Header/Footer tab of the Page Setup dialog. I tell you about that next.

ADDING BUILT-IN HEADERS & FOOTERS

To add custom headers & footers

1. In the Page Setup dialog, click the Header/Footer tab to display its options (**Figure 8**).

2. To add a header, click the Custom Header button to display the Header dialog (**Figure 11**).

3. Enter the text or codes that you want to appear in the header in the Left section, Center section, and Right section text boxes. You can use the buttons in **Table 1** to format selected text or insert codes for dynamic information. **Figure 12** shows an example.

4. Click OK to save your settings. The settings appear in the Page Setup dialog (**Figure 13**).

5. To add a footer, click the Custom Footer button. This displays the Footer dialog, which looks just like the Header dialog.

6. Repeat steps 3 and 4 for the footer.

7. Click OK in the Page Setup dialog to save your settings.

✔ Tips

- In step 3, to enter an ampersand (&) character in a header or footer, type && where you want it to appear.

- To specify the starting page number to be printed in the header or footer, enter a value in the First page number text box of the Page tab of the Page Setup dialog (**Figure 2**).

- *Dynamic information* changes automatically. For example the page number changes on each page and the print date changes each day you print the file. Using the buttons or codes for dynamic information (**Table 1**) ensures header and footer contents are accurate.

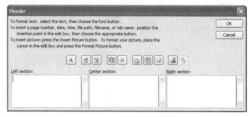

Figure 11 The Header dialog.

Table 1

Buttons for Inserting Dynamic Information into Headers or Footers	
Button	**Use**
A	Use the Font button to format selected text. I tell you about the Font dialog in **Chapter 6**.
	Use the Page Number button to insert the *&[Page]* code. This inserts the page number.
	Use the Total Pages button to insert the *&[Pages]* code. This inserts the total pages number.
	Use the Date button to insert the *&[Date]* code. This inserts the print date.
	Use the Time button to insert the *&[Time]* code. This inserts the print time.
	Use the Path & File button to insert the *&[Path]&[File]* code. This inserts the complete workbook pathname.
	Use the Filename button to insert the *&[File]* code. This inserts the workbook name.
	Use the Sheet Name button to insert the *&[Tab]* code. This inserts the sheet name.
	Use the Insert Picture button to insert the *&[Picture]* code. This inserts a picture you specify.
	Use the Format Picture button to format an inserted picture.

Figure 12 An example of a custom header entered into the Header dialog.

Figure 13 Here's the header from **Figure 12** in the Page Setup dialog.

To remove headers & footers

1. In the Page Setup dialog, click the Header/Footer tab to display its options (**Figure 8**).

2. To remove a header, choose (none) from the Header drop-down list (**Figure 9**). The header disappears from the dialog.

3. To remove a footer, choose (none) from the Footer drop-down list (**Figure 9**). The footer disappears from the dialog.

4. Click OK to save your settings.

To set sheet options

1. In the Page Setup dialog, click the Sheet tab to display its options (**Figure 14**).
2. To print less than the entire worksheet, enter a range in the Print area box (**Figure 15**).
3. To display column or row titles on all pages of a lengthy report, enter row or column (or both) ranges in the Rows to repeat at top or Columns to repeat at left boxes (**Figure 15**). **Figures 16** through **18** show how this affects the printout.
4. Turn on check boxes in the dialog to set additional print options as desired:
   - ▲ **Gridlines** prints worksheet gridlines.
   - ▲ **Black and white** prints the worksheet in black and white. This can save time if you print on a color printer.
   - ▲ **Draft quality** reduces printing time by omitting gridlines and most graphics.
   - ▲ **Row and column headings** prints the column letters and row numbers with the worksheet.
5. To print worksheet comments, choose an option other than (None) from the Comments drop-down list (**Figure 19**).
6. To specify how cells containing errors should be printed, choose an option from the Cell errors as drop-down list (**Figure 20**).
7. Select a Page order option for a long or wide worksheet:
   - ▲ **Down, then over** prints all rows of the first few columns first, then prints rows from subsequent columns.
   - ▲ **Over, then down** prints all columns of the first bunch of rows first, then prints columns from subsequent rows.
8. Click OK to save your settings.

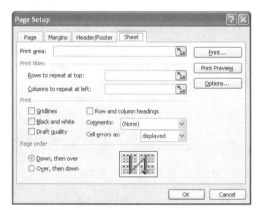

Figure 14 The Sheet tab of the Page Setup dialog.

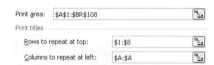

Figure 15 This example shows the proper way to enter ranges for the Print area and Print titles.

Payments Table

	5.00%	5.25%	5.50%	5.75%	6.00%
$5,000	$53.03	$53.65	$54.26	$54.88	$55.51
$10,000	$106.07	$107.29	$108.53	$109.77	$111.02
$15,000	$159.10	$160.94	$162.79	$164.65	$166.53
$20,000	$212.13	$214.58	$217.05	$219.54	$222.04
$25,000	$265.16	$268.23	$271.32	$274.42	$277.55
$30,000	$318.20	$321.88	$325.58	$329.31	$333.06

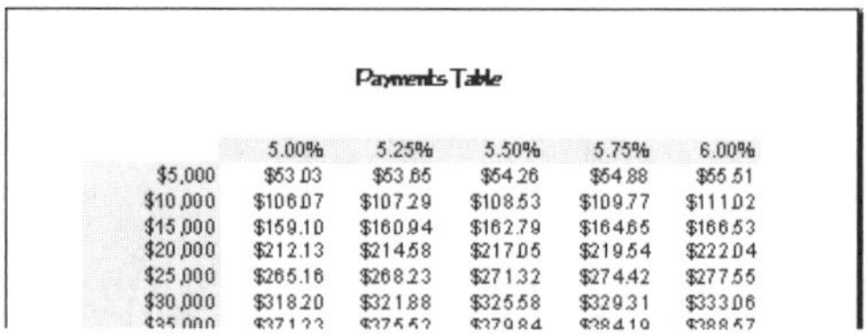

Figure 16 Here's the first page of a lengthy report.

Payments Table

$175,000	$1,856.15	$1,877.60	$1,899.21	$1,920.96	$1,942.86
$180,000	$1,909.18	$1,931.25	$1,953.47	$1,975.85	$1,998.37
$185,000	$1,962.21	$1,984.90	$2,007.74	$2,030.73	$2,053.88
$190,000	$2,015.24	$2,038.54	$2,062.00	$2,085.62	$2,109.39
$195,000	$2,068.28	$2,092.19	$2,116.26	$2,140.50	$2,164.90
$200,000	$2,121.31	$2,145.83	$2,170.53	$2,195.38	$2,220.41
$205,000	$2,174.34	$2,199.48	$2,224.79	$2,250.27	$2,275.92
$210,000	$2,227.38	$2,253.13	$2,279.05	$2,305.15	$2,331.43

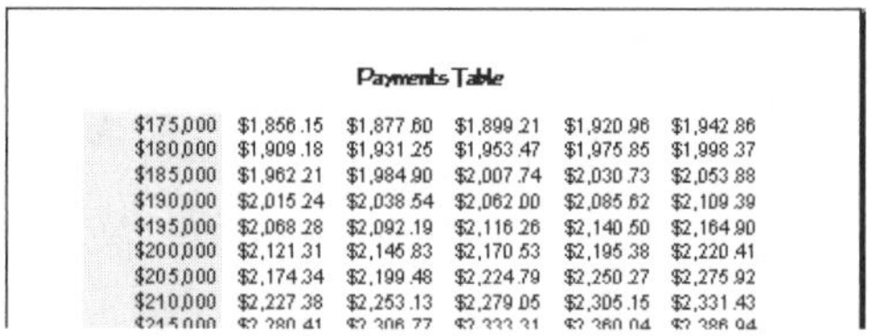

Figure 17 Without page titles, the headings don't appear on subsequent pages.

Payments Table

	5.00%	5.25%	5.50%	5.75%	6.00%
$175,000	$1,856.15	$1,877.60	$1,899.21	$1,920.96	$1,942.86
$180,000	$1,909.18	$1,931.25	$1,953.47	$1,975.85	$1,998.37
$185,000	$1,962.21	$1,984.90	$2,007.74	$2,030.73	$2,053.88
$190,000	$2,015.24	$2,038.54	$2,062.00	$2,085.62	$2,109.39
$195,000	$2,068.28	$2,092.19	$2,116.26	$2,140.50	$2,164.90
$200,000	$2,121.31	$2,145.83	$2,170.53	$2,195.38	$2,220.41

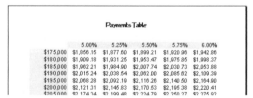

Figure 18 But with page titles set as they are in Figure 15, headings appear on every page.

Figure 19
The Comments drop-down list.

Figure 20
The Cell errors as drop-down list.

Figure 21
Use options under the Print Area submenu to set or clear a print area.

✔ Tips

- In steps 2 and 3, you can enter each range manually by typing it into the text box or have Excel enter it automatically for you by clicking in the text box, then selecting the range in the worksheet window.

- You can use the Collapse Dialog button 🔲 to collapse the dialog so you can see the worksheet behind it. You can then use the Expand Dialog button 🔲 to restore the dialog so you can finish working with it.

- You can also specify the range of cells to print by selecting the range in the worksheet, then choosing File > Print Area > Set Print Area (**Figure 21**). The Clear Print Area command clears any previously set print area.

- I tell you about worksheet comments in **Chapter 11**.

To set chart options

1. In the Page Setup dialog, click the Chart tab to display its options (**Figure 22**).

2. Select one of the Printed chart size options:

   ▲ **Use full page** expands the chart so it fills the page. The size of chart objects may change, relative to each other.

   ▲ **Scale to fit page** expands the chart proportionally until it fills the space between one set of opposite margins.

   ▲ **Custom** prints the chart with the size you specified.

3. Turn on Printing quality check boxes as desired:

   ▲ **Draft quality** omits graphics from printouts. This increases printing speed and uses less printer memory.

   ▲ **Print in black and white** prints the chart in black and white with patterns replacing colors.

4. Click OK to save your settings.

✔ Tip

■ For the largest possible image, make sure Landscape is the selected orientation in the Page tab of the Page Setup dialog (**Figure 2**). I tell you about orientation earlier in this chapter.

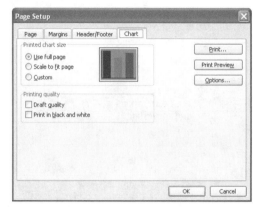

Figure 22 The Chart tab of the Page Setup dialog.

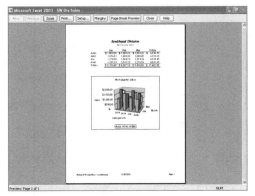

Figure 23 A worksheet with embedded chart in Print Preview.

Print Preview

Excel's Print Preview feature lets you see what a report will look like before you print it. If a report doesn't look perfect, you can use Setup, Margins, and Page Break Preview buttons right inside the Print Preview dialog to make adjustments. When you're ready to print, click the Print button.

To preview a report

Choose File > Print Preview (**Figure 3**).

Or

Click the Print Preview button ⬚ on the Standard toolbar.

Or

Click the Print Preview button in the Page Setup or Print dialog.

A preview of the current sheet appears (**Figure 23**). It reflects all Page Setup dialog settings.

✔ Tips

- To view the other pages of the report, click the Next or Previous button. (These buttons do not appear for one-page reports.)

- To zoom in to see report detail, click the Zoom button or click the mouse pointer (a magnifying glass) on the area you want to magnify.

- To open the Print dialog and print, click the Print button. I tell you about the Print dialog later in this chapter.

- To change Page Setup dialog options, click the Setup button.

- To close the Print Preview dialog, click the Close button.

PRINT PREVIEW

To change margin options & column widths

1. In the Print Preview window, click the Margins button. Handles for margins, header and footer locations, and column widths appear around the report preview (**Figure 24**).

2. Position the mouse pointer over the handle or guideline for the margin, header, footer, or column you want to change. The mouse pointer turns into a line with two arrows coming out of it (**Figure 25**).

3. Press the mouse button and drag to make the change. A measurement for your change appears in the status bar as you drag.

4. Release the mouse button to complete the change. The report reformats automatically.

✔ Tips

■ The changes you make by dragging handles in the Print Preview dialog will be reflected in the appropriate text boxes of the Page Setup dialog.

■ I tell how to change margins and header and footer locations with the Page Setup dialog earlier in this chapter. I tell you how to change column widths in the worksheet window or with the Column Width dialog in **Chapter 6**.

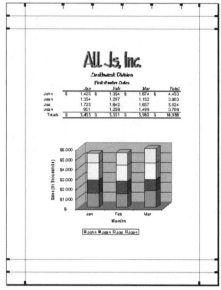

Figure 24 When you click the Margins button, handles for margins, header, footer, and columns appear.

Figure 25
Position the mouse pointer on a handle and drag to change the measurement.

Figure 26
Choosing Page Break
Preview from the
View menu.

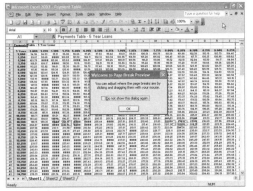

Figure 27 Page Break Preview view, with its instruction
dialog.

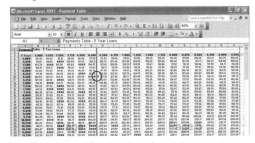

Figure 28 Drag a page break to change it.

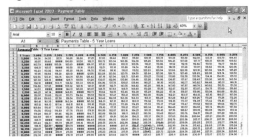

Figure 29 When you move one page break, the ones
beyond it also move.

To set page breaks

1. In normal view, choose View > Page Break
   Preview (**Figure 26**).

   or

   In the Print Preview window (**Figure 23**),
   click the Page Break Preview button.

   The sheet appears in Page Break Preview
   view (**Figure 27**).

2. Position the mouse pointer over one of
   the dashed, blue page break lines. The
   mouse pointer turns into a box with two
   triangles in its corners.

3. Press the mouse button and drag to make
   the change. A dark line moves with the
   mouse pointer (**Figure 28**).

4. Release the mouse button. The page
   break shifts to the new position and turns
   into a solid blue line. Any automatic page
   break to its right or below it also shifts
   (**Figure 29**).

5. To return to Normal view, choose View >
   Normal.

   or

   To return to Print Preview, choose File >
   Print Preview (**Figure 3**) or click the Print
   Preview button 🔲 on the Standard toolbar.

✔ Tips

- The first time you use the Page Break
  Preview feature, a dialog with instructions
  appears (**Figure 27**). Click OK to dismiss
  the dialog before you can drag page
  breaks. Turn on the check box within the
  dialog if you don't want to see it again.

- You may need to scroll within the window
  to see all page breaks for a large worksheet.

- You can use this feature to change both
  vertical and horizontal page breaks.

The Print Dialog

You use the Print dialog (**Figure 30**) to set options for a print job and send it to the printer.

To print

1. Choose File > Print (**Figure 3**) or press ⌃Ctrl ⌃P.

   or

   Click the Print button in the Page Setup dialog (**Figure 2**) or Print Preview window (**Figure 23**).

   The Print dialog appears (**Figure 30**).

2. If desired, choose a different printer from the Name drop-down list near the top of the dialog.

3. Select a Print range option:

   ▲ **All** prints all pages in the report.

   ▲ **Pages** enables you to enter a page range. Enter the first and last page to print in the From and To text boxes.

4. Select a Print what option:

   ▲ **Selection** prints only the selected cells, sheet, or object.

   ▲ **Active sheet(s)** prints the currently selected sheets.

   ▲ **Entire workbook** prints all nonblank sheets in the workbook file.

5. Enter the number of copies you want to print in the Number of copies box. If you enter a value greater than 1, you can turn on the Collate check box to have Excel automatically collate copies as it prints.

6. Click OK. Excel sends the document to the printer.

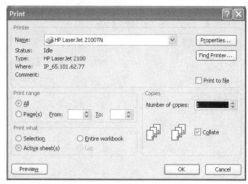

Figure 30 The Print dialog.

✔ Tips

■ Clicking the Print button 🖨 on the Standard toolbar sends the document directly to the printer without displaying the Print dialog.

■ You can click the Properties button in the Print dialog to display a dialog full of options for your printer. Consult the documentation that came with your printer to learn more about these options.

PRINTING

Figure 31 The Print to File dialog enables you to specify a name for a .PRN file created from an Excel worksheet.

To print to a .PRN file

1. Choose File > Print (**Figure 3**) or press Ctrl P.

   or

   Click the Print button in the Page Setup dialog (**Figure 2**) or Print Preview window (**Figure 23**).

   The Print dialog appears (**Figure 30**).

2. Turn on the Print to file check box.

3. Click OK.

4. In the Print to File dialog that appears (**Figure 31**), enter a name for the .PRN file in the Output File Name box.

5. Click OK. The document is saved as a .PRN file on disk in the same location as the original Excel file.

✔ Tip

- ■ A .PRN file is a plain text file that includes all of the information that would normally be printed. .PRN files are sometimes used to share worksheet information with DOS computer programs or to print worksheets from DOS.

Working with Lists

10

List Basics

Microsoft Excel's list or database features and functions help make it a flexible tool for organizing, maintaining, and reporting data. With Excel, you can use a form to enter data into a list, filter information, sort records, and automatically generate subtotals. You can use Excel's calculating, formatting, charting, and printing features on your list, too.

In Excel, a *list* is any group of worksheet data with unique labels in the first row. You don't need to do anything special to identify a list—Excel is smart enough to know one when it sees it. **Figure 1**, for example, shows the first few rows of a list that Excel can recognize as a database.

A list is organized into fields and records. A *field* is a category of information. In **Figure 1**, *Product Code, Department*, and *Cost* are the first three fields. A *record* is a collection of fields for one thing. In **Figure 1**, *row 2* shows the record for the item with product code *KWA424F* and *row 3* shows the record for *PFS2220U*.

✔ Tips

- Fields are always in columns while records are always in rows.

- In Excel, you can use the words *list* and *database* interchangeably—they refer to the same thing.

- Excel 2003 includes several advanced features for working with lists, including the ability to publish them on a Share-Point server and to view lists on servers. A discussion of these features is beyond the scope of this book.

	A	B	C	D	E	F	G	H	I
1	Product Code	Department	Cost	Sale Price	Reorder Point	Qty on Hand	Time to Order?	Resale Value	Markup
2	KWA424F	Men's Accessories	12.26	70.99	10	472		33,507	579%
3	PFS2220U	Garden	20.63	119.99	190	192		23,038	582%
4	DNO263N	Girls Clothes	17.83	62.99	180	303		19,086	353%
5	XWE114X	Books	6.73	10.99	10	185		2,033	163%
6	FOX112Y	Misses Clothes	4.48	12.99	120	143		1,858	290%
7	IXC94G	Lingerie	12.75	47.99	10	30		1,440	376%
8	MIC28W	Toys	0.47	1.99	160	66	Reorder Now!	131	423%
9	EZH2224N	Baby Clothes	18.56	101.99	120	45	Reorder Now!	4,590	550%
10	WHN27O	Computers	10.34	27.99	50	276		7,725	271%

Figure 1 The first few rows of a worksheet that Excel can automatically recognize as a list.

To enter data in a list

1. In a worksheet window, enter unique column titles for each of the fields in your list (**Figure 2**). These will be the field names.

2. Beginning with the row immediately below the one containing the column titles, enter the data for each record (**Figure 3**). Be sure to put the proper information in each column.

✔ Tips

- Use only one cell for each column title. If the field name is too long to fit in the cell, use the Wrap text (**Figure 4**) or Shrink to fit alignment option for the cell. I tell you about alignment options in **Chapter 6**.
- Do not skip rows when entering information. A blank row indicates the end of the database above it.
- You can format your list any way you like (**Figure 4**). Formatting does not affect the way Excel works with the list data.
- A quick way to enter data into a list is to press Tab to move from cell to cell. Then, when you finish entering data in the last column of the row, press Enter to advance to the first column of the next row.
- Your list can include formulas. Excel treats the results of the formulas like any other field.

	A	B	C
1	First Name	Last Name	Phone Number
2			
3			

Figure 2 Enter unique field names in the first row of the list.

	A	B	C
1	First Name	Last Name	Phone Number
2	Nancy	Drew	555-4256
3	Sherlock	Holmes	555-4584
4	Lew	Archer	555-6235
5	Sam	Spade	555-6845
6	Peter	Whimsey	555-1248
7	Jessica	Fletcher	555-1253
8	John	Aabbott	555-9871
9			

Figure 3 Enter the data, one record per row.

	A	B	C
1	**First Name**	**Last Name**	**Phone Number**
2	Nancy	Drew	555-4256
3	Sherlock	Holmes	555-4584
4	Lew	Archer	555-6235
5	Sam	Spade	555-6845
6	Peter	Whimsey	555-1248
7	Jessica	Fletcher	555-1253
8	John	Aabbott	555-9871
9			

Figure 4 Formatting a list doesn't affect the way Excel works with data.

486	OOJ21J	Office Supplies	15.93
487	NZX114Z	Hardware	0.19
488	MUG2511Z	Toys	5.40
489	QNT1920P	Bed & Bath	19.08
490	ZEM816P	Pets	17.54
491	IHA1820S	Lingerie	19.27
492	MDD98B	Toys	22.24
493	GYM29L	Junior Clothes	15.46
494	WOQ714V	Computers	24.89
495	IHA232R	Lingerie	10.75
496	JZY28D	Women's Accessorie	17.34
497	HAA218C	Big & Tall Men's Cloth	5.76
498	ZIY1422G	Pets	24.18
499	YXV1017L	Music	1.78
500	DOK411C	Girls Clothes	10.94
501	VTI2226Z	Electronics	22.05
502	NIB1992H	Hardware	

Figure 5 When the first few characters you type match an existing entry in the column, Excel fills in the remaining characters for you.

486	OOJ21J	Office Supplies	15.93	84.99
487	NZX114Z	Hardware	0.19	1.99
488	MUG2511Z	Toys	5.40	27.99
489	QNT1920P	Bed & Bath	19.08	114.99
490	ZEM816P	Pets	17.54	89.99
491	IHA1820S	Lingerie	19.27	115.99
492	MDD98B	Toys	22.24	65.99
493	GYM29L	Junior Clothe	15.46	64.99
494	WOQ714V	Computers	✂ Cut	
495	IHA232R	Lingerie		
496	JZY28D	Women's Acc	🗐 Copy	
497	HAA218C	Big & Tall Men	📋 Paste	
498	ZIY1422G	Pets		
499	YXV1017L	Music	🗐 Format Cells...	
500	DOK411C	Girls Clothes	Pick From Drop-down List...	
501	VTI2226Z	Electronics		
502	NIB1992H	Hardware	Look Up...	

Figure 6 Right-click on the cell to display a shortcut menu of options.

486	OOJ21J	Office Supplies	15.93
487	NZX114Z	Hardware	0.19
488	MUG2511Z	Toys	5.40
489	QNT1920P	Bed & Bath	19.08
490	ZEM816P	Pets	17.54
491	IHA1820S	Lingerie	19.27
492	MDD98B	Toys	22.24
493	GYM29L	Junior Clothes	15.46
494	WOQ714V	Computers	24.89
495	IHA232R		10.75
496	JZY28D	Hardware	17.34
497	HAA218C	Housewares	5.76
498	ZIY1422G	Junior Clothes	24.18
499	YXV1017L	Lingerie	1.78
		Men's Accessories	
500	DOK411C	Men's Clothes	10.94
501	VTI2226Z	Misses Clothes	22.05
		Music	
502	NIB1992H	Hardware	

Figure 7 The Pick From Drop-down list command displays a list of column entries to choose from.

To enter data with AutoComplete

1. Enter list data as instructed above. If the first few characters that you type into a cell match an existing entry in the same column, Excel automatically fills in the remaining characters for you (**Figure 5**).

2. To accept the entry, press Enter.

   or

   To choose from a list of entries, right-click on the cell to display a shortcut menu (**Figure 6**), choose Pick From Drop-down list, and then choose the entry you want from the drop-down list that appears (**Figure 7**).

   or

   To enter something different, continue typing to complete the entry. That entry is automatically added to the AutoComplete list Excel maintains for that column.

USING AUTOCOMPLETE

Designating a Range as a List

Although Excel can recognize data entered in list format (as described on page 200) as a list, you can take advantage of additional list management features by designating a range of cells containing list data as a list. For example, when you indicate that cells in a worksheet contain a list, you can filter, sort, and expand the list without affecting other worksheet cells. This is especially useful when your list resides on a worksheet with other information.

✔ Tip

■ I explain how to filter, sort, and expand lists later in this chapter.

To designate a range as a list

1. Position the cell pointer anywhere within the list (**Figure 8**).

2. Choose Data > List > Create List (**Figure 9**) or press Ctrl L.

3. The Create List dialog appears and Excel displays a marquee around the cells it thinks you want to include in your list (**Figure 10**). If necessary, drag to select a different range of cells.

4. Toggle the check box to indicate whether the list includes column headings.

5. Click OK.

   Excel places a blue border called a *list frame* around the cells in the list and displays AutoFilter pop-up menu buttons for each column (**Figure 11**).

✔ Tip

■ AutoFilter menus only appear when a cell in a list is selected (**Figure 11**).

Figure 8 Position the cell pointer anywhere in the list.

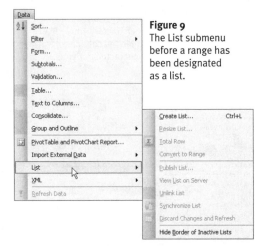

Figure 9
The List submenu before a range has been designated as a list.

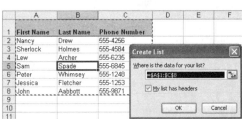

Figure 10 The Create List dialog with the selected list cells behind it.

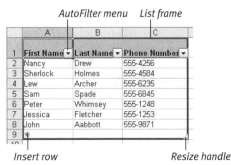

Figure 11 A range of cells designated as a list.

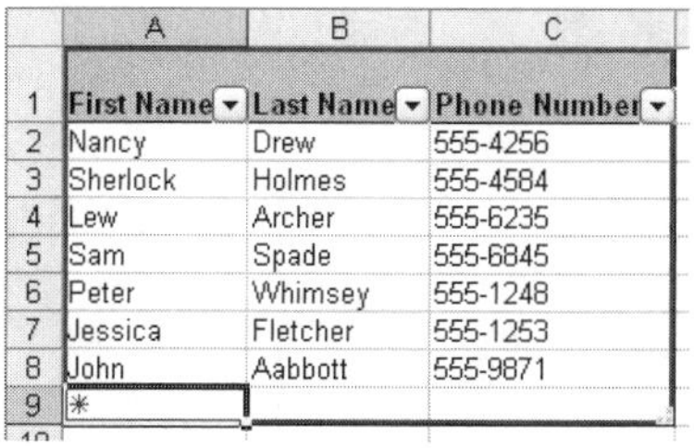

Figure 12 Click in the first cell of the insert row.

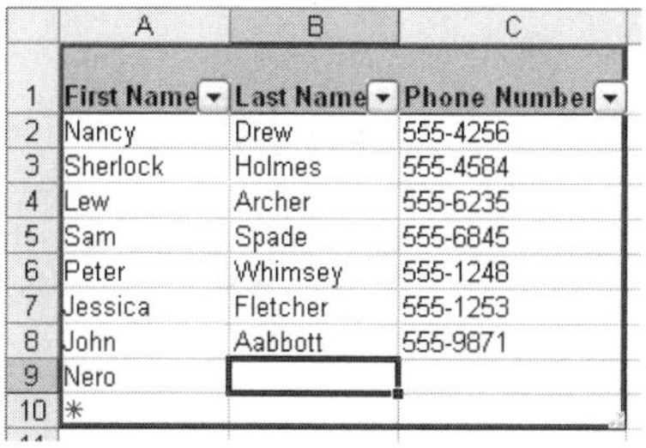

Figure 13 As you enter data into the insert row, a new insert row appears beneath it.

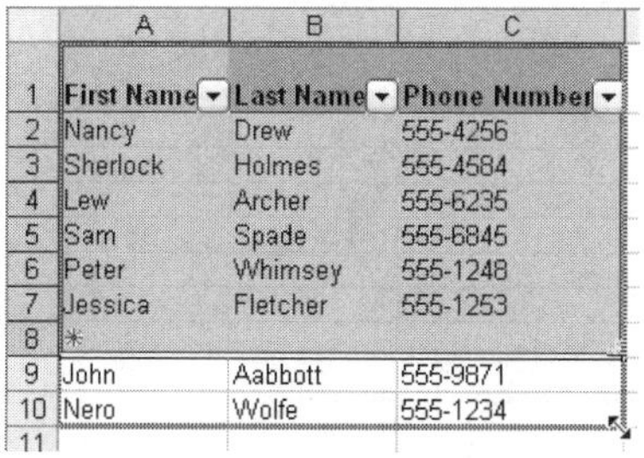

Figure 14 Drag the resize handle to change the size of the list frame.

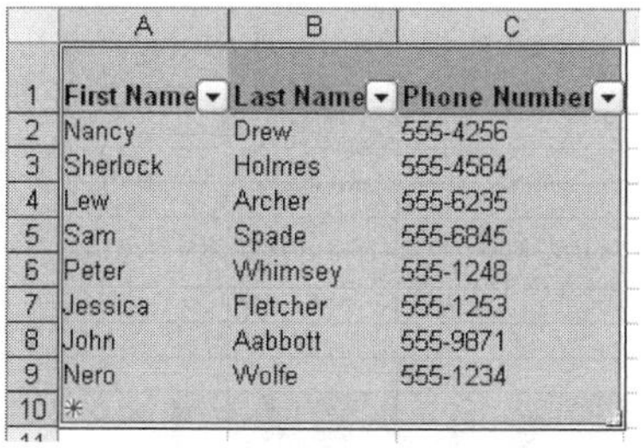

Figure 15 When you release the mouse button, the list frame's size changes.

To insert data at the end of a list

1. If necessary, click any cell in the list to activate the list.

2. Click in the first cell of the insert row (**Figure 12**).

3. Enter the data into the cells of that row. As you enter data into the second column, the list frame expands to add a new insert row below the current row (**Figure 13**).

4. Repeat steps 2 and 3 for each record you want to add.

To change the size of a list range

1. If necessary, click any cell in the list to activate the list.

2. Drag the resize handle at the bottom right corner of the list frame to increase (**Figure 14**) or decrease the size of the frame. When you release the mouse button, the frame's size changes (**Figure 15**).

✔ Tip

■ This feature is especially useful if you add records in cells beneath a list and want them included in the list.

To add totals to a list

1. Position the cell pointer anywhere within the list (**Figure 16**).

2. Choose Data > List > Total Row (**Figure 17**).

   Excel instantly adds a total row with column totals for each column containing numerical values (**Figure 18**).

✔ Tips

- The totals in the total row automatically change when values in the database change.

- Another way to add totals to a list is with the Subtotals command on the Data menu. This command, which works only with normal ranges, is discussed near the end of this chapter.

To convert a list to a normal range

1. Position the cell pointer anywhere within the list (**Figure 11**).

2. Choose Data > List > Convert to Range (**Figure 17**).

3. Click Yes in the confirmation dialog that appears (**Figure 19**). Excel converts the list to a normal range of cells (**Figure 8**).

✔ Tip

- If the list you are converting to a range contains a total row, Excel keeps the totals in the row immediately beneath the list.

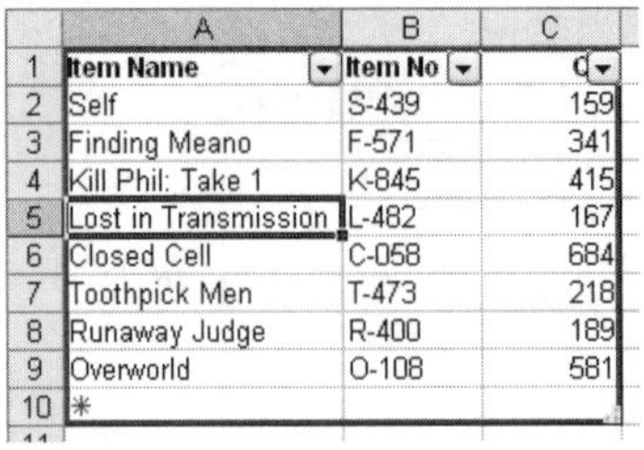

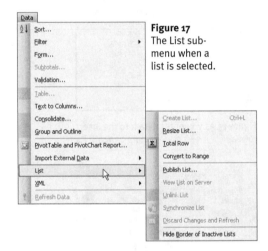

Figure 16 A list with textual and numerical values.

Figure 17
The List submenu when a list is selected.

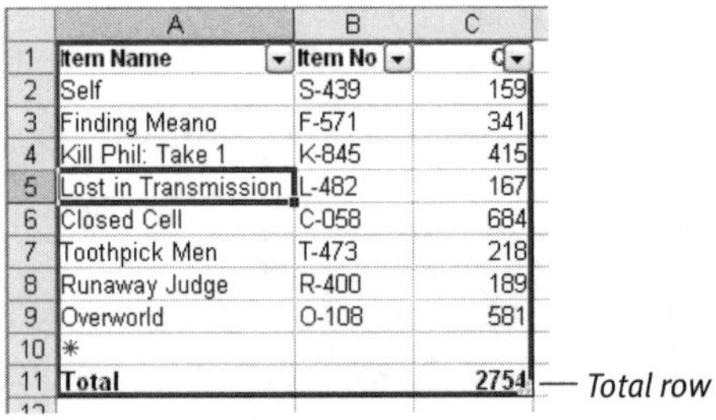

Figure 18 Excel instantly inserts a total row at the bottom of the list.

— *Total row*

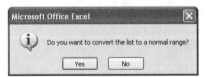

Figure 19 You must confirm that you want to convert a list to a normal range of cells.

ADDING TOTALS, CONVERTING LISTS TO RANGES

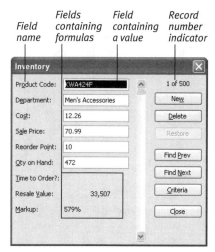

Field name | *Fields containing formulas* | *Field containing a value* | *Record number indicator*

Figure 20 The data form offers another way to enter, edit, delete, and find records.

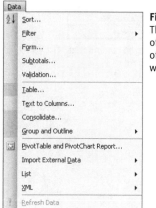

Figure 21
The Data menu offers a number of commands for working with lists.

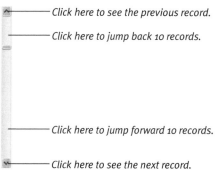

— *Click here to see the previous record.*

— *Click here to jump back 10 records.*

— *Click here to jump forward 10 records.*

— *Click here to see the next record.*

Figure 22 Use the scroll bar in the data form to browse records.

Using the Data Form

Excel's data form feature creates a dialog with custom text boxes for fields (**Figure 20**). You can use this dialog to enter, edit, delete, and find records in a database.

✔ Tip

■ The data form works with a list in a normal range of cells or in a designated list. I tell you about these two types of lists earlier in this chapter.

To open the data form

1. Select any cell in the list.

2. Choose Data > Form (**Figure 21**).

To browse records

Use the scroll bar (**Figure 22**) as follows:

◆ To see the next record, click the down arrow on the scroll bar.

◆ To see the previous record, click the up arrow on the scroll bar.

◆ To jump ahead 10 records, click the scroll bar beneath the scroll box.

◆ To jump back 10 records, click the scroll bar above the scroll box.

To enter, edit, and delete data

To create a new record, click the New button and enter the information into the empty text boxes for each field (**Figure 23**).

Or

To edit a record, locate the record you want to edit and make changes in the appropriate text boxes.

Or

To delete a record, locate the record you want to delete and click the Delete button. Then click OK in the confirmation dialog that appears (**Figure 24**).

✔ Tips

- Excel records your changes when you move to another record or click the Close button to close the form.

- If a field contains a formula, Excel carries the formula forward from the previous record and performs the calculation.

- The AutoComplete feature, which I discussed earlier in this chapter, is not available when you add or modify records with the data form.

Figure 23 Use this form to enter data for a new record.

Figure 24 Use this dialog to confirm that you want to delete a record.

Figure 25 The data form turns into a criteria form when you click the Criteria button.

Figure 26 Enter the search criteria in the field in which you expect to find a match.

Table 1

Comparison Operators

Operator	Meaning
=	Equal To
<>	Not Equal To
>	Greater Than
>=	Greater Than or Equal To
<	Less Than
<=	Less Than or Equal To

Table 2

Wildcard Characters

Character	Meaning
?	Any single character
*	Any group of characters

To find records

1. In the data form, click the Criteria button. A criteria form appears (**Figure 25**).

2. Enter search criteria in the field(s) in which you expect to find a match (**Figure 26**).

3. Click the Find Next button to move forward through the list for records that match the criteria.

   or

   Click the Find Prev button to move backward through the list for records that match the criteria.

   Excel beeps when it reaches the end or beginning of the matches.

✔ Tips

- You can enter criteria in any combination of fields. If you enter criteria into multiple fields, Excel looks for records that match all criteria.

- The more fields you enter data into, the more specific you make the search and the fewer matches you'll find.

- You can use comparison operators (**Table 1**) and wildcard characters (**Table 2**) in conjunction with criteria. For example, *>100* finds records with values greater than 100 in the field in which the criteria is entered.

- You can use Excel's AutoFilter feature to quickly locate and display all records that match search criteria. I explain how next.

FINDING RECORDS

AutoFilter

The AutoFilter feature puts menus in the titles of each column (**Figures 11** and **27**). You can use these menus to choose criteria for a column and display only those records that match the criteria.

✔ Tip

- The AutoFilter feature works with a list in a normal range of cells or in a designated list. I tell you about these two types of lists earlier in this chapter.

To display AutoFilter menus

1. Select any cell in the list.

2. Choose Data > Filter > AutoFilter (**Figure 28**). Excel scans the data and creates menus for each field (**Figure 27**).

✔ Tip

- It is not necessary to manually display AutoFilter menus for a designated list; menus appear automatically as shown in **Figure 11**.

To find records with AutoFilter

Use the AutoFilter menu for a column (**Figure 29**) to choose the criteria you want to match in that column.

Only the records matching the criteria you selected are displayed (**Figure 30**).

✔ Tips

- To display all of the records, choose Data > Filter > Show All (**Figure 28**) or choose (Show All) from the AutoFilter menu you used to filter the data (**Figure 15**).

- To filter data by more than one column, choose the criteria you want from each column. The records that are displayed will match all criteria.

AutoFilter menu

Figure 27 The AutoFilter feature works with drop-down lists in the titles of each column.

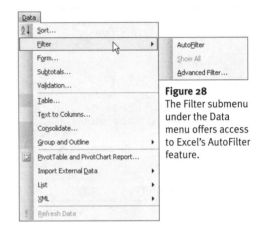

Figure 28 The Filter submenu under the Data menu offers access to Excel's AutoFilter feature.

Figure 29 Choose search criteria from the AutoFilter menu. This menu is for the Department column.

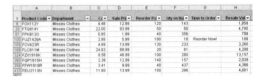

Figure 30 Excel displays only the records that match the criteria you chose.

Figure 31 Use the Top 10 AutoFilter to find the top or bottom number or percent of items.

Figure 32 The Custom AutoFilter dialog.

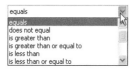

Figure 33
Use this drop-down list to select a comparison operator.

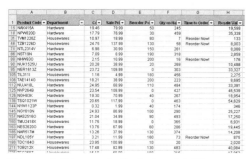

Figure 34 In this example, the Custom AutoFilter was used to find all inventory items in the Hardware or Housewares department.

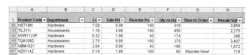

Figure 35 This example adds another filter to Figure 34: Sale Price less than 10.

To use the Top 10 AutoFilter

1. Choose (Show Top 10…) from the Auto-Filter menu for the field by which you want to filter information (**Figure 29**).

2. In the Top 10 AutoFilter dialog (**Figure 31**), set options to display the top or bottom items or percent based on the field you selected.

3. Click OK. Excel filters the list and displays only the records that match the settings you entered.

✔ Tip

- The Top 10 AutoFilter does not work for columns that contain text.

To set a custom AutoFilter

1. Choose (Custom …) from the AutoFilter menu for the field for which you want to set criteria (**Figure 29**). The Custom AutoFilter dialog (**Figure 32**) appears.

2. Use the drop-down lists (**Figure 33**) to choose one or two comparison operators.

3. Use the drop-down lists or text boxes to enter one or two criteria.

4. Select the And or Or option button to tell Excel whether it should match both criteria (And) or either criteria (Or).

5. Click OK. Excel filters the records to show only those matching the criteria you entered (**Figure 34**).

✔ Tip

- Criteria can include wildcard characters (**Table 2**).

To use multiple AutoFilters

Set criteria for multiple fields as desired. Excel displays only the records that match all of the filters (**Figure 35**).

Advanced Filters

Advanced filters enable you to specify even more criteria than you can with AutoFilters. First set up a criteria range, then use the Advanced Filter dialog to perform the search.

To use advanced filters

1. Create a criteria range by copying the data labels in the list to a blank area of the worksheet and then entering the criteria in the cells beneath it (**Figure 36**).

2. Choose Data > Filter > Advanced Filter (**Figure 28**) to display the Advanced Filter dialog (**Figure 37**).

3. Select one of the option buttons to tell Excel what to do with the matches:

   ▲ **Filter the list, in place** tells Excel to replace the original list with a list of the matches. Keep in mind that this option overwrites the contents of the database.

   ▲ **Copy to another location** creates a list of matches in a new location.

4. In the List range text box, confirm that the correct cell references for your list have been entered.

5. In the Criteria range text box, enter the cell references for the range containing your criteria (including the field labels).

6. If you selected the Copy radio button in step 3 above, enter a cell reference for the first cell of the new list in the Copy to text box.

7. To omit duplicate records from the results list, turn on the Unique records only check box.

8. Click OK. Excel searches for records that match the criteria and either replaces the original list or creates a new list with the matches (**Figure 38**).

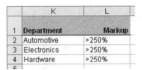

Figure 36 Create a criteria range with field names and values that you want to match.

Figure 37 The Advanced Filter dialog, all set up to filter a list.

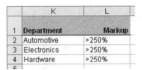

Figure 38 The criteria in **Figure 36** yielded these results.

✔ Tip

■ You can enter a range into any of the text boxes in the Advanced Filter dialog by selecting the range you want to enter.

ADVANCED FILTERS

	A	B	C
1	First Name ▼	Last Name ▼	Phone Number ▼
2	Nancy	Drew	555-4256
3	Sherlock	Holmes	555-4584
4	Lew	Archer	555-6235
5	Sam	Spade	555-6845
6	Peter	Whimsey	555-1248
7	Jessica	Fletcher	555-1253
8	John	Aabbott	555-9871
9	Nero	Wolfe	555-1234
10	✳		

Figure 39 Start by selecting any cell in the column you want to sort by.

	A	B	C
1	First Name ▼	Last Name ▼	Phone Number ▼
2	Jessica	Fletcher	555-1253
3	John	Aabbott	555-9871
4	Lew	Archer	555-6235
5	Nancy	Drew	555-4256
6	Nero	Wolfe	555-1234
7	Peter	Whimsey	555-1248
8	Sam	Spade	555-6845
9	Sherlock	Holmes	555-4584
10	✳		

Figure 40 In this example, clicking the Sort Ascending button puts the records in alphabetical order by first name.

Sorting

You can sort lists by any column(s). Excel will quickly put database information in the order you specify.

✔ Tips

- The sorting feature works with a list in a normal range of cells or in a designated list. I tell you about these two types of lists earlier in this chapter.

- When you sort data in a designated list, the contents of cells in adjacent columns are not disturbed.

- You can sort an entire list, a filtered list, or a list created with the Advanced Filter dialog.

- If the results of a sort are not what you expected, choose Edit > Undo, press Ctrl Z, or click the Undo button 🔄 on the Standard toolbar to restore the original sort order.

To sort a list with Sort buttons

1. Select a cell in the column for the field by which you want to sort (**Figure 39**).

2. Click the Sort Ascending button 📊 to sort from lowest to highest value or the Sort Descending button 📊 to sort from highest to lowest value. (Both buttons are on the Standard toolbar.)

   The data is sorted by the selected column (**Figure 40**).

To sort a list with the Sort dialog

1. Select any cell in the list (**Figure 41**).

2. Choose Data > Sort (**Figure 21**) to display the Sort dialog (**Figure 42**).

3. Choose a primary sort field from the Sort By drop-down list (**Figure 43**).

4. Select a sort order option:

   ▲ **Ascending** is lowest to highest.

   ▲ **Descending** is highest to lowest.

5. If desired, repeat steps 3 and 4 for a secondary and tertiary sort field using options in the Then by areas.

6. If the list has column titles, select the Header row option; otherwise, select the No header row option.

7. Click OK. Excel sorts the list as you specified (**Figure 44**).

✔ Tips

- The two Then by fields in the sort dialog are "tie-breakers" and are only used if the primary sort field has more than one record with the same value. **Figures 42** and **44** show how they can be used.

- If you make the wrong selection in step 6, you could sort column headings along with the rest of the list. Undo the sort and try again.

- If you select a cell in the column by which you want to sort, that column is automatically referenced in the Sort dialog when you open it.

- To sort by more than three columns, sort by the least important columns first, then by the most important ones. For example, to sort a list by columns A, B, C, D, and E, you'd sort first by columns D and E, then by columns A, B, and C.

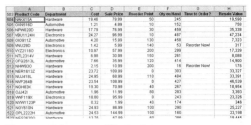

Figure 41 Select any cell in the list.

Figure 42 The Sort dialog with a primary and secondary sort set up.

Figure 43 The Sort by (or Then by) drop-down list lists all database fields.

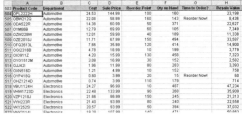

Figure 44 The beginning of the list in **Figure 41** sorted as shown in **Figure 42**.

SORTING LISTS

Table 3

| Valid *function_num* Values for the SUBTOTAL Function ||
Number	Function Name
1	AVERAGE
2	COUNT
3	COUNTA
4	MAX
5	MIN
6	PRODUCT
7	STDEV
8	STDEVP
9	SUM
10	VAR
11	VARP

Subtotals

Excel's Subtotal feature enters formulas with the SUBTOTAL function in sorted database lists. The SUBTOTAL function returns a subtotal for a sorted list. It uses the following syntax:

SUBTOTAL(*function_num,ref*)

The function_num argument is a number that specifies which function to use. **Table 3** shows the valid values. (I tell you about most of these functions in **Chapter 5**.) The ref argument is the range of cells to subtotal.

✔ Tip

- You can only use the Subtotal feature on a list in a normal range of cells. If you're working with a designated list, use the total row feature instead. I explain the difference between these types of lists and how to insert a total row earlier in this chapter.

To subtotal a list

1. Sort the list by the field(s) for which you want subtotals and select any cell in the list (**Figure 45**).

2. Choose Data > Subtotals (**Figure 21**) to display the Subtotal dialog (**Figure 46**).

3. Choose the name of the field to be grouped for subtotaling from the At each change in drop-down list. The field you select will probably be one of the fields you sorted by.

4. Choose a function from the Use function drop-down list (**Figure 47**).

5. In the Add subtotal to scrolling list, turn on the check box for each field you want to add a subtotal to.

6. If desired, use the check boxes at the bottom of the dialog to set other options.

7. Click OK. Excel turns the list into an outline and enters row titles and subtotals (**Figure 48**).

✔ Tips

- To remove subtotals, click the Remove All button in the Subtotal dialog (**Figure 46**).

- Excel's outline feature groups information into different levels. You can show or hide information based on its level.

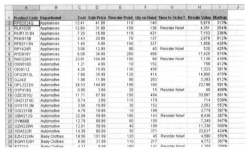

Figure 45 Sort the list by the field you want to subtotal.

Figure 46 The Subtotal dialog.

Figure 47 Use this drop-down list to choose a function for the Subtotal. In most cases, you'll choose Sum.

Outline buttons & bars   =SUBTOTAL(9,F2:F9)

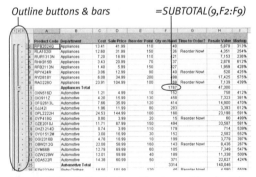

Figure 48 Here's the list from **Figure 45** with subtotals as set in **Figure 46**.

ADDING SUBTOTALS TO LISTS

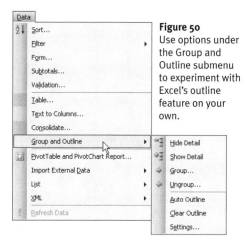

Figure 49 Here's the outline from **Figure 48** with some of the detail hidden.

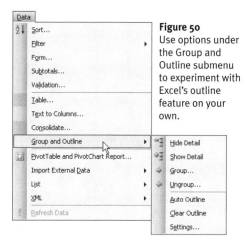

Figure 50
Use options under the Group and Outline submenu to experiment with Excel's outline feature on your own.

To work with a subtotal outline

Click outline symbols on the left side of the window to display or hide detail:

■ Click a minus sign button to collapse the outline for that section.

■ Click a plus sign button to expand the outline for that section.

■ Click one of the outline level numbers to collapse or expand the entire outline to that level.

Figure 49 shows an outline created by the Subtotals command partially collapsed. Note how the outline buttons and bars are set to the left of the data.

✔ Tip

■ You can create an outline for virtually any spreadsheet data. Although creating outlines is beyond the scope of this book, here's a hint to get you started if you decide to explore this feature: Use commands on the Group and Outline submenu under the Data menu (**Figure 50**) to create and clear groups and outlines.

Database Functions

Excel includes several database and list management functions. (SUBTOTAL, which I discuss earlier in this chapter, is one of them.) Here are a few of the most commonly used ones, along with their syntax:

DSUM(*database,field,criteria*)

DAVERAGE(*database,field,criteria*)

DCOUNT(*database,field,criteria*)

DCOUNTA(*database,field,criteria*)

DMAX(*database,field,criteria*)

DMIN(*database,field,criteria*)

The database argument is the cell references for a range containing the database or list. The field argument is the name of the field you want to summarize. The criteria argument is either the data you want to match or a range containing the data you want to match.

Figure 51 shows an example of these database functions in action, using the criteria range in **Figure 36**.

✔ Tips

- Each database function corresponds to a mathematical or statistical function and performs the same kind of calculation—but on records matching criteria only. I tell you about other functions in **Chapter 5**.

- You can enter database functions with the Insert Function and Function Arguments dialogs. I tell you how to use these dialogs in **Chapter 5**.

DSUM	595.05	=DSUM($A$1:$I$501,"Cost",$K$1:$L$4)
DAVERAGE	12.396875	=DAVERAGE($A$1:$I$501,"Cost",$K$1:$L$4)
DCOUNT	48	=DCOUNT($A$1:$I$501,"Cost",$K$1:$L$4)
DCOUNTA	48	=DCOUNTA($A$1:$I$501,"Cost",$K$1:$L$4)
DMAX	24.95	=DMAX($A$1:$I$501,"Cost",$K$1:$L$4)
DMIN	0.11	=DMIN($A$1:$I$501,"Cost",$K$1:$L$4)

Figure 51 These formulas use database functions to summarize information based on criteria. The database is the 500-record list used throughout this chapter. The field is the Cost field, which is found in column C of the database. The criteria range is the range illustrated in **Figure 36**.

Working with Others

Collaboration Features

In office environments, a document is often the product of multiple people. In the old days, a draft worksheet or financial report would be printed and circulated among reviewers. Along the way, it would be marked up with colored ink and covered with sticky notes full of comments. Some poor soul would have to make sense of all the markups and notes to create a clean document. The process was time consuming and was sometimes repeated through several drafts to fine-tune the document for publication.

Microsoft Excel, which is widely used in office environments, includes many features that make the collaboration process easier:

- ◆ **Properties** stores information about the document's creator and contents.

- ◆ **Comments** enables reviewers to enter notes about the document. The notes don't print—unless you want them to.

- ◆ **Revision Tracking** enables reviewers to edit the document while keeping the original document intact. Changes can be accepted or rejected to finalize the document.

- ◆ **Document Protection** limits how a document can be changed.

- ◆ **Save options** protect documents from being opened or modified.

- ◆ **Workbook sharing** enables multiple users to access a workbook file simultaneously via network.

Document Properties

The Properties dialog (**Figures** 2 and 4) enables you to store information about a document. This information can be viewed by anyone who opens the document.

✔ Tips

- The Properties dialog is organized into tabs for storing information. I cover the Summary and Statistics tabs here; explore the other tabs on your own.

- Information in the Properties dialog is also used by Excel's internal Search feature. A discussion of Search is beyond the scope of this book, however, you can explore it on your own by choosing File > Search (**Figure 1**).

To open the Properties dialog

1. Open the document for which you want to view or edit properties.

2. Choose File > Properties (**Figure 1**).

To enter summary information

1. Open the Properties dialog.

2. If necessary, click the Summary tab to display its options (**Figure 2**).

3. Enter or edit information in each field as desired:

   ▲ **Title** is the title of the document. This does not have to be the same as the file name.

   ▲ **Subject** is the subject of the document.

   ▲ **Author** is the person who created the document. This field may already be filled in based on information stored in the General tab of the Options dialog.

Figure 1
The File menu.

Figure 2 The Summary tab of the Properties dialog offers text boxes for entering information about the document.

DOCUMENT PROPERTIES

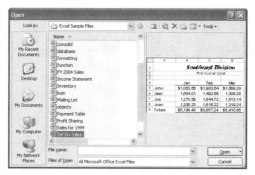

Figure 3 When you create a preview picture, it appears in the Open dialog.

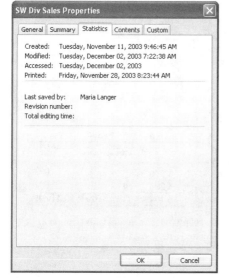

Figure 4 The Statistics tab of the Properties dialog provides additional information about the document.

▲ **Manager** is the person responsible for the document content.

▲ **Company** is the organization for which the author or manager works.

▲ **Category** is a category name assigned to the document. It can be anything you like.

▲ **Keywords** are important words related to the document.

▲ **Comments** are notes about the document.

▲ **Hyperlink base** is an Internet address or path to a folder on a hard disk or network volume. This option works in conjunction with hyperlinks inserted in the document.

4. To create a document preview image that will appear in the Preview area of the Open dialog (**Figure 3**), turn on the Save preview picture check box.

5. Click OK to save your entries.

✔ Tips

■ It is not necessary to enter information in any Summary tab text boxes (**Figure 2**).

■ I tell you more about the General tab of the Options dialog in **Chapter 15**.

To view document statistics

1. Open the Properties dialog.

2. If necessary, click the Statistics tab to display its information (**Figure 4**).

3. When you are finished viewing statistics, click OK to dismiss the dialog.

✔ Tip

■ Information in the Statistics tab (**Figure 4**) cannot be changed.

Comments

Comments are annotations that you and other document reviewers can add to a document. These notes can be viewed onscreen but don't print unless you want them to.

To insert a comment

1. Select the cell for which you want to insert a comment (**Figure 5**).

2. Choose Insert > Comment (**Figure 6**).

   Two things happen: A comment marker (a tiny red triangle) appears in the upper-right corner of the cell and a box with your name and a blinking insertion point appears (**Figure 7**).

3. Type your comment into the box. It can be as long or as short as you like (**Figure 8**).

4. When you are finished, click anywhere else in the worksheet window. Your comment is saved and the box disappears.

✔ Tip

- Word gets your name from the General tab of the Options dialog. I tell you more about that in **Chapter 15**.

Figure 5 Start by selecting the cell you want to enter a comment for.

3			
4		Jan	Fe
5	John	$1,063.66	$1,9(
6	Jean	1,654.01	1,4
7	Joe	1,270.59	1,8
8	Joan	1,206.23	1,6
9	Totals	$5,194.49	$6,8!

Figure 6 Choose Comment from the Insert menu.

Insert
- Cells...
- Rows
- Columns
- Worksheet
- Chart...
- Symbol...
- Page Break
- Function...
- Name ▸
- Comment
- Picture ▸
- Diagram...
- Object...
- Hyperlink... Ctrl+K

	A	B	C	D
3				
4		Jan	Feb	Mar
5	John	$1,063.66		2(
6	Jean	1,654.01	Maria Langer:	2(
7	Joe	1,270.59		1
8	Joan	1,206.23		2
9	Totals	$5,194.49	$6,857.24	$5,410.95

Figure 7 Excel prepares to accept your comment.

	A	B	C	D
3				
4		Jan	Feb	Mar
5	John	$1,063.66		2(
6	Jean	1,654.01	Maria Langer: This was a new monthly	2(
7	Joe	1,270.59	sales record for the	1
8	Joan	1,206.23	company!	2
9	Totals	$5,194.49	$6,857.24	$5,410.95

Figure 8 Enter your comment in the box.

	A	B	C	D
3				
4		Jan	Feb	Mar
5	John	$1,063.66	$1,003.64 $1,660	2(
6	Jean	1,65⊕01	Maria Langer: This was a new monthly	2(
7	Joe	1,270.59	sales record for the	1
8	Joan	1,206.23	company!	2
9	Totals	$5,194.49	$6,857.24	$5,410.95

Figure 9 When you position the mouse pointer over a cell with a comment marker, the comment appears.

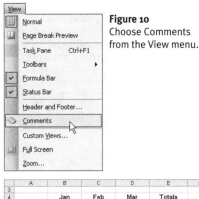

Figure 10
Choose Comments
from the View menu.

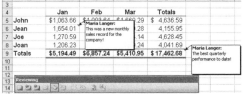

Figure 11 All comments for visible cells appear, along
with the Reviewing toolbar.

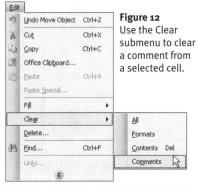

Figure 12
Use the Clear
submenu to clear
a comment from
a selected cell.

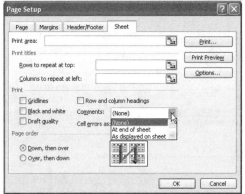

Figure 13 Use the Comments drop-down list in the
Page Setup dialog to set up comments for printing.

To view comments

Position the mouse pointer over a cell with a
comment marker. A box appears containing
the name of the person who wrote the comment and the comment itself (**Figure 9**).

Or

Choose View > Comments (**Figure 10**). All
comments for visible cells appear in yellow
boxes (**Figure 11**).

✔ Tip

■ When you display Comments as instructed
above, the Reviewing toolbar may appear
(**Figure 11**). It includes buttons for Excel's
Comments and Revisions features.

To delete a comment

1. Select the cell containing the comment
you want to remove.

2. Choose Edit > Clear > Comments (**Figure
12**). The comment marker and comment
are removed.

To print comments

1. Follow the instructions in **Chapter 9** to
prepare the sheet for printing and open
the Page Setup dialog.

2. Choose an option from the Comments
drop-down list in the Sheet tab (**Figure 13**).

3. Click Print.

4. In the Print dialog that appears, click OK
to print the sheet and its comments.

✔ Tip

■ I tell you more about the Page Setup dialog
and printing in **Chapter 9**.

VIEWING, DELETING, & PRINTING COMMENTS

Revision Tracking

Excel's revision tracking feature enables multiple reviewers to edit a document without actually changing it. Instead, each reviewer's markups are displayed in the document window. At the conclusion of the reviewing process, someone with final say over document content reviews all of the edits and either accepts or rejects each of them. The end result is a final document that incorporates the accepted changes.

To turn revision tracking on or off

1. Choose Tools > Track Changes > Highlight Changes (**Figure 14**).

2. In the Highlight Changes dialog that appears (**Figure 15**), toggle check boxes to set up the revision tracking feature:

   ▲ **Track changes while editing** enables the revision tracking feature. Turn on this check box to track changes. Turn off this check box to disable the revision tracking feature.

   ▲ **When** enables you to choose which changes should be tracked based on when the changes were made. If you turn on this check box, choose an option from the drop-down list (**Figure 16**).

   ▲ **Who** enables you to specify which changes should be tracked based on who made them. If you turn on this check box, choose an option from the drop-down list (**Figure 17**).

   ▲ **Where** enables you to specify which changes should be tracked based on which cells the changes were made in. If you turn on this check box, enter a range of cells in the text box beside it.

   ▲ **Highlight changes on screen** displays revision marks in the document window.

Figure 14
Use commands on the Track Changes sub-menu to set up and use Excel's revision tracking feature.

Figure 15 The Highlight Changes dialog lets you enable and configure the revision tracking feature.

Figures 16 & 17
Use these two drop-down lists to specify which changes to track based on when they were made (top) or who made them (bottom).

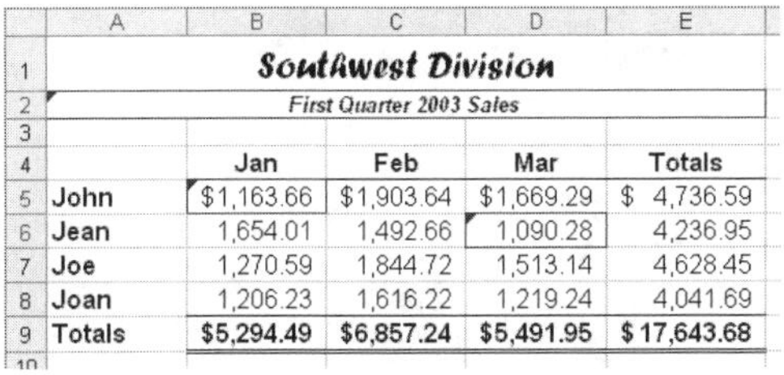

	A	B	C	D	E
1	Southwest Division				
2	First Quarter 2003 Sales				
3					
4		Jan	Feb	Mar	Totals
5	John	$1,163.66	$1,903.64	$1,669.29	$ 4,736.59
6	Jean	1,654.01	1,492.66	1,090.28	4,236.95
7	Joe	1,270.59	1,844.72	1,513.14	4,628.45
8	Joan	1,206.23	1,616.22	1,219.24	4,041.69
9	Totals	$5,294.49	$6,857.24	$5,491.95	$ 17,643.68

Figure 18 When you edit the document, the cells you change are marked.

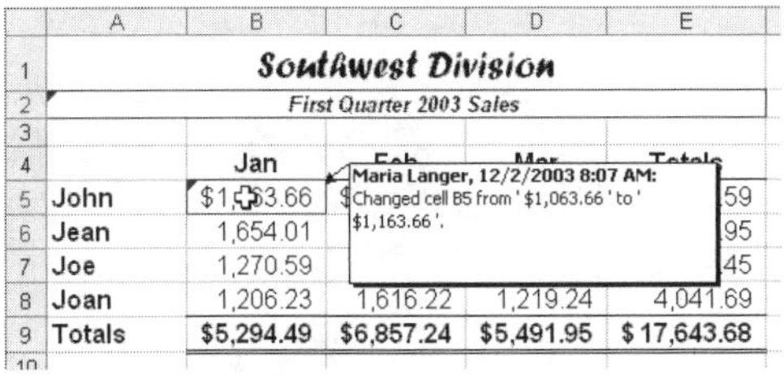

Figure 19 Point to a revision mark to display information about it.

▲ **List changes on a new sheet** records changes in a separate History worksheet. This option is only available after you have saved the workbook file as a shared workbook.

3. Click OK.
4. If prompted, save the workbook file.

✔ Tip

■ Turning on revision tracking also shares the workbook file. I tell you more about workbook sharing later in this chapter.

To track changes

1. Turn on revision tracking as instructed on the previous page.
2. Make changes to the document.

   The cells you changed get a colored border around them and a color-coordinated triangle appears in the upper-left corner (**Figure 18**).

✔ Tip

■ If the document is edited by more than one person, each person's revision marks appear in a different color. This makes it easy to distinguish one editor's changes from another's.

To view revision information

Point to a revision mark. A box with information about the change appears (**Figure 19**).

✔ Tip

■ This is a handy way to see who made a change and when it was made.

To accept or reject revisions

1. Choose Tools > Track Changes > Accept or Reject Changes (**Figure 14**).

2. If prompted, save the workbook file.

3. The Select Changes to Accept or Reject dialog appears (**Figure 20**). Set options to select the changes to review. The options work like those in the Highlight Changes dialog (**Figure 15**).

4. Click OK.

5. Excel selects the first change and displays the Accept or Reject Changes dialog (**Figure 21**).

   ▲ To accept the currently selected change, click the Accept button. Excel selects the next change.

   ▲ To reject the currently selected change, click the Reject button. The cell reverts to its original contents and Excel selects the next change.

   ▲ To accept all changes, click the Accept All button. Skip the remaining step.

   ▲ To reject all changes, click the Reject All button. All changed cells in the selection revert to their original contents. Skip the remaining step.

6. Repeat step 5 for each change Excel selects.

   When Excel has reached the end of the document, the Accept or Reject Changes dialog disappears.

✖ Caution!

■ The Undo command will not work after you click the Accept All or Reject All button in step 5. Use these two buttons with care!

Figure 20 The Select Changes to Accept or Reject dialog.

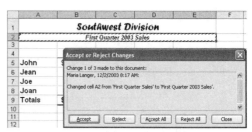

Figure 21 Excel selects the changed cell and displays information about the change in the Accept or Reject Changes dialog.

To remove revision marks

1. Choose Tools > Track Changes > Highlight Changes (**Figure 14**).

2. In the Highlight Changes dialog (**Figure 15**), turn off the Track Changes while editing check box and click OK.

   The revision marks disappear.

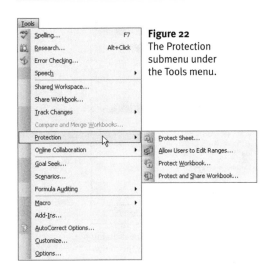

Figure 22
The Protection submenu under the Tools menu.

Document Protection

Excel's document protection features enable you to limit the types of changes others can make to a document. There are four types of protection:

◆ **Protect Sheet** protects against certain types of changes to worksheets and locked worksheet cells.

◆ **Allow Users to Edit Ranges** protects against changes to specific ranges of worksheet cells.

◆ **Protect Workbook** protects workbook structure and windows.

◆ **Protect and Share Workbook** enables you to share the workbook but only with change tracking enabled.

You set up all protection options using commands on the Protection submenu under the Tools menu (**Figure 22**).

✔ Tips

■ I explain how revision tracking works earlier in this chapter.

■ In addition to document protection, you can password protect a document to prevent it from being opened or changed. I explain how later in this chapter.

To protect a sheet

1. Choose Tools > Protection >Protect Sheet (**Figure** 22).

2. In the Protect Sheet dialog that appears (**Figure** 23), turn on check boxes for the types of changes you want to allow.

3. If desired, enter a password in the Password text box.

4. Click OK.

5. If you entered a password, the Confirm Password dialog appears (**Figure** 24). Enter the password again and click OK.

✔ Tips

- Entering a password in the Protect Sheet dialog (**Figure** 23) is optional. If you do not use a password, however, the document can be unprotected by anyone.

- If you enter a password in the Protect Sheet dialog (**Figure** 23), don't forget it! If you can't remember the password, you can't unprotect the document!

- If you try to change a protected item, Excel displays a dialog reminding you that the item is protected (**Figure** 25).

Figure 23 Use the Protect Sheet dialog to set protection options for the active worksheet.

Figure 24 If you entered a password in the Protect Sheet dialog, you'll have to enter it again to turn on protection.

Figure 25 Excel tells you when you're trying to edit a protected item.

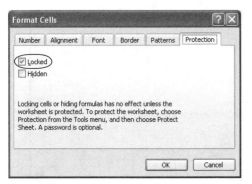

Figure 26 Turn off the Locked check box to allow modification to selected cells in a protected sheet.

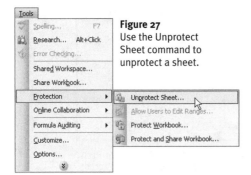

Figure 27
Use the Unprotect
Sheet command to
unprotect a sheet.

To turn off protection for selected cells

1. If the sheet is already protected, turn off protection.

2. Select the cells you want to allow modification to.

3. Choose Format > Cells to display the Format Cells dialog and click the Protection tab (**Figure 26**).

4. Turn off the Locked check box.

5. Click OK.

When you protect the sheet's contents, the unlocked cells can be modified.

✔ Tip

- I tell you more about the Format Cells dialog in **Chapter 6**.

To unprotect a sheet

1. Choose Tools > Protection > Unprotect Sheet (**Figure 27**).

2. If protection is enforced with a password, enter the password in the dialog that appears and click OK.

UNLOCKING CELLS, UNPROTECTING SHEETS

To allow users to edit ranges of a protected sheet

1. If necessary, follow the instructions on the previous page to unprotect the worksheet.

2. Choose Tools > Protection >Allow Users to Edit Ranges (**Figure 22**). The Allow Users to Edit Ranges dialog appears (**Figure 28**).

3. To add an editable range of cells, click New to display the New Range dialog (**Figure 29**).

4. Enter information into each text box:
   - ▲ **Title** is a name for the range.
   - ▲ **Refers to cells** is the cell reference for the range.
   - ▲ **Range password** is the password to allow editing the range of cells.

5. Click OK.

6. If you entered a password in step 4, the Confirm Password dialog appears (**Figure 24**). Enter the password again and click OK.

7. Repeat steps 2 through 5 for each range you want to add. The ranges appear in the Allow Users to Edit Ranges dialog (**Figure 30**).

8. Click OK.

9. Follow the instructions on the previous page to protect the worksheet.

Figure 28 The Allow Users to Edit Ranges dialog before any ranges have been defined.

Figure 29 The New Range dialog with information for a range already entered.

Figure 30 Ranges you add appear in the Allow Users to Edit Ranges dialog.

	A	B	C	D
1	Permissions for	[SW Div Sales.xls]SW Div Sales		
2				
3	Range Title	Range of Cells	Password Protected	Users and Groups
4	March Amounts	=$D$5:$D$8	No	-
5	Jean Sales	=$B$6:$D$6	Yes	-

Figure 31 Excel can record permission information in a worksheet.

Figure 32 Enter the password assigned to the range to modify a cell within it.

✔ Tips

- In step 4, an easy way to enter the cell reference is to move the dialog aside and select the range in the worksheet window.

- Not entering a password in step 4 is the same as simply unlocking the cell. I explain how to turn off protection for selected cells earlier in this section.

- You can modify or delete the settings for a range by selecting the range name in the Allow Users to Edit Ranges dialog (**Figure 30**) and clicking either the Modify or the Delete button.

- If you turn on the Paste permissions information into a new workbook check box in the Allow Users to Edit Ranges dialog (**Figure 30**), Excel creates a worksheet with a summary of permissions settings (**Figure 31**).

- If you attempt to edit a cell that is part of a password-protected range in a protected worksheet, the Unlock Range dialog appears (**Figure 32**). Enter the appropriate password and click OK to edit the cell.

- Excel 2003 enables you to use the new permissions feature to further customize who can modify cell contents. Although this advanced feature is far beyond the scope of this book, you can experiment with it by clicking the Permissions button in the Allow Users to Edit Ranges (**Figure 30**) or New Range (**Figure 29**) dialogs.

To protect a workbook

1. Choose Tools > Protection >Protect Workbook (**Figure 22**).

2. In the Protect Workbook dialog that appears (**Figure 33**), turn on check boxes for the type of protection you want:

   ▲ **Structure** prevents workbook sheets from being inserted, deleted, moved, hidden, unhidden, or renamed.

   ▲ **Windows** protects workbook windows from being moved, resized, hidden, unhidden, or closed.

3. If desired, enter a password in the Password text box.

4. Click OK.

5. If you entered a password in step 3, enter the password again in the Confirm Password dialog that appears (**Figure 24**) and click OK.

✔ Tip

■ With workbook protection options enabled, Excel disables any menu commands or shortcut keys that you would use to make unallowed changes.

To unprotect a workbook

1. Choose Tools > Protection > Unprotect Workbook (**Figure 34**).

2. If protection is enforced with a password, enter the password in the dialog that appears and click OK.

Figure 33
Use the Protect Workbook dialog to protect a workbook's structure or windows.

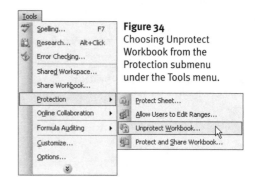

Figure 34
Choosing Unprotect Workbook from the Protection submenu under the Tools menu.

Figure 35
Use the Protect Shared Workbook dialog to allow others to share the workbook, but only with change tracking enabled.

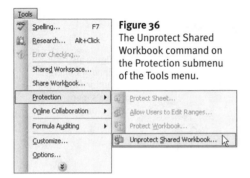

Figure 36
The Unprotect Shared Workbook command on the Protection submenu of the Tools menu.

To protect a workbook for sharing & change tracking

1. Choose Tools > Protection >Protect and Share Workbook (**Figure 22**).

2. In the Protect Shared Workbook dialog that appears (**Figure 35**), turn on the Sharing with track changes check box.

3. If desired, enter a password in the Password text box.

4. Click OK.

5. If you entered a password in step 3, enter the password again in the Confirm Password dialog that appears (**Figure 24**) and click OK.

6. When prompted to save the workbook, click OK. Excel turns on change tracking and workbook sharing.

✔ Tip

- I tell you about workbook sharing later in this chapter and about change tracking earlier in this chapter.

To turn off workbook sharing & change tracking protection

1. Choose Tools > Protection > Unprotect Shared Workbook (**Figure 36**).

2. If protection is enforced with a password, enter the password in the dialog that appears and click OK.

Save Options & Password Protection

Excel's save options enable you to set up passwords to prevent a document from being opened or from being modified.

To set save options

1. Choose File > Save As (**Figure 1**).

2. In the Save As dialog that appears (**Figure 37**), choose General Options from the Tools menu in the toolbar (**Figure 38**).

3. Set options in the Save Options dialog (**Figure 39**) as desired:

   ▲ **Always create backup** tells Excel to save the previous version of the file as a backup when saving the current version. (The old file is named "Backup of *filename.*")

   ▲ **Password to open** is the password that must be entered in order to open the file.

   ▲ **Password to modify** is the password that must be entered in order to save changes to the file.

   ▲ **Read-only recommended** tells Excel to recommend that the file be opened as a read-only file when the user tries to open it.

4. Click OK.

5. If you entered a password in step 3, a dialog appears, asking you to confirm it (**Figure 23**). Re-enter the password and click OK. (If you entered two passwords, this dialog appears twice.)

✔ Tips

■ Clicking the Advanced button in the Save Options dialog enables you to set encryption options for the file, further enhancing security for sensitive files.

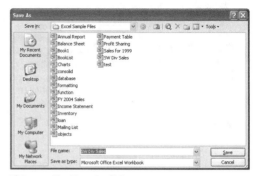

Figure 37 The Save As dialog.

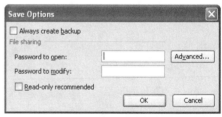

Figure 38 Choose General Options from the Tools menu on the toolbar.

Figure 39 Use the Save Options dialog to set all kinds of options for protecting a file.

■ I tell you more about saving files in **Chapter 4**.

Figure 40 Use a dialog like this to enter a password to open a file.

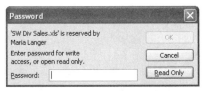

Figure 41 Use a dialog like this to enter a password to open a file for modification.

Figure 42 If read-only access is recommended for a file, Excel displays a dialog like this one when you open it.

Figure 43 Excel displays a dialog like this if you try to save a file that is opened for read-only access.

Figure 44 Not sure if a document is open as a read-only file? Just look in the title bar.

To open a file that has save options set

Open the file as usual. Then:

◆ If the file requires a password to open it, a dialog like the one in **Figure 40** appears. Enter the password and click OK.

◆ If the file requires a password for modification, a dialog like the one in **Figure 41** appears. You have two choices:

▲ Enter the password and click OK.

▲ Click Read Only to open the file as a read-only file.

◆ If the file was set up so read-only access is recommended, a dialog like the one in **Figure 42** appears, asking if you want to open the file as a read-only file. You have three choices:

▲ Click Cancel to not open the file at all.

▲ Click No to open the file as a regular file.

▲ Click Yes to open the file as a read-only file.

✔ Tip

■ If a file is opened for read-only access only, you cannot save changes to the file—a dialog like the one in **Figure 43** appears if you try. You can identify a file opened as a read-only file by the words "Read-Only" in the document window's title bar (**Figure 44**).

Workbook Sharing

Excel's workbook sharing feature enables multiple people to work on the same workbook at the same time. This feature is designed for work environments with networked computer systems.

To share a workbook

1. Choose Tools > Share Workbook (**Figure 45**).

2. In the Share Workbook dialog that appears, click the Editing tab to display its options (**Figure 46**).

3. Turn on the check box beside Allow changes by more than one user at the same time.

4. Click OK. A dialog prompts you to save the workbook.

5. Click OK.

✔ Tip

- You can identify a workbook that has sharing enabled by the word "Shared" in its title bar (**Figure 47**).

To open a shared workbook

1. Choose File > Open (**Figure 1**).

2. Use the Open dialog that appears (**Figure 3**) to open the network volume on which the workbook resides, then locate, select, and open the file.

Figure 45
To enable or disable workbook sharing, choose Share Workbook from the Tools menu.

Figure 46 Sharing a workbook is as easy as turning on a check box.

Figure 47 You can identify a shared workbook by the word "Shared" in its title bar.

ENABLING WORKBOOK SHARING

Figure 48 The Share Workbook dialog lists all users who have the workbook file open.

Figure 49 This warning appears when you remove a user from sharing a workbook file.

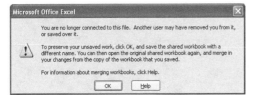

Figure 50 When a user is removed from sharing a workbook file, he sees this message when he attempts to save changes to the file.

To stop sharing a workbook

1. Choose Tools > Share Workbook (**Figure 45**).

2. In the Share Workbook dialog that appears, click the Editing tab to display its options (**Figure 48**).

3. To stop a specific user from sharing the workbook, select the user's name in the user list and click the Remove User button. Then click OK in the warning dialog that appears (**Figure 49**).

   or

   To stop all users from sharing the workbook, turn off the check box beside Allow changes by more than one user at the same time.

4. Click OK.

5. A dialog may prompt you to save the workbook. Click OK.

✔ Tips

■ The Share Workbook dialog for a file lists all of the users who have the file open (**Figure 48**).

■ If you remove a user from workbook sharing, when he tries to save the workbook, a dialog like the one in **Figure 50** appears, telling him that he is no longer sharing the workbook and offering instructions on how to save his changes.

Using Other Programs

Using Excel with Other Programs

Microsoft Excel works well with a number of other programs. These programs can expand Excel's capabilities:

◆ OLE objects created with other Microsoft Office and Windows programs can be inserted into Excel documents.

◆ Excel documents can be inserted into documents created with other Microsoft Office programs.

◆ Excel documents can be e-mailed to others using Microsoft Outlook.

This chapter explains how you can use Excel with some of these other programs.

✔ Tip

■ This chapter provides information about programs other than Microsoft Excel. To follow instructions for a specific program, that program must be installed on your computer.

OLE Objects

An *object* is all or part of a file created with an OLE-aware program. *OLE* or *Object Linking and Embedding* is a Microsoft technology that enables you to insert a file as an object within a document (**Figure 1**)—even if the file was created with a different program. Clicking or double-clicking the inserted object starts the program that created it so you can modify its contents.

Excel's Object command enables you to insert OLE objects in two different ways:

◆ **Create and insert a new OLE object.** This method starts a specific OLE-aware program so you can create an object.

◆ **Insert an existing OLE object.** This method enables you to locate, select, and insert an existing file as an object.

✔ Tips

■ All Microsoft programs are OLE-aware. Many software programs created by other developers are also OLE-aware; check the documentation that came with a specific software package for details.

■ Excel comes with a number of OLE-aware programs that can be used to insert objects. The full Microsoft Office package includes even more of these programs.

■ You can learn more about inserting text and multimedia elements in **Chapter 7**.

	A	B	C	D	E
1	Southwest Division				
2	1st Quarter Commission Calculations				
3					
4			January	February	March
5	Sales		$1,000.00	$1,250.00	$1,485.00
6	Cost		400.00	395.00	412.00
7	Profit		$ 600.00	$ 855.00	$1,073.00
8					
9	Owner	Percent	Jan Share	Feb Share	Mar Share
10	John	50%	$ 300.00	$ 427.50	$ 536.50
11	Jean	20%	120.00	171.00	214.60
12	Joe	15%	90.00	128.25	160.95
13	Joan	15%	90.00	128.25	160.95
14		100%	$ 600.00	$ 855.00	$1,073.00
15					
16	Commissions Breakdown				
17					
18	Commissions are based on ownership percentages. Each				
19	month, the total sales and expenses are calculated. The next				
20	profit is multiplied by each owner's percentage of ownership				
21	to arrive at a commission total. Commission checks are cut				
22	and distributed within two weeks of month-end. Any				
23	adjustments for returns, etc. are carried forward to the				
24	following month.				
25					
26	All accounting is handled by Jenny in the Accounting				
27	Department. She can be reached at x1234.				
28					

Figure 1 A Microsoft Word Document object inserted in a Microsoft Excel document.

Figure 2
Choose Object from the Insert menu.

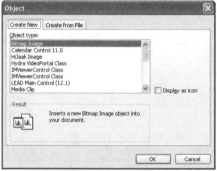

Figure 3 The Object dialog. The options in the Object type list vary depending on the software installed in your computer.

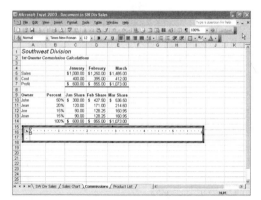

Figure 4 A frame containing a Microsoft Word object inserted into an Excel document. The menu bar and toolbars are also for Word.

To insert a new object

1. Select a cell near where you want the object to appear.

2. Choose Insert > Object (**Figure 2**) to display the Object dialog.

3. If necessary, click the Create New tab to display its options (**Figure 3**).

4. In the Object type list, click to select the type of object that you want to insert.

5. Click OK.

    Excel starts the program that you selected. It may take a moment for it to appear. **Figure 4** shows a frame for a Microsoft Word document in the Excel worksheet window. The Word menu bar and toolbars appear at the top of the program window.

6. Use the program to create the object that you want.

7. When you are finished creating the object, click outside the object. The object's frame and any toolbars or menus that appeared disappear and you can continue working with Excel.

8. If necessary, resize the object and drag it into position in the Excel document (**Figure 1**).

✔ Tips

■ Some of the programs that come with Excel and appear in the Object dialog may not be fully installed. If that is the case, Excel will prompt you to insert the program CD to install the software.

■ Some OLE-aware programs may display a dialog or similar interface. Use the controls within the dialog to create and insert the object.

INSERTING NEW OBJECTS

To insert an existing object

1. Select the cell where you want the object to appear.

2. Choose Insert > Object (**Figure** 2) to display the Object dialog.

3. Click the Create from File tab to display its options (**Figure** 5).

4. Click the Browse button.

5. Use the Browse dialog that appears (**Figure** 6) to locate and select the file that you want to insert. Then click Insert.

6. The pathname for the file appears in the Object dialog. Click OK. The file is inserted as an object in the document.

✔ Tip

■ To insert a file as an object, the program that created the file must be properly installed on your computer or accessible through a network connection. Excel displays a dialog if the program is missing.

To customize an inserted object

Follow the instructions in the previous two sections to create and insert a new object or insert an existing object. In the Object dialog (**Figure** 3 or 5), turn on check boxes as desired:

◆ **Link to File** creates a link to the object's file so that when it changes, the object inserted within the Excel document can change. This option is only available when inserting an existing file as an object.

◆ **Display as icon** (**Figure** 7) displays an icon that represents the object rather than the object itself. Double-clicking the icon opens the object and displays its contents.

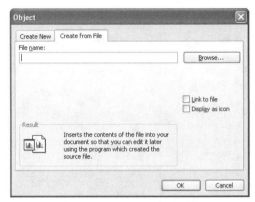

Figure 5 The Create from File tab of the Object dialog.

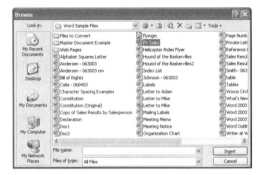

Figure 6 Use this dialog to select the file you want to insert.

Figure 7 An inserted Microsoft Word 2003 document displayed as an icon.

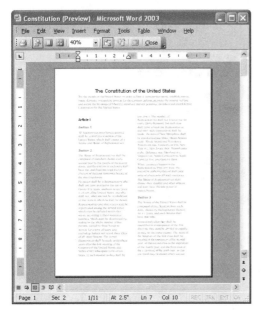

Figure 8 Word processing software like Word is most often used to create formatted documents.

Using Word with Excel

Word is the word processing component of Microsoft Office. A *word processor* is a program for creating formatted text-based documents (**Figure 8**). Word can also create mailing labels, merge static text with data (a data merge or mail merge), and create documents with pictures and other graphic elements.

You can use Word with Excel to:

◆ Include information from a Word document in an Excel document (**Figure 1**).

◆ Perform a Word data merge with an Excel list as a data source.

✔ Tips

■ Because performing a data merge is primarily a function of Word rather than Excel, it is not covered in detail in this book.

■ To learn more about using Word 2003, pick up a copy of *Microsoft Word 2003 for Windows: Visual QuickStart Guide*, a Peachpit Press book by Maria Langer.

To include Word document content in an Excel document

To insert a Word document as an object in an Excel document, consult the section about OLE objects earlier in this chapter.

Or

1. In the Word document, select the text that you want to include in the Excel document (**Figure 9**).

2. Choose Edit > Copy (**Figure 10**), press Ctrl C, or click the Copy button  on the Standard toolbar.

3. Switch to Excel and either:

   ▲ Double-click in the cell where you want the content to appear to position the insertion point there (**Figure 11**).

   ▲ Create a text box to hold the content and position the insertion point inside the text box (**Figure 12**).

4. Choose Edit > Paste (**Figure 13**), press Ctrl V, or click the Paste button on the Standard toolbar. The selection appears in the selected cell (**Figure 14**) or text box (**Figure 15**).

✔ Tip

■ You can also use drag-and-drop editing to drag a Word document selection into an Excel document. I tell you how in **Chapter 3**.

Replacement for Jane Jones
Team for Product X marketing development

First Quarter Sales
First Quarter 2004 sales look very good. The following chart graphically represents performance, broken down by salesperson.

Figure 9 Select the text you want to include.

Figure 10 Choose Copy from Word's Edit menu.

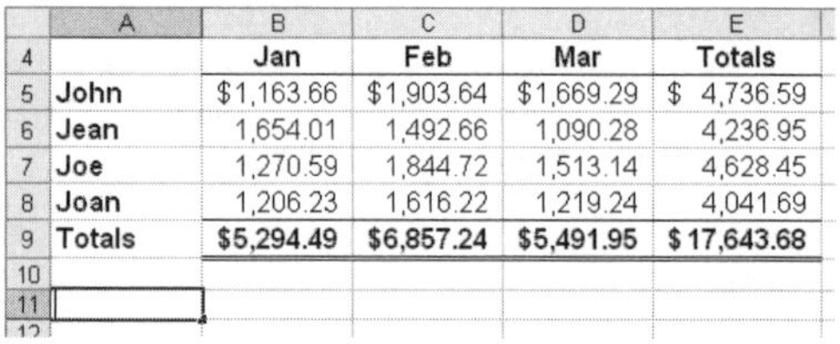

	A	B	C	D	E
4		Jan	Feb	Mar	Totals
5	John	$1,163.66	$1,903.64	$1,669.29	$ 4,736.59
6	Jean	1,654.01	1,492.66	1,090.28	4,236.95
7	Joe	1,270.59	1,844.72	1,513.14	4,628.45
8	Joan	1,206.23	1,616.22	1,219.24	4,041.69
9	Totals	$5,294.49	$6,857.24	$5,491.95	$ 17,643.68
10					
11					

Figures 11 & 12 Position the insertion point in a cell (above) or text box (below).

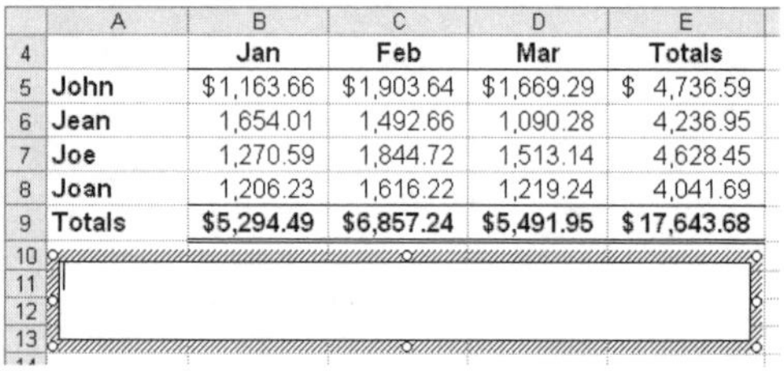

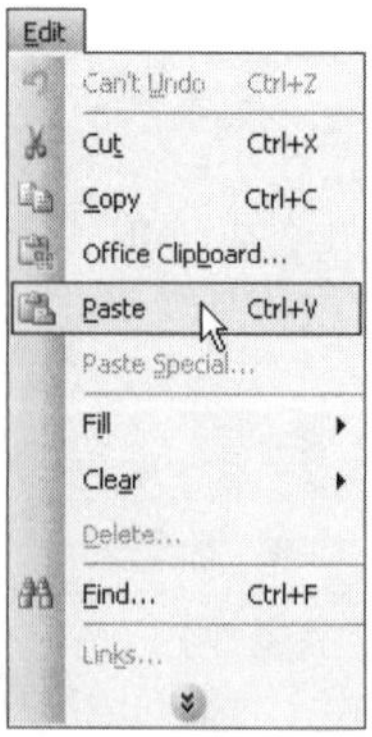

	A	B	C	D	E
4		Jan	Feb	Mar	Totals
5	John	$1,163.66	$1,903.64	$1,669.29	$ 4,736.59
6	Jean	1,654.01	1,492.66	1,090.28	4,236.95
7	Joe	1,270.59	1,844.72	1,513.14	4,628.45
8	Joan	1,206.23	1,616.22	1,219.24	4,041.69
9	Totals	$5,294.49	$6,857.24	$5,491.95	$ 17,643.68
10					
11					
12					
13					

Figure 13 Choose Paste from Excel's Edit menu.

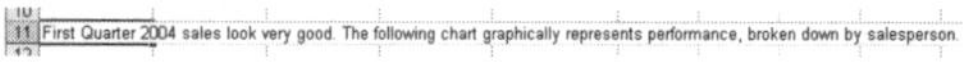

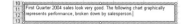
First Quarter 2004 sales look very good. The following chart graphically represents performance, broken down by salesperson.

Figures 14 & 15 The text is pasted into the cell (above) or the text box (below).

First Quarter 2004 sales look very good. The following chart graphically represents performance, broken down by salesperson.

Figure 16 Start with an Excel list, like this one.

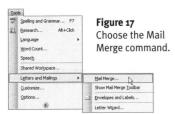

Figure 17 Choose the Mail Merge command.

Figure 18 The third step of the Mail Merge task pane.

Figure 19 Use this dialog to locate, select, and open the Excel file you want to use for the merge.

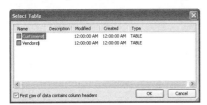

Figure 20 If the Select Table dialog appears, use it to indicate which worksheet contains the data.

To use an Excel list as a data source for a Word data merge

1. Follow the instructions in **Chapter 10** to create an Excel list and enter data into it (**Figure 16**).

2. Switch to Word and choose Tools > Letters and Mailings > Mail Merge (**Figure 17**).

3. Follow the steps in the Mail Merge task pane. In step 3 (**Figure 18**), select the Use an existing list option.

4. Click the Browse link and then use the Select Data Source dialog that appears (**Figure 19**) to locate, select, and open the Excel file containing the list you want to use for the merge.

5. If the Select Table dialog appears (**Figure 20**), select the worksheet containing the data you want to use. If the first row of the Excel worksheet contains column headings, make sure the check box for First row of data contains column headers is turned on. Then click OK.

6. The Mail Merge Recipients dialog appears (**Figure 21**). It contains all of the data from the Excel list. Use the Mail Merge task pane to complete the merge.

✔ Tip

■ Because performing a data merge is a function of Word rather than Excel, it is not covered in detail in this book.

Figure 21 The Mail Merge Recipients dialog.

Using Outlook with Excel

Outlook is the e-mail, newsgroup, and personal information management software component of Microsoft Office. *E-mail software* enables you to send and receive electronic mail messages (**Figure 22**). *Personal information management software* enables you to store and organize address book (**Figure 23**) and calendar (**Figure 24**) data.

You can use Outlook with Excel to e-mail an Excel document to a friend, family member, or co-worker.

✔ Tip

- To learn more about using Outlook, consult the documentation that came with the program or its onscreen help feature.

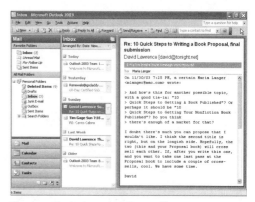

Figure 22 Outlook can handle e-mail, ...

Figure 23 ... address book information, ...

Figure 24 ... and calendar events.

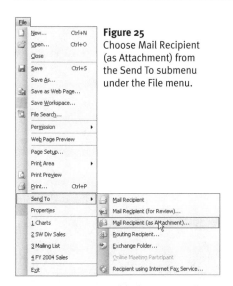

Figure 25
Choose Mail Recipient (as Attachment) from the Send To submenu under the File menu.

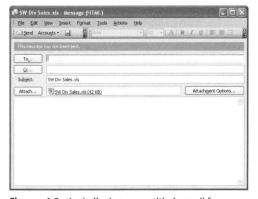

Figure 26 Outlook displays an untitled e-mail form.

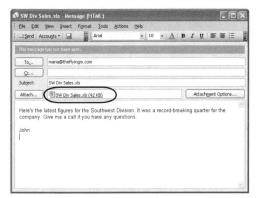

Figure 27 Here's what a finished message might look like. Note that the name of the Excel document being sent appears in the Attachments area.

To send an Excel document via e-mail

1. Display the Excel document you want to send via e-mail.

2. Choose File > Send To > Mail Recipient (as Attachment) (**Figure 25**).

3. Excel runs Outlook and displays an empty e-mail window with the To field selected (**Figure 26**). Enter the e-mail address for the person you want to send the document to.

4. If desired, edit the contents of the Subject field.

5. In the message body, enter a message to accompany the file. **Figure 27** shows an example.

6. To send the message, click the Send button. Outlook connects to the Internet and sends the message.

7. Switch back to Excel to continue working with the document.

✔ Tips

- These instructions assume that Outlook is the default e-mail program as set in the Internet Options control panel. If a different program has been set as the default e-mail program, ignore steps 3 through 6 and send the message as you normally would with your e-mail program.

- Outlook (or your default e-mail program) must be properly configured to send and receive e-mail messages. Check the program's documentation or onscreen help if you need assistance with setup.

Advanced Techniques

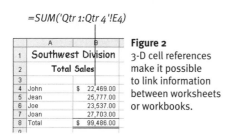

	A	B	C	D	E
1		Southwest Division			
2		First Quarter Sales			
3		Jan	Feb	Mar	Total
4	John	$ 1,254.00	$ 1,256.00	$ 2,435.00	$ 4,945.00
5	Jean	1,865.00	1,736.00	3,495.00	7,096.00
6	Joe	1,614.00	1,284.00	2,509.00	5,407.00
7	Joan	1,987.00	2,740.00	2,890.00	7,617.00
8	Totals	$ 6,720.00	$ 7,016.00	$ 11,329.00	$ 25,065.00

Figure 1 The reference to the selected range would be a lot easier to remember if it had a name like *FirstQtrSales* rather than just *A4:D7*.

=SUM('Qtr 1:Qtr 4'!E4)

	A	B
1	Southwest Division	
2	Total Sales	
3		
4	John	$ 22,469.00
5	Jean	25,777.00
6	Joe	23,537.00
7	Joan	27,703.00
8	Total	$ 99,486.00

Figure 2 3-D cell references make it possible to link information between worksheets or workbooks.

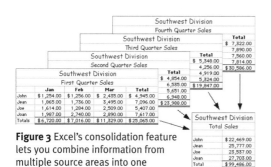

Figure 3 Excel's consolidation feature lets you combine information from multiple source areas into one destination area—with or without live links.

Advanced Techniques

Microsoft Excel has many advanced features that you can use to tap into Excel's real power. In this chapter, I tell you about some of the advanced techniques I think you'll find most useful in your day-to-day work with Excel:

◆ **Names** (**Figure 1**) let you assign easy-to-remember names to cell references. You can then use the names in place of cell references in formulas.

◆ **3-D cell references** (**Figure 2**) let you write formulas with links to other worksheets and workbooks.

◆ **Consolidations** (**Figure 3**) let you summarize information from several source areas into one destination area.

◆ **Custom views** enable you to create predefined views of workbook contents that can include a variety of settings.

◆ **Macros** let you automate repetitive tasks and build custom Excel-based applications.

✔ Tip

■ This chapter builds on information in previous chapters. It's a good idea to have a solid understanding of the information covered up to this point in this book before exploring the features in this chapter.

Names

The trouble with using cell references in formulas is that they're difficult to remember. To make matters worse, cell references can change if cells above or to the left of them are inserted or deleted.

Excel's Names feature eliminates both problems by letting you assign easy-to-remember names to individual cells or ranges of cells in your workbooks. The names, which you can use in formulas, don't change, no matter how much worksheet editing you do.

✔ Tips

- Excel can automatically recognize many column and row labels as cell or range names. I tell you about this feature on the next page.

- Names can be up to 255 characters long and can include letters, numbers, periods, question marks, and underscore characters (_). The first character must be a letter. Names cannot contain spaces or "look" like cell references.

- If you enter an incorrect name reference in a formula, one of two things happens:

  - ▲ Excel's Formula AutoCorrect feature offers to fix it (**Figure 4**)—if Excel can "guess" what name you meant to type.

  - ▲ A *#NAME?* error value appears in the cell (**Figure 5**).

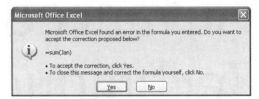

Figure 4 The Formula AutoCorrect feature can sometimes help you fix incorrectly entered name references.

Figure 5 If a name reference in a formula is not correct, a *#NAME?* error appears in the cell.

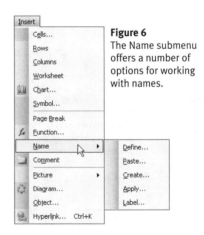

Figure 6
The Name submenu offers a number of options for working with names.

Figure 7 Use the Define Name dialog to set a name for one or more cells. As you can see, the name of the worksheet is part of the cell reference.

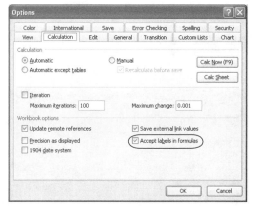

Figure 8 To use labels as names, make sure the Accept labels in formulas check box is turned on.

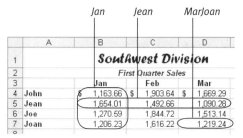

Figure 9 Examples of labels automatically recognized as range and cell names.

To define a name

1. Select the cell(s) you want to name (**Figure 1**).

2. Choose Insert > Name > Define (**Figure 6**).

3. In the Define Name dialog that appears, Excel may suggest a name in the text box. You can enter a name you prefer (**Figure 7**).

4. The cell reference in the Refers to text box should reflect the range you selected in step 1. To enter a different range, delete the range that appears in the text box and either type in a new range or reselect the cell(s) in the worksheet window.

5. Click OK.

✔ Tip

- To define more than one name, follow the above steps for the first name but click the Add button in step 5. Then repeat steps 3 through 5 for each name you want to define. When you're finished, click OK.

To use labels as names

Make sure the Accept labels in formulas check box is turned on in the Calculation tab of the Options dialog (**Figure 8**). (See **Chapter 15** for more information about setting options.)

✔ Tips

- The Accept labels in formulas option is turned off by default.

- Here's how Excel applies labels to ranges and cells (**Figure 9**):

  ▲ To refer to a column, use the label at the top of the column.

  ▲ To refer to a row, use the label at the left end of the row.

  ▲ To refer to a cell, use the label at the top of the column and the label at the left end of the row.

DEFINING NAMES, USING LABELS AS NAMES

To create names

1. Select the cells containing the ranges you want to name as well as text in adjoining cells that you want to use as names (**Figure 10**).

2. Choose Insert > Name > Create (**Figure 6**).

3. In the Create Names dialog (**Figure 11**), turn on the check box(es) for the cells that contain the text you want to use as names.

4. Click OK.

   Excel uses the text in the cells you indicated as names for the adjoining cells. You can see the results if you open the Define Name dialog (**Figure 12**).

✔ Tip

■ This is a quick way to create a lot of names all at once.

To delete a name

1. Choose Insert > Name > Define (**Figure 6**).

2. In the Define Name dialog (**Figure 12**), click to select the name in the scrolling list that you want to delete.

3. Click Delete. The name is removed from the list.

4. Repeat steps 2 and 3 to delete other names as desired.

5. Click OK to dismiss the Define Name dialog.

✔ Tip

■ Deleting a name does not delete the cells to which the name refers.

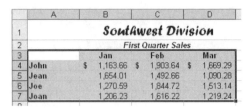

Figure 10 To use the Create Names dialog, you must first select the cells you want to name, as well as adjoining cells with text you want to use as names.

Figure 11
In the Create Names dialog, tell Excel which cells contain the text for names.

Figure 12 Look in the Define Name dialog to see how many names were added.

CREATING & DELETING NAMES

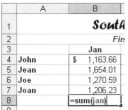

Figure 13
Once a range has been named, it can be used instead of a cell reference in a formula.

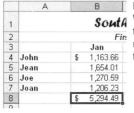

Figure 14
When you complete the formula, the result appears in the cell.

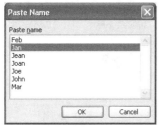

Figure 15
Use the Paste Name dialog to select and paste in a name.

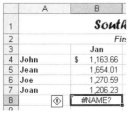

Figure 16
If you delete a name used in a formula, a *#NAME?* error results.

To enter a name in a formula

1. Position the cellpointer in the cell in which you want to write the formula.

2. Type in the formula, replacing any cell reference with the corresponding name (**Figure 13**).

3. Press [Enter] or click the Enter button ☑ on the formula bar.

   Excel performs the calculation just as if you'd typed in a cell reference (**Figure 14**).

✔ Tips

- You can use the Paste Name command to enter a name for you. Follow the steps above, but when it's time to type in the name, choose Insert > Name > Paste (**Figure 6**). Use the Paste Name dialog that appears (**Figure 15**) to select and paste in the name you want. The Paste Name command even works when you use the Formula Palette to write formulas. I tell you about the Formula Palette in **Chapter 5**.

- When you delete a name, Excel responds with a *#NAME?* error in each cell that contains a formula referring to that name (**Figure 16**). These formulas must be rewritten.

To apply names to existing formulas

1. Select the cells containing formulas for which you want to apply names. If you want to apply names throughout the worksheet, click any single cell.

2. Choose Insert > Name > Apply (**Figure 6**).

3. In the Apply Names dialog (**Figure 17**), select the names that you want to use in place of the cell reference. To select or deselect a name, click on it.

4. Click OK.

   Excel rewrites the formulas with the appropriate names from those you selected. **Figure 18** shows an example of formulas changed by selecting *Jan*, *Feb*, and *Mar* in **Figure 17**.

✔ Tips

■ If only one cell is selected, Excel applies names based on your selection(s) in the Apply Names dialog instead of the selected cell.

■ If you turn off the Ignore Relative/Absolute check box in the Apply Names dialog (**Figure 17**), Excel matches the type of reference. I tell you about relative and absolute references in **Chapter 3**.

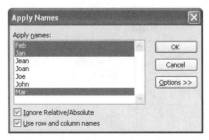

Figure 17 Select the names that you want to apply to formulas in your worksheet.

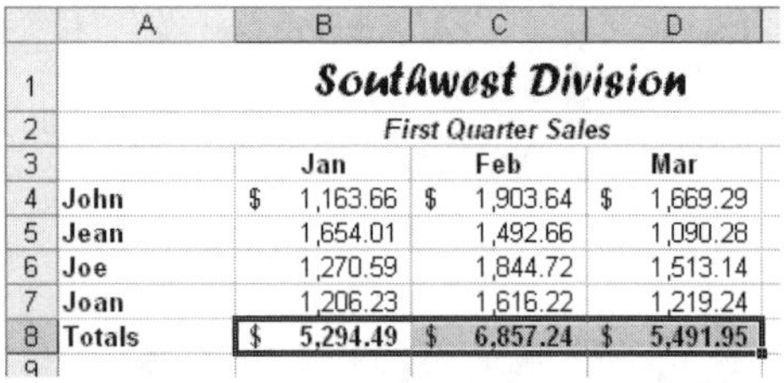

	A	B	C	D
1		*Southwest Division*		
2		*First Quarter Sales*		
3		Jan	Feb	Mar
4	John	$ 1,163.66	$ 1,903.64	$ 1,669.29
5	Jean	1,654.01	1,492.66	1,090.28
6	Joe	1,270.59	1,844.72	1,513.14
7	Joan	1,206.23	1,616.22	1,219.24
8	Totals	$ 5,294.49	$ 6,857.24	$ 5,491.95
9				

Figure 18
Excel applies the names you selected to formulas that reference their ranges.

Cell	Before	After
B8	=SUM(B4:B7)	=SUM(Jan)
C8	=SUM(C4:C7)	=SUM(Feb)
D8	=SUM(D4:D7)	=SUM(Mar)

APPLYING NAMES TO EXISTING FORMULAS

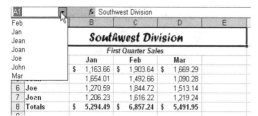

Figure 19 The Name drop-down list on the left end of the formula bar lets you select named ranges quickly.

Figure 20 If you prefer, you can type in a name and press Enter to select it.

Figure 21 Choose the Go To command under the Edit menu.

To select named cells

Choose the name of the cell(s) you want to select from the Name drop-down list on the far-left end of the formula bar (**Figure 19**).

Or

1. Click the Name box at the far-left end of the formula bar to select it.

2. Type in the name of the cells you want to select (**Figure 20**).

3. Press Enter.

Or

1. Choose Edit > Go To (**Figure 21**).

2. In the Go To dialog (**Figure 22**), click to select the name of the cell(s) you want in the Go to scrolling list.

3. Click OK.

✔ Tip

■ When named cells are selected, the name appears in the cell reference area at the far-left end of the formula bar.

Figure 22 Select the name of the cell(s) you want to select from the Go to scrolling list.

3-D References

3-D cell references let you write formulas that reference cells in other worksheets or workbooks. The links are live—when a cell's contents change, the results of formulas in cells that reference it change.

Excel offers several ways to write formulas with 3-D cell references:

- **Use cell names.** I tell you about cell names in the first part of this chapter. **Figure 23** shows an example.

- **Type them in.** When you type in a 3-D cell reference, you must include the name of the sheet (in single quotes, if the name contains a space), followed by an exclamation point (!) and cell reference. If the reference is for a cell in another workbook, you must also include the workbook name, in brackets. **Figures 24, 25,** and **26** show examples.

- **Click on them.** You'll get the same results as if you had typed the references, but Excel does all the typing for you. (This is the method I prefer.)

- **Use the Paste Special command.** The Paste Link button in the Paste Special dialog lets you paste a link between cells in different sheets of a workbook or different workbooks.

✔ Tips

- When you delete a cell, Excel displays a *#REF!* error in any cells that referred to it. The cells containing these errors must be revised to remove the error.

- Do not make references to an unsaved file. If you do and you close the file with the reference before saving (and naming) the file it refers to, Excel won't be able to update the link.

=SUM(John,Joan,Joe,Jean)

Figure 23 This example uses the SUM function to add the contents of the cells named *John, Joan, Joe,* and *Jean* in the same workbook.

='Results for Year'!$B$9

Figure 24 This example refers to cell *B9* in a worksheet called *Results for Year* in the same workbook.

=SUM('Qtr 1:Qtr 4'!E9)

Figure 25 This example uses the SUM function to add the contents of cell *E9* in worksheets starting with *Qtr 1* and ending with *Qtr 4* in the same workbook.

=[Sales]'Results for Year'!$B$9

Figure 26 This example refers to cell *B9* in a worksheet called *Results for Year* in a workbook called *Sales.*

```
=TotalSales
```

```
='Inventory Records'!InventoryValue
```

Figures 27 & 28 Two examples of 3-D references utilizing names. The first example refers to a name in the same workbook. The second example refers to a name in a different workbook.

PMT	▼ X ✓ ƒx	='Qtr 1'!E8		
	A	B	C	D	E
1		Southwest Division			
2		First Quarter Sales			
3		Jan	Feb	Mar	Total
4	John	$ 1,254.00	$ 1,256.00	$ 2,435.00	$ 4,945.00
5	Jean	1,865.00	1,736.00	3,495.00	7,096.00
6	Joe	1,614.00	1,284.00	2,509.00	5,407.00
7	Joan	1,987.00	2,740.00	2,890.00	7,617.00
8	Totals	$ 6,720.00	$ 7,016.00	$ 11,329.00	$ 25,0⟨⟩00

Figure 29 After typing an equal sign in the cell in which you want the reference to go, you can select the cell(s) you want to reference.

To reference a named cell or range in another worksheet

1. Select the cell in which you want to enter the reference.

2. Type an equal sign (=).

3. If the sheet containing the cells you want to reference is in another workbook, type the name of the workbook (within single quotes, if the name contains a space) followed by an exclamation point (!).

4. Type the name of the cell(s) you want to reference (**Figures** 27 and 28).

5. Press [Enter] or click the Enter button ☑ on the formula bar.

✔ Tip

■ If the name you want to reference is in the same workbook, you can paste it in by choosing Insert > Name > Paste (**Figure 6**). I tell you how to use the Paste Name dialog earlier in this chapter.

To reference a cell or range in another worksheet by clicking

1. Select the cell in which you want to enter the reference.

2. Type an equal sign (=).

3. If the sheet containing the cells you want to reference is in another workbook, switch to that workbook.

4. Click on the sheet tab for the worksheet containing the cell you want to reference.

5. Select the cell(s) you want to reference (**Figure 29**).

6. Press [Enter] or click the Enter button ☑ on the formula bar.

To reference a cell or range in another worksheet by typing

1. Select the cell in which you want to enter the reference.

2. Type an equal sign (=).

3. If the sheet containing the cells you want to reference is in another workbook, type the name of the workbook within brackets ([ ]).

4. Type the name of the sheet followed by an exclamation point (!).

5. Type the cell reference for the cell(s) you want to reference.

6. Press Enter or click the Enter button ✓ on the formula bar.

✔ Tip

■ If the name of the sheet includes a space character, the sheet name must be enclosed within single quotes in the reference. See **Figures** 24, 25, and 26 for examples.

To reference a cell with the Paste Special command

1. Select the cell you want to reference.

2. Choose Edit > Copy (**Figure 21**), press Ctrl C, or click the Copy button 📋 on the Standard toolbar.

3. Switch to the worksheet in which you want to put the reference.

4. Select the cell in which you want the reference to go.

5. Choose Edit > Paste Special (**Figure 21**).

6. In the Paste Special dialog (**Figure 30**), click the Paste Link button.

Figure 30 You can click the Paste Link button in the Paste Special dialog to paste a reference to cells you copied.

✔ Tips

- Do not press [Enter] after using the Paste Special command! Doing so pastes the contents of the Clipboard into the cell, overwriting the link.

- Using the Paste Link button to paste a range of cells creates a special range called an *array*. Each cell in an array shares the same cell reference and cannot be changed unless all cells in the array are changed.

To write a formula with 3-D references

1. Select the cell in which you want to enter the formula.

2. Type an equal sign (=).

3. Use any combination of the following techniques until the formula is complete.

   ▲ To enter a function, use the Formula Palette or type in the function. I tell you how to use the Formula Palette in **Chapter 5**.

   ▲ To enter an operator, type it in. I tell you about using operators in **Chapter 2**.

   ▲ To enter a cell reference, select the cell(s) you want to reference or type the reference in. If typing the reference, be sure to include single quotes, brackets, and exclamation points as discussed on the previous page.

4. Press [Enter] or click the Enter button ☑ on the formula bar.

WRITING FORMULAS WITH 3-D REFERENCES

To write a formula that sums the same cell on multiple, adjacent sheets

1. Select the cell in which you want to enter the formula.

2. Type =SUM((**Figure 31**).

3. If the cells you want to add are in another workbook, switch to that workbook.

4. Click the sheet tab for the first worksheet containing the cell you want to sum.

5. Hold down Shift and click on the sheet tab for the last sheet containing the cell you want to sum. All tabs from the first to the last become selected (**Figure 32**). The formula in the formula bar should look something like the one in **Figure 33**.

6. Click the cell you want to sum (**Figure 34**). The cell reference is added to the formula (**Figure 35**).

7. Type).

8. Press Enter or click the Enter button ☑ on the formula bar.

✔ Tips

- Use this technique to link cells of identically arranged worksheets. This results in a "3-D worksheet" effect.

- Although you can use this technique to consolidate data, the Consolidate command, which I discuss later in this chapter, automates consolidations with or without links.

Figure 31 Type the beginning of a formula with the SUM function ...

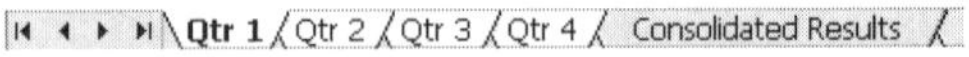

| ◄ ◄ ► ►| \ Qtr 1 / Qtr 2 / Qtr 3 / Qtr 4 / Consolidated Results / |

Figure 32 ... select all of the tabs for sheets that contain the cells you want to sum ...

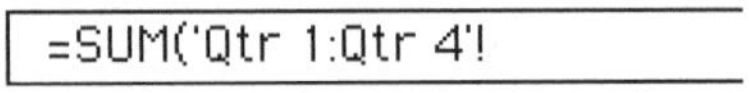

=SUM('Qtr 1:Qtr 4'!

Figure 33 ... so the sheet names are appended as a range in the formula bar.

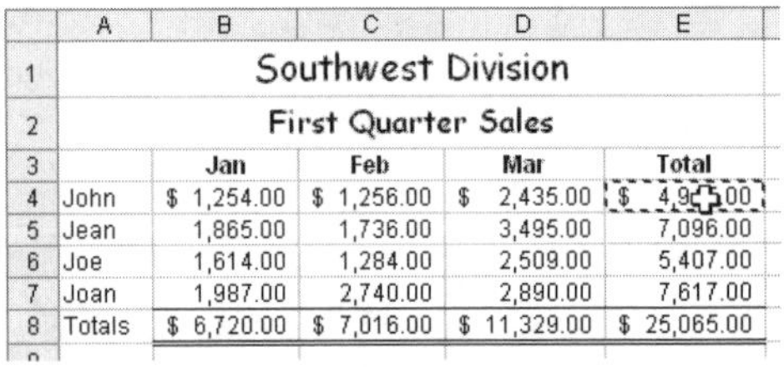

	A	B	C	D	E
1		Southwest Division			
2		First Quarter Sales			
3		Jan	Feb	Mar	Total
4	John	$ 1,254.00	$ 1,256.00	$ 2,435.00	$ 4,945.00
5	Jean	1,865.00	1,736.00	3,495.00	7,096.00
6	Joe	1,614.00	1,284.00	2,509.00	5,407.00
7	Joan	1,987.00	2,740.00	2,890.00	7,617.00
8	Totals	$ 6,720.00	$ 7,016.00	$ 11,329.00	$ 25,065.00

Figure 34 Then click on the cell you want to add ...

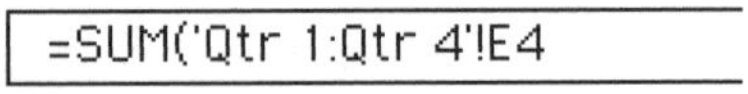

=SUM('Qtr 1:Qtr 4'!E4

Figure 35 ... so that its reference is appended to the formula in the formula bar.

Figure 36 This dialog appears if you open a workbook that contains links to another workbook.

Opening Workbooks with Links

When you open a workbook that has a link to another workbook file, a dialog like the one in **Figure 36** appears.

◆ If you click Update, Excel checks the other file and updates linked information. If Excel can't find the other workbook, it tells you.

◆ If you click Don't Update, Excel does not check the data in the other file.

✔ Tip

■ As the dialog in Figure 36 explains, links can be used to acces information on your computer without your permission. As a result, you should not update links in a file if you don't trust the source of the file, especially if you weren't expecting the file to include links.

Consolidations

The Consolidate command lets you combine data from multiple sources. Excel lets you do this in two ways:

◆ **Consolidate based on the arrangement of data.** This is useful when data occupies the same number of cells in the same arrangement in multiple locations (**Figure 3**).

◆ **Consolidate based on identifying labels or categories.** This is useful when the arrangement of data varies from one source to the next.

✔ Tip

■ With either method, Excel can create links to the source information so the consolidation changes automatically when linked data changes.

To consolidate based on the arrangement of data

1. Select the cell(s) where you want the consolidated information to go (**Figure 37**).

2. Choose Data > Consolidate (**Figure 38**).

3. In the Consolidate dialog (**Figure 39**), choose a function from the Function drop-down list (**Figure 40**).

4. Switch to the worksheet containing the first cell(s) to be included in the consolidation. The reference is entered into the Reference text box.

5. Select the cell(s) you want to include in the consolidation (**Figure 41**). The reference is entered into the Reference text box.

6. Click Add.

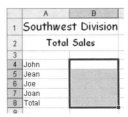

Figure 37
Select the cells in which you want the consolidated data to go.

Figure 38
Choose Consolidate from the Data menu.

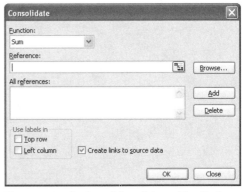

Figure 39 Use the Consolidate dialog to identify the cells you want to combine.

Figure 40
Choose a function for the consolidation from the Function drop-down list.

	A	B	C	D	E
1	Southwest Division				
2	First Quarter Sales				
3		Jan	Feb	Mar	Total
4	John	$ 1,254.00	$ 1,256.00	$ 2,435.00	$ 4,945.00
5	Jean	1,865.00	1,736.00	3,495.00	7,096.00
6	Joe	1,614.00	1,284.00	2,509.00	5,407.00
7	Joan	1,987.00	2,740.00	2,890.00	7,617.00
8	Totals	$ 6,720.00	$ 7,016.00	$ 11,329.00	$ 25,065

Figure 41 Enter references for cells in the Consolidate dialog by selecting them in the worksheet.

Figure 42 The cells you want to consolidate are listed in the All references scrolling list in the Consolidate dialog.

1 2		A	B
	1	Southwest Division	
	2	Total Sales	
	3		
+	8	John	$ 22,469.00
+	13	Jean	25,777.00
+	18	Joe	23,537.00
+	23	Joan	27,703.00
+	28	Total	$ 99,486.00
	29		

Figure 43
Excel combines the data in the cell(s) you originally selected.

7. Repeat steps 4, 5, and 6 for all of the cells that you want to include in the consolidation. When you're finished, the All references scrolling list in the Consolidate dialog might look something like **Figure 42**.

8. To create links between the source data and destination cell(s), turn on the Create links to source data check box.

9. Click OK.

   Excel consolidates the information in the originally selected cell(s) (**Figure 43**).

✔ Tips

- For this technique to work, each source range must have the same number of cells with data arranged in the same way.

- If the Consolidate dialog contains references when you open it, you can clear them by selecting each one and clicking the Delete button.

- If you turn on the Create links to source data check box, Excel creates an outline (**Figure 43**) with links to all source cells. You can expand or collapse the outline by clicking the outline buttons. I tell you more about outlines in **Chapter 10**.

To consolidate based on labels

1. Select the cell(s) in which you want the consolidated information to go. As shown in **Figure 44**, you can select just a single starting cell.

2. Choose Data > Consolidate (**Figure 38**).

3. In the Consolidate dialog (**Figure 39**), choose a function from the Function drop-down list (**Figure 40**).

4. Switch to the worksheet containing the first cell(s) to be included in the consolidation. The reference is entered into the Reference text box.

5. Select the cell(s) you want to include in the consolidation, including any text that identifies data (**Figure 45**). The text must be in cells adjacent to the data. The reference is entered into the Reference text box.

6. Click Add.

7. Repeat steps 4, 5, and 6 for all cells you want to include in the consolidation. **Figures 46** and **47** show the other two ranges included for the example. When you're finished, the Consolidate dialog might look something like **Figure 48**.

8. Turn on the appropriate check box(es) in the Use labels in area to tell Excel where identifying labels for the data are.

9. Click OK.

Excel consolidates the information in the originally selected cell(s) (**Figure 49**).

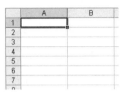

Figure 44
Select the destination cell(s).

	A	B
1		**Widgets**
2	John	$ 1,254.00
3	Jean	1,865.00
4	Joe	1,614.00
5	Joan	1,987.00
6	Total	$ 6,720.00

Figures 45, 46, & 47
Select the cell(s) you want to include in the consolidation.

	A	B
1		**Wing Nuts**
2	John	$ 1,254.00
3	Jean	1,865.00
4	Jerry	1,984.00
5	Joe	1,614.00
6	Jack	1,420.00
7	Joan	1,987.00
8	Total	$ 10,124.00

	A	B
1		**Screw Balls**
2	John	$ 1,254.00
3	Jason	$ 2,745.00
4	Jean	1,865.00
5	Joe	1,614.00
6	Jack	2,412.00
7	Joan	1,987.00
8	Total	$ 11,877.00

Figure 48 The Consolidate dialog records all selections and enables you to specify where the data labels are.

	A	B
1	John	$ 3,762.00
2	Jason	$ 2,745.00
3	Jean	5,595.00
4	Jerry	1,984.00
5	Joe	4,842.00
6	Jack	3,832.00
7	Joan	5,961.00

Figure 49
The final consolidation accounts for all data.

Figure 50 Create a view you'd like to save.

Figure 51
Choose Custom Views from the View menu.

Figure 52 The Custom Views dialog.

Figure 53 Use the Add View dialog to name and set options for a view.

Custom Views

Excel's custom views feature lets you create multiple *views* of a workbook file. A view includes the window size and position, the active cell, the zoom percentage, hidden columns and rows, and print settings. Once you set up a view, you can choose it from a dialog to see it quickly.

✔ Tip

- Including print settings in views makes it possible to create and save multiple custom reports for printing.

To add a custom view

1. Create the view you want to save. **Figure 50** shows an example.

2. Choose View > Custom Views (**Figure 51**).

3. In the Custom Views dialog (**Figure 52**), click the Add button.

4. In the Add View dialog (**Figure 53**), enter a name for the view in the Name text box.

5. Turn on the appropriate Include in view check boxes:

   ▲ **Print settings** includes current Page Setup and other printing options in the view.

   ▲ **Hidden rows, columns and filter settings** includes current settings for hidden columns and rows, as well as filter selections.

6. Click OK.

To switch to a view

1. Switch to the sheet containing the view you want to see.

2. Choose View > Custom Views (**Figure 51**).

3. In the Custom Views dialog (**Figure 54**), select the view you want to see from the Views scrolling list.

4. Click Show.

   Excel changes the window so it looks just like it did when you created the view.

To delete a view

1. Switch to the sheet containing the view you want to delete.

2. Choose View > Custom Views (**Figure 51**).

3. In the Custom Views dialog (**Figure 54**), select the view you want to delete from the Views scrolling list.

4. Click Delete.

5. In the confirmation dialog that appears (**Figure 55**), click Yes.

6. Follow steps 3 through 5 to delete other views if desired.

7. Click Close to dismiss the Custom Views dialog without changing the view.

✔ Tip

■ Deleting a view does not delete the information contained in the view. It simply removes the reference to the information from the Views list in the Custom Views dialog (**Figure 54**).

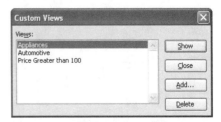

Figure 54 To see or delete a view, select the name of the view in the Custom Views dialog, then click Show or Delete.

Figure 55 When you click the Delete button to delete a view, Excel asks you to confirm that you really do want to delete it.

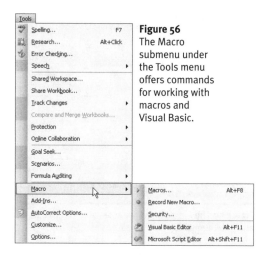

Figure 56 The Macro submenu under the Tools menu offers commands for working with macros and Visual Basic.

Figure 57 Enter a name and set options for a new macro in the Record Macro dialog.

Figure 58 When you're finished recording macro steps, click the Stop Recording button on the tiny Stop Recording toolbar.

Macros

A macro is a series of commands that Excel can perform automatically. You can create simple macros to automate repetitive tasks, like entering data or formatting cells.

Although macros are created with Excel's built-in Visual Basic programming language, you don't need to be a programmer to create them. Excel's Macro Recorder will record your keystrokes, menu choices, and dialog settings as you make them and will write the programming code for you. This makes macros useful for all Excel users, even beginners.

✔ Tip

- The macro feature makes it possible to create highly customized workbook files, complete with special dialogs, menus, and commands. A discussion of these capabilities, however, is far beyond the scope of this book.

To record a macro

1. Choose Tools > Macro > Record New Macro (**Figure 56**) to display the Record Macro dialog (**Figure 57**).

2. Enter a name for the macro in the Macro name text box.

3. If desired, enter a keystroke to use as a shortcut key in the Ctrl+Shift+ text box.

4. If desired, edit the description automatically entered in the Description text box.

5. Click OK.

6. Perform all the steps you want to include in your macro. Excel records them all— even the mistakes—so be careful!

7. When you're finished recording macro steps, click the Stop Recording button ▣ on the tiny Stop Recording toolbar (**Figure 58**).

To run a macro

Press the keystroke you specified as a short-cut key for the macro when you created it.

Or

1. Choose Tools > Macro > Macros (**Figure 56**).

2. In the scrolling list of the Macro dialog (**Figure 59**), select the macro you want to run.

3. Click Run.

   Excel performs each macro step, just the way you recorded it.

✔ Tips

- Save your workbook *before* running a macro for the first time. You may be surprised by the results and need to revert the file to the way it was before you ran the macro. Excel's Undo command cannot undo the steps of a macro, so reverting to the last saved version of the file is the only way to reverse macro steps.

- Excel stores each macro as a *module* within the workbook. View and edit a macro by selecting it in the Macro dialog and clicking the Edit button. **Figure 60** shows an example. I don't recommend editing macro code unless you have at least a general understanding of Visual Basic!

- More advanced uses of macros include the creation of custom functions and applications that work within Excel.

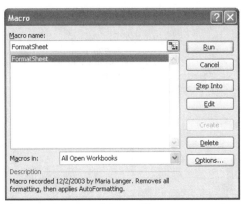

Figure 59 The Macro dialog enables you to run, edit, and delete macros.

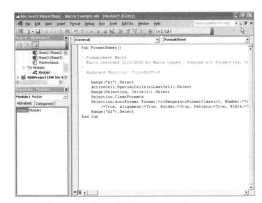

Figure 60 Here's the code for a macro that removes cell formatting, then applies AutoFormatting.

Web
Publishing

Web Publishing

The World Wide Web has had a huge impact on publishing since 1995. Web pages, which can include text, graphics, and hyperlinks, can be published on the Internet or an intranet, making them available to audiences 24 hours a day, 7 days a week. They provide information quickly and inexpensively to anyone who needs it.

Microsoft Excel's Save as Web Page command enables you to save worksheets and charts as HTML documents, making it easy to publish Excel data on the Web.

✔ Tips

- This chapter explains how to create Web pages from Excel documents. Modifying the HTML underlying those pages is beyond the scope of this book.

- *HTML (or HyperText Markup Language)* is a system of codes for defining Web pages.

- Web pages are normally viewed with *Web browser* software. Microsoft Internet Explorer and Netscape Navigator are two examples of Web browsers.

- To access the Internet, you need an Internet connection, either through an organizational network or dial-up connection. Setting up a connection is beyond the scope of this book; consult the documentation that came with your System or Internet access software for more information.

- To publish a Web page, you need access to a Web server. Contact your Network Administrator or Internet Service Provider (ISP) for more information.

- A *hyperlink (or link)* is text or a graphic that, when clicked, displays other information from the Web.

- An *intranet* is like the Internet, but it exists only on the internal network of an organization and is usually closed to outsiders.

Creating Web Pages

Excel has built-in Web publishing features that make it easy to publish Excel data on the Web:

◆ Save Excel documents as standard Web pages (**Figure 1**). This enables you to publish formatted worksheets and charts on the Web so the information can be shared with others.

◆ Publish Excel documents as interactive Web pages (**Figure 2**). This enables you to publish spreadsheet solutions on the Web in a format that allows the information to be edited and formatted by others who access it with a Web browser.

✔ Tips

■ You can use Excel's Web Page Preview command to see what a workbook will look like when published as a Web page without actually saving it as a Web page (**Figure 1**). I explain how on the next page.

■ The interactive features of a spreadsheet published on the Web with Excel are only available when the spreadsheet is accessed with Microsoft Internet Explorer 4.01 and the user has Microsoft Office (or Excel) installed on his computer.

■ When you publish an Excel document as an interactive Web page, some features—such as graphics, text boxes, patterns, and some other formatting options—do not appear on the Web.

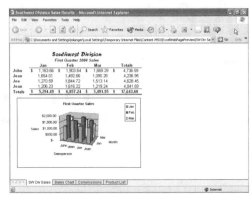

Figure 1 A workbook saved as Web pages. Note the sheet tabs at the bottom of the window; click a tab to view another sheet on a separate Web page.

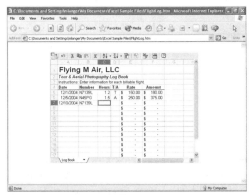

Figure 2 A worksheet saved as an interactive Web page. As you can see, when you enter data into cells, formulas in other cells immediately calculate results.

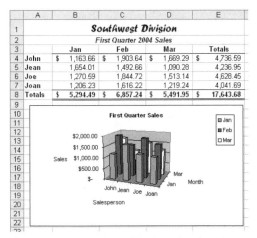

Figure 3 Here's a simple workbook ready to be converted into Web pages.

Figure 4
The File menu.

To preview a workbook as Web pages

1. Open the workbook that you want to preview as a Web page (**Figure 3**).

2. Choose File > Web Page Preview (**Figure 4**). Excel launches your default Web browser and displays the current worksheet as a Web page (**Figure 1**).

3. To see other workbook sheets as Web pages, click the corresponding sheet tabs at the bottom of the Web page window.

4. When you are finished previewing the workbook as Web pages, choose File > Close to close the Web browser window or File > Exit to exit the Web browser software.

✔ Tip

- **Figure 1** shows what the Web page looks like with Microsoft Internet Explorer 6.0, which is the default Web browser on my system. If your system has a different default Web browser, the page may look different.

PREVIEWING WORKBOOKS AS WEB PAGES

To save a workbook as Web pages

1. Open or activate the workbook that you want to save as a Web page (**Figure 3**).

2. Choose File > Save as Web Page (**Figure 4**).

3. A Save As dialog like the one in **Figure 5** appears. Check to be sure that Web Page is selected from the Save as type drop-down list.

4. Use the top portion of the dialog to select a disk location for the Web page and its supporting images.

5. In the File name text box, enter a name for the Web page. Make sure it follows the naming conventions of your Web server.

6. Select one of the Save options to specify what you want to save as a Web page:

   ▲ **Entire Workbook** is all the sheets in the workbook.

   ▲ **Selection** is the currently displayed sheet or, if multiple cells were selected when you opened the Save As dialog, the cell reference for the selection.

7. To enter a title for the Web page, click the Change Title button. Then enter a new title in the Set Page Title dialog that appears (**Figure 6**) and click OK.

8. Click Save.

9. If the workbook, sheet, or selection includes features that cannot be saved as part of a Web page, a dialog like the one in **Figure 7** appears. Click Yes.

   Excel creates the HTML, image, and other supporting files required to display the Excel document as Web pages. All supporting files are saved in a folder with the same name as the Web page file (**Figure 8**).

Figure 5 Use this Save As dialog to save the workbook or selection as Web pages.

Figure 6 The Set Page Title dialog enables you to enter a custom page title for the Web page.

Figure 7 This dialog appears if a worksheet includes features that can't be saved as part of a Web page.

Figure 8 Excel creates all the HTML, image, and other supporting files necessary to view the workbook, sheet, or selection as Web pages.

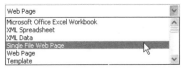

Figure 9 Choose Single File Web Page from the Save as type drop-down list.

✔ Tips

- If you're not sure about the file naming conventions of your Web server, ask your System Administrator, Webmaster, or ISP.

- You can further customize the appearance of a Web page created by Excel by modifying its HTML code with your favorite Web authoring program or HTML editor.

- Excel can also create single-file Web pages in which all files for a page, including images, are embedded in a single *MIME encapsulated aggregate HTML (MHTML)* file. This format, which is supported by Internet Explorer 4.0 and later, is handy for sending Web pages to others via e-mail. To create a single-file Web page, in step 3, choose Single File Web Page from the Save as type drop-down list (**Figure 9**).

To publish an Excel worksheet as an interactive Web page

1. Open or activate the workbook that you want to publish as an interactive Web page (**Figure 10**).

2. Activate the sheet you want to publish.

3. Choose File > Save as Web Page (**Figure 4**).

4. A Save As dialog like the one in **Figure 5** appears. Make sure Web Page is selected from the Save as type drop-down list.

5. Use the top portion of the dialog to select a disk location for the Web page and its supporting images.

6. In the File name text box, enter a name for the Web page. Make sure it follows the naming conventions of your Web server.

7. To enter a title for the Web page, click the Change Title button. Then enter a new title in the Set Page Title dialog that appears (**Figure 6**) and click OK.

8. Select the Save option for Selection and turn on the Add interactivity check box (**Figure 11**).

9. Click the Publish button to display the Publish as Web Page dialog (**Figure 12**).

10. Choose an option from the Choose drop-down list (**Figure 13**):

   ▲ **Previously published items** displays a list of items in the workbook that have already been published. This enables you to update or republish these items. If you choose this option, be sure to select the desired item.

   ▲ **Range of cells** enables you to publish less than an entire sheet. If you choose this option, enter the desired range of cells in the box beneath the menu (**Figure 14**).

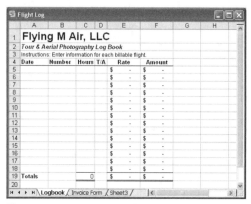

Figure 10 Here's a simple worksheet for publishing on the Web.

Figure 11 Turn on the Add interactivity check box.

Figure 12 The Publish as Web Page dialog.

Figure 13 Use this menu to choose what you want to publish.

Figure 14 If you choose Range of cells, enter the range beneath the drop-down list.

▲ **Items on *Sheet Name*** enables you to select a specific sheet if you did not do so in step 2.

11. Confirm that the Add interactivity with check box is turned on. Then choose an option from the menu beside it:

   ▲ **Spreadsheet functionality** makes the sheet work like a regular worksheet file.

   ▲ **PivotTable functionality** makes the sheet work like a PivotTable.

   ▲ **Chart functionality** makes the sheet work like a chart. This option is automatically selected when you publish a chart sheet or a chart embedded in a worksheet.

12. To preview the page after it is saved, turn on the Open published web page in browser check box.

13. Click the Publish button.

   The sheet (or a selected portion of it) is saved as an interactive Web page in the location you specified. If you turned on the Open published web page in browser check box in step 12, the page is displayed in a Web browser window (**Figure 2**).

✔ Tips

■ In step 10, if you choose Entire workbook from the Choose drop-down list, you cannot include interactive features.

■ In step 10, if you choose Range of cells from the Choose drop-down list, you can click in the box beneath it and then select the range of cells you want to publish. This is usually easier than typing in the cell references.

■ PivotTables are an advanced feature of Excel that is beyond the scope of this book.

PUBLISHING AS INTERACTIVE WEB PAGES

To automatically save a workbook as Web pages

1. Follow the steps in the previous two sections to prepare a workbook or worksheet to be saved as a Web page.

2. If necessary, click the Publish button in the Save As dialog to display the Publish as Web Page dialog (**Figure 12**).

3. Turn on the check box for AutoRepublish every time this workbook is saved.

4. Click Publish.

✔ Tip

- This feature is especially useful if you can save your Web pages directly to a Web server. This way, the pages are automatically updated—with no additional work on your part—when changed or revised.

	A	B	C	D	E
1			*Southwest Division*		
2			*First Quarter 2004 Sales*		
3					
4		Jan	Feb	Mar	Totals
5	John	$ 1,163.66	$ 1,903.64	$ 1,669.29	$ 4,736.59
6	Jean	1,654.01	1,492.66	1,090.28	4,236.95
7	Joe	1,270.59	1,844.72	1,513.14	4,628.45
8	Joan	1,206.23	1,616.22	1,219.24	4,041.69
9	Totals	$ 5,294.49	$ 6,857.24	$ 5,491.95	$ 17,643.68
10					
11	For questions about this workbook, contact John Aabbott				
12	E-Mail John				
13					

Figure 15 A hyperlink appears as colored, underlined text. When you point to it, the mouse pointer turns into a hand with a pointing finger and a box with the link's URL or ScreenTip (as shown here) appears.

Hyperlinks

A *hyperlink* is text or a graphic that, when clicked, displays other information. Excel enables you to create two kinds of hyperlinks:

◆ A link to a *URL* (*Uniform Resource Locator*), which is the Internet address of a document or individual. Excel makes it easy to create links to two types of URLs:

  ▲ **http://** links to a Web page on a Web server.

  ▲ **mailto:** links to an e-mail address.

◆ A link to another document on your hard disk or network.

By default, hyperlinks appear as colored, underlined text (**Figure 15**).

✔ Tips

■ Although you can create a link to any document on your hard disk or accessible over a local area network or the Internet, clicking the link will only open the document if you have a program capable of opening it—such as the program that created it.

■ Clicking a cell that contains a hyperlink opens the linked location. To select a cell containing a hyperlink, point to the cell, press the mouse button, and hold the mouse button down until the cell is selected.

HYPERLINKS

To insert a hyperlink

1. Select the cell or object that you want to convert to a hyperlink (**Figure 16**).

2. Choose Insert > Hyperlink (**Figure 17**), press `Ctrl K`, or click the Insert Hyperlink button 🔳 on the Standard toolbar.

   The Insert Hyperlink dialog appears (**Figure 18**).

3. Choose one of the Link to buttons on the left side of the dialog:

   ▲ **Existing File or Web Page** (**Figure 18**) enables you to link to a file on disk or a Web page. If you select this option, you can either select one of the files or locations that appears in the list or type a path or URL in the Address box (**Figure 19**).

   ▲ **Place in This Document** (**Figure 20**) enables you to link to a specific location in the current document. If you select this option, choose a heading or enter a cell reference.

   ▲ **Create New Document** (**Figure 21**) enables you to create and link to a new document. If you select this option, you can either enter a pathname for the document or click the Change button and use the Create New Document dialog that appears to create a new document.

   ▲ **E-mail Address** (**Figure 22**) enables you to link to an e-mail address. If you select this option, you can either enter the e-mail address in the E-mail address box or select one of the recently used e-mail addresses in the list.

4. Click OK to save your settings and dismiss the Insert Hyperlink dialog.

   The selected cell or object turns into a hyperlink (**Figure 15**).

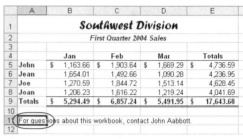

Figure 16 Select the cell you want to convert to a hyperlink.

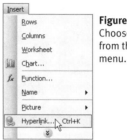

Figure 17 Choose Hyperlink from the Insert menu.

Figure 18 The Insert Hyperlink dialog for inserting a link to an existing file or Web page.

Figure 19 Use the Address text box to enter the URL for the link location.

Figure 20 The Insert Hyperlink dialog for inserting a link to a place in the current document.

Figure 21 The Insert Hyperlink dialog for inserting a link to a new document.

Figure 22 The Insert Hyperlink dialog for inserting a link to an e-mail address.

Figure 23 Use this dialog to set up a custom ScreenTip for a hyperlink.

✔ Tips

- The Text to display box near the top of the Insert Hyperlink dialog (**Figures 18, 20, 21,** and **22**) determines what text appears as the link in the worksheet cell.

- To specify what should appear in the ScreenTip box when you point to the hyperlink, click the ScreenTip button in the Insert Hyperlink dialog (**Figures 18, 20, 21,** and **22**). Then enter the text you want to appear in the Set Hyperlink ScreenTip dialog (**Figure 23**) and click OK. **Figure 15** shows an example of a custom ScreenTip. Keep in mind that this feature is not compatible with all Web browsers.

To follow a hyperlink

1. Position the mouse pointer on the hyperlink. The mouse pointer turns into a pointing finger and a ScreenTip appears in a box nearby (**Figure 15**).

2. Click once.

    If the hyperlink points to an Internet URL, Excel starts your default Web browser, connects to the Internet, and displays the URL.

    or

    If the hyperlink points to a location in the current file, that location appears.

    or

    If the hyperlink points to a file on your hard disk or another computer on the network, the file opens.

    or

    If the hyperlink points to an e-mail address, Excel starts your default e-mail program and prepares a preaddressed new message form.

Figure 24 Use the Edit Hyperlink dialog to modify or remove a hyperlink.

To modify or remove a hyperlink

1. Select the cell or object containing the hyperlink. (You can select a cell with a hyperlink by pointing to it and then holding down the mouse button until the mouse pointer turns into a fat plus sign.)

2. Choose Insert > Hyperlink (**Figure 17**), press [Ctrl][K], or click the Insert Hyperlink button 🖳 on the Standard toolbar.

   The Edit Hyperlink dialog appears (**Figure 24**).

3. To change the link information, make changes as discussed earlier in this section.

   or

   To remove the link, click the Remove Link button.

4. Click OK.

Setting
Excel Options 15

The Options Dialog

Microsoft Excel's Options dialog offers thirteen categories of options that you can set to customize the way Excel works for you:

◆ **View** options control Excel's on-screen appearance.

◆ **Calculation** options control the way Excel calculates formulas.

◆ **Edit** options control editing.

◆ **General** options control general Excel operations.

◆ **Transition** options control options for Excel users who also work with other spreadsheet programs.

◆ **Custom Lists** options enable you to create or modify series lists.

◆ **Chart** options control the active chart and chart tips.

◆ **Color** options control standard, chart fill, and chart line colors.

◆ **International** options control number handling, printing, and right-to-left settings useful when working with non-U.S. files.

◆ **Save** options control Excel's AutoRecover feature.

◆ **Error Checking** options control Excel's error checking feature.

Continued on next page...

Continued from previous page.

◆ **Spelling** options control Excel's spelling check feature.

◆ **Security** options control passwords to protect Excel files, as well as digital signatures, privacy options, and macro security.

✔ Tips

■ Excel's default options settings are discussed and illustrated throughout this book.

■ Some of the options settings affect only the active sheet or workbook file while others affect all Excel operations. If you want a setting to affect a specific sheet or file, be sure to open and activate it before opening the Options dialog.

To set options

1. Choose Tools > Options (**Figure 1**) to display the Options dialog (**Figure 2**).

2. Click the tab to display the category of options that you want to set.

3. Set options as desired.

4. Repeat steps 2 and 3 for other categories of options that you want to set.

5. Click OK to save your settings.

✔ Tip

■ I illustrate and discuss all Options dialog settings throughout this chapter.

Figure 1
To open the Options dialog, choose Options from the Tools menu.

SETTING OPTIONS

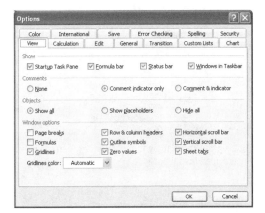

Figure 2 The View tab of the Options dialog. Some of the window options are not available when a chart sheet is active.

View Options

The View tab of the Options dialog (**Figure 2**) offers options in four categories: Show, Comments, Objects, and Window options.

✔ Tip

■ The available options in the View tab vary depending on the type of sheet that is active when you open the Options dialog. When a chart sheet is active, many of the Window options are gray.

Show

Show options determine what Excel elements appear on screen:

◆ **Startup Task Pane** displays the Getting Started task pane when you start Excel.

◆ **Formula bar** displays the formula bar above the document window.

◆ **Status bar** displays the status bar at the bottom of the screen.

◆ **Windows in Taskbar** displays a Taskbar icon for each open Excel document window.

Comments

The Comments area enables you to select one of three options for displaying comments:

◆ **None** does not display comments or comment indicators.

◆ **Comment indicator only** displays a small red triangle in the upper-right corner of a cell containing a comment. When you point to the cell, the comment appears in a box.

◆ **Comment & indicator** displays cell comments in boxes as well as a small red triangle in the upper-right corner of each cell containing a comment.

Objects

The Objects area enables you to select one of three options for displaying graphic objects, buttons, text boxes, drawn objects, and pictures:

◆ **Show all** displays all objects.

◆ **Show placeholders** displays gray rectangles as placeholders for pictures and charts. This can speed up scrolling through a window with many graphic objects.

◆ **Hide all** does not display any objects. Excel will not print objects with this option selected.

Window options

Window options determine how various Excel elements are displayed in the active window.

◆ **Page breaks** displays horizontal and vertical page breaks.

◆ **Formulas** displays formulas instead of formula results (**Figure 3**). The Formula Auditing toolbar also appears. You may find this feature useful to document and check your worksheets.

◆ **Gridlines** displays the boundaries of cells as lines.

◆ **Gridlines color** is a drop-down list (**Figure 4**) for selecting a gridline color. Automatic (the default option) displays gridlines in gray.

◆ **Row & column headers** displays the numeric row headings and alphabetical column headings.

◆ **Outline symbols** displays outline symbols when the worksheet includes an outline.

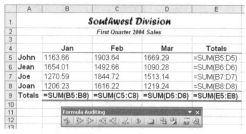

Figure 3 You can display formulas rather than their results in worksheet cells.

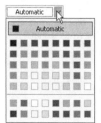

Figure 4 Use the Gridlines color drop-down list to select a color for a worksheet's gridlines.

◆ **Zero values** displays a 0 (zero) in cells that contain zero values. Turning off this check box instructs Excel to leave a cell blank if it contains a zero value.

◆ **Horizontal scroll bar** displays a scroll bar along the bottom of the window.

◆ **Vertical scroll bar** displays a scroll bar along the right side of the window.

◆ **Sheet tabs** displays tabs at the bottom of the window for each sheet in the workbook file.

VIEW OPTIONS

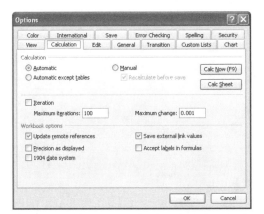

Figure 5 The default settings for the Calculation tab of the Options dialog.

Calculation Options

Calculation options (**Figure 5**) control the way formulas are calculated (or recalculated) in a worksheet. There are three groups of options: Calculation, Iteration, and Workbook options.

Calculation

The Calculation area enables you to select one of three options for specifying how formulas should be calculated:

◆ **Automatic** tells Excel to recalculate all dependent formulas whenever you change a value, formula, or name.

◆ **Automatic except tables** is the same as Automatic, but does not recalculate data tables. With this option selected, you must click the Calc Now button or press F9 to recalculate data tables.

◆ **Manual** recalculates formulas only when you click the Calc Now button or press F9. With this option selected, you can turn on the **Recalculate before save** check box to ensure that the worksheet is recalculated each time you save it.

The Calculation area also offers two buttons for calculating formulas:

◆ **Calc Now (F9)** recalculates all open worksheets and updates all open chart sheets. You can also access this option by pressing F9.

◆ **Calc Sheet** recalculates the active worksheet and updates linked charts or updates the active chart sheet.

CALCULATION OPTIONS

Iteration

The Iteration check box enables you to set limits for the number of times Excel tries to resolve circular references or complete goal seeking calculations. To use this advanced option, turn on the check box, then enter values in the two text boxes below it:

◆ **Maximum iterations** is the maximum number of times Excel should try to resolve circular references or solve goal seeking problems.

◆ **Maximum change** is the maximum amount of result change below which iteration stops.

Workbook options

Workbook options control calculation in the active workbook file.

◆ **Update remote references** calculates formulas with references to documents created with other applications.

◆ **Precision as displayed** permanently changes values stored in cells from 15-digit precision to the precision of the applied formatting. This may result in rounding.

◆ **1904 date system** changes the starting date from which all dates are calculated to January 2, 1904. This is the date system used on Macintosh computers. Wintel computers begin dates at January 1, 1900. Turning on this option enhances compatibility with Excel for Mac OS.

◆ **Save external link values** saves copies of values from linked documents within the workbook file. If many values are linked, storing them can increase file size; turning off this option can reduce file size.

◆ **Accept labels in formulas** allows you to use column and row headings to identify ranges of cells.

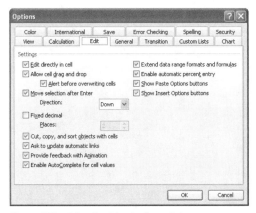

Figure 6 The Edit tab of the Options dialog.

Figure 7
Use the Direction drop-down list to select a direction in which to move the cellpointer when you press (Enter).

Edit Options

Edit options (**Figure 6**) control the way certain editing tasks work:

◆ **Edit directly in cell** enables you to edit a cell's value or formula by double-clicking the cell. With this option turned off, you must edit a cell's contents in the formula bar.

◆ **Allow cell drag and drop** enables you to copy or move cells by dragging them to a new location. With this option turned on, you can also turn on the **Alert before overwriting cells** check box to have Excel warn you if a drag-and-drop operation will overwrite the contents of destination cells.

◆ **Move selection after Enter** tells Excel to move the cellpointer when you press (Enter). With this option turned on, you can use the **Direction** drop-down list (**Figure 7**) to choose a direction: Down, Right, Up, or Left.

◆ **Fixed decimal** instructs Excel to automatically place a decimal point when you enter a value. Turn on the check box and enter a value in the **Places** text box. A positive value moves the decimal to the left; a negative value moves the decimal to the right.

◆ **Cut, copy, and sort objects with cells** keeps objects (such as graphics) with cells that you cut, copy, filter, or sort.

◆ **Ask to update automatic links** prompts you to update links when you open a workbook containing links to other files.

Continued on next page...

Continued from previous page.

◆ **Provide feedback with Animation** displays worksheet movement when you insert or delete cells. Turning on this option may slow Excel's performance on some systems.

◆ **Enable AutoComplete for cell values** turns on the AutoComplete feature for entering values in cells based on entries in the same column.

◆ **Extend data range formats and formulas** tells Excel that it should copy the formats and formulas in list cells to new rows added at the bottom of the list.

◆ **Enable automatic percent entry** tells Excel to multiply by 100 all numbers less than 1 that you enter in cells formatted with a Percentage format.

◆ **Show Paste Options buttons** displays the button for the Paste Options menu after you use a Paste or Fill command.

◆ **Show Insert Options buttons** displays the button for the Insert Options menu after you use an Insert command.

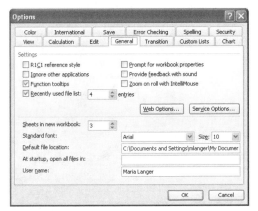

Figure 8 The General tab of the Options dialog.

Figure 9 You can use the Summary tab of the Properties dialog to enter information about the file the first time you save it. You can also open this dialog by choosing Properties from the File menu.

General Options

General options (**Figure 8**) control the general operation of Excel.

Settings

The Settings options offer check boxes to set a variety of options:

◆ **R1C1 reference style** changes the style of cell references so both rows and columns have numbers.

◆ **Ignore other applications** prevents the exchange of data with other applications that use Dynamic Data Exchange (DDE).

◆ **Function tooltips** displays information about function arguments as you enter a function.

◆ **Recently used file list** enables you to specify the number of recently opened files that should appear near the bottom of the File menu. Turn on the check box and enter a value in the **Entries** text box. This feature is handy for quickly reopening recently accessed files.

◆ **Prompt for workbook properties** displays the Properties dialog (**Figure 9**) the first time you save a file. You can use this dialog to enter summary information about a file.

◆ **Provide feedback with sound** plays sounds at certain events, such as opening, saving, and printing files and displaying error messages. If this option is turned on in one Microsoft Office application, it is automatically turned on in all Office applications.

Continued on next page...

GENERAL OPTIONS

Continued from previous page.

♦ **Zoom on roll with IntelliMouse** instructs Excel to zoom in or out (rather than scroll) when you roll the wheel on a Microsoft IntelliMouse. This command only works with IntelliMouse or other compatible pointing devices.

Other options

The bottom half of the General tab lets you set a variety of other workbook options:

♦ **Sheets in new workbook** enables you to specify the number of worksheets that should be included in each new workbook you create. Enter a value in the text box.

♦ **Standard font** enables you to select the default font for worksheets and charts.

♦ **Default file location** allows you to specify the default location in which new workbook files should be saved.

♦ **At startup, open all files in** enables you to specify a folder in which Excel should look for files when it starts. Any files in that folder will automatically open when you start Excel.

♦ **User name** is the name that appears when Excel displays a user name.

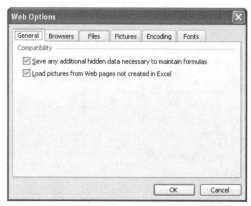

Figure 10 The General tab of the Web Options dialog.

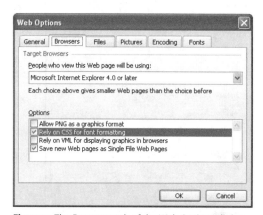

Figure 11 The Browsers tab of the Web Options dialog.

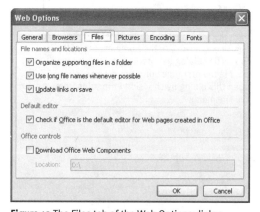

Figure 12 The Files tab of the Web Options dialog.

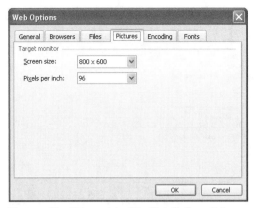

Figure 13 The Pictures tab of the Web Options dialog.

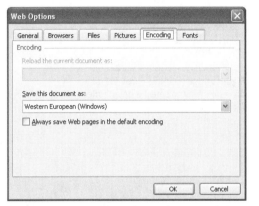

Figure 14 The Encoding tab of the Web Options dialog.

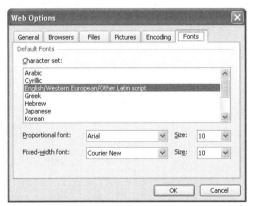

Figure 15 The Fonts tab of the Web Options dialog.

Web Options

Clicking the Web Options button displays the Web Options dialog, which you can use to edit the default settings for saving workbooks as Web pages.

◆ **General** options (**Figure 10**) control compatibility with other programs and browsers.

◆ **Browsers** options (**Figure 11**) control various compatibility and formatting options for Web pages created by Excel.

◆ **Files** options (**Figure 12**) control file naming and locations and the default editor for Web pages.

◆ **Pictures** options (**Figure 13**) control the size and resolution of the typical target monitor.

◆ **Encoding** options (**Figure 14**) control how a Web page is coded when saved.

◆ **Fonts** options (**Figure 15**) control the character set and default fonts.

Transition Options

Transition options (**Figure 16**) offer options to help you transition between Excel and other spreadsheet software packages, such as Lotus 1-2-3. Options are broken down into three groups: default file format, Settings, and Sheet options.

Default file format

The **Save Excel files as** enables you to specify the default file format for every Excel file you save. Choose an option from the drop-down list (**Figure 17**). The option you select will automatically appear in the Save As dialog. You can override this choice if desired when you save a file. This option is useful if you often share the Excel files you create with people who use a different version of Excel or some other spreadsheet or database application.

Settings

Settings options provide options to make Excel work more like Lotus 1-2-3.

◆ **Microsoft Office Excel menu key** allows you to specify the keyboard key that will activate Excel's menu bar. Enter a key in the text box.

◆ **Transition navigation keys** activates the Lotus 1-2-3 keystrokes for worksheet navigation, entries, and other actions.

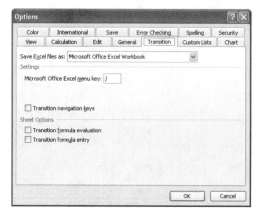

Figure 16 The Transition tab of the Options dialog.

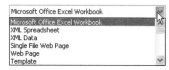

Figure 17 Use the Save Excel files as drop-down list to select a default file format in which to save files.

TRANSITION OPTIONS

Sheet options

Sheet options control the way formula transitions work.

◆ **Transition formula evaluation** instructs Excel to evaluate Lotus 1-2-3 formulas without changing them. This option may be extremely helpful if you often open files created with Lotus 1-2-3.

◆ **Transition formula entry** converts formulas entered in Lotus 1-2-3 release 2.2 syntax to Excel syntax and changes the behavior of Excel-defined names to Lotus-defined names. This makes it possible for a Lotus 1-2-3 user to use Excel with less retraining.

TRANSITION OPTIONS

Custom Lists Options

The Custom Lists options (**Figure 18**) enable you to create, modify, and delete custom lists. Once created, you can use the AutoFill feature I discuss in **Chapter 3** to enter list contents into cells.

✔ Tip

■ You cannot modify or delete the predefined lists in the Custom lists scrolling list (**Figure 18**).

To create a custom list

1. In the Custom Lists tab of the Options dialog, select NEW LIST in the Custom lists scrolling list (**Figure 18**).

2. Enter the list contents in the List entries area (**Figure 19**). Be sure to press [Enter] after each item.

3. Click Add.

   The list appears in the Custom lists scrolling list (**Figure 20**).

To import cell contents as a custom list

1. In the Custom Lists tab of the Options dialog, select NEW LIST in the Custom lists scrolling list (**Figure 18**).

2. Click in the Import list from cells text box.

3. In the worksheet window, drag to select the cells containing the values you want to use as a custom list (**Figure 21**).

4. Click Import.

   The list appears in the Custom lists scrolling list (**Figure 20**).

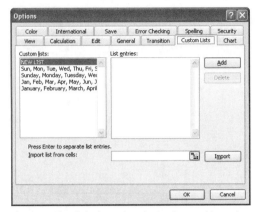

Figure 18 The default settings in the Custom Lists tab of the Options dialog.

Figure 19 Enter the values you want to include in the list, one per line.

Figure 20 The list appears in the Custom lists scrolling list.

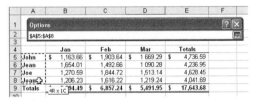

	Jan	Feb	Mar	Totals
John	$ 1,163.66	$ 1,903.64	$ 1 669.29	$ 4,736.59
Jean	1,654.01	1,492.66	1 090.28	4,236.95
Joe	1,270.59	1,844.72	1,513.14	4,628.45
Joan	1,206.23	1,616.22	1,219.24	4,041.69
Totals	94.49	$ 6,857.24	$ 5,491.95	$ 17,643.68

Figure 21 Select the cells containing the values you want to appear in the custom list.

Figure 22 Excel displays this dialog when you delete a custom list.

To modify a custom list

1. In the Custom Lists tab of the Options dialog, select the list you want to modify in the Custom lists scrolling list.

2. Edit the list contents as desired in the List entries area.

3. Click Add.

   The custom list changes.

To delete a custom list

1. In the Custom Lists tab of the Options dialog, select the list you want to delete in the Custom lists scrolling list.

2. Click Delete.

3. A confirmation dialog like the one in **Figure 22** appears. Click OK.

   The list disappears from the Custom list scrolling list.

✔ Tip

- Deleting a custom list does not delete any data from your workbook files. It simply removes the list from the Custom Lists tab of the Options dialog so you can no longer use it with the AutoFill feature.

CUSTOM LISTS OPTIONS

Chart Options

Chart options (**Figure 23**) let you set options for the active chart and chart tips.

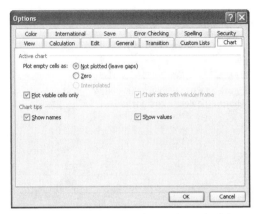

Figure 23 The default settings in the Chart tab of the Options dialog.

Active chart

Active chart options affect the active chart only. Be sure to activate the chart for which you want to set these options before opening the Options dialog.

◆ **Plot empty cells as** enables you to select one of two or three options to specify how Excel should plot empty cells:

▲ **Not plotted (leave gaps)** tells Excel not to plot the cell values at all. This leaves gaps in the chart.

▲ **Zero** tells Excel to plot empty cells as zeros, thus including a zero data point for each empty cell.

▲ **Interpolated** tells Excel to interpolate data points for blank cells and fill in the chart gaps with connecting lines. This option is not available for all chart types.

◆ **Plot visible cells only** tells Excel to plot only the cells that are displayed on the work-sheet. If one or more cells are in hidden columns or rows, they are not plotted.

◆ **Chart sizes with window frame** resizes the chart in a chart sheet window so it fills the window, no matter how the window is sized. This option is not available for charts embedded in worksheets.

Chart tips

Chart tips options enable you to specify what displays in chart tips.

◆ **Show names** displays the names of data points.

◆ **Show values** displays the values of data points.

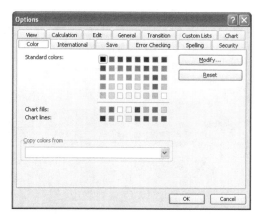

Figure 24 The default settings in the Color tab of the Options dialog.

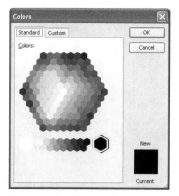

Figure 25 Use the Standard tab ...

Figure 26 ... or the Custom tab of the Colors dialog to select a new color.

Color Options

The Color tab of the Options dialog (**Figure 24**) enables you to set the color palettes used within the Excel workbook file.

◆ **Standard colors** are the colors that appear in color drop-down lists throughout Excel.

◆ **Chart fills** are the first eight colors Excel uses as chart fills.

◆ **Chart lines** are the first eight colors Excel uses as chart lines.

To modify the color palette

1. Click the color that you want to change to select it.

2. Click the Modify button to display the Colors dialog.

3. In the Standard (**Figure 25**) or Custom (**Figure 26**) tab of the Colors dialog, click to select a color.

4. Click OK. The selected color changes.

5. Repeat steps 1 through 4 for each color you want to change.

To copy colors from another workbook file

1. Before opening the Options dialog, open the workbook file into which you want to copy colors.

2. Open the Color tab of the Options dialog.

3. From the Copy colors from drop-down list, choose the workbook file from which you want to copy colors.

   The palette changes to reflect the colors from the other workbook file.

To reset the color palette

Click the Reset button. The colors change back to the default colors.

International Options

The International tab of the Options dialog (**Figure 27**) enables you to set options for working with other countries and languages.

Number handling

Number handling options enable you to specify the way separators are displayed in numbers.

◆ **Decimal separator** enables you to specify the character to be used as a decimal separator. You must turn off the **Use system separators** option to set this option.

◆ **Thousands separator** enables you to specify the character to be used as a thousands separator. You must turn off the **Use system separators** option to set this option.

◆ **Use system separators** tells Excel to use the separator options specified in the Regional and Language Options control panel.

Printing

The Printing area has only one option. **Allow A4/Letter paper resizing** enables you to print onto A4-sized letter paper, which is commonly used outside the U.S.

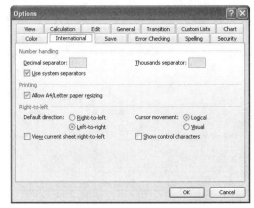

Figure 27 The default settings in the International tab of the Options dialog.

Right-to-left

The Right-to-left options enable you to specify settings for languages that read from right-to-left (instead of from left-to-right).

♦ **Default direction** controls the default direction of text: Right-to-left or Left-to-right.

♦ **Cursor movement** controls the movement of the cursor within text that contains both left-to-right and right-to-left sections. Logical moves the cursor the same direction as the arrow key being pressed and Visual moves the cursor forward or backward in the direction that text is read.

♦ **View current sheet right-to-left** sets the current worksheet so that cells are displayed from right-to-left. For example, cell A1 would appear in the upper-right corner of the worksheet rather than the upper-left. (This sounds like a great setting for playing a practical joke on a co-worker, but you didn't read that here.)

♦ **Show control characters** controls the display of special characters for bi-directional text.

INTERNATIONAL OPTIONS

Save Options

Save options (**Figure 28**) control how Excel's AutoRecover feature works. AutoRecover makes it possible to recover unsaved work in the event that Excel exits unexpectedly before you can save changes to a file.

Settings

Settings control default AutoRecover settings for all workbook files.

◆ **Save AutoRecover info every** enables you to set a frequency for automatically saving a special document recovery file.

◆ **AutoRecover save location** enables you to specify a directory for saving document recovery files.

Workbook options

Workbook options control the AutoRecover feature for the currently active workbook file. There's only one option: **Disable AutoRecover** turns off the AutoRecover feature for the workbook.

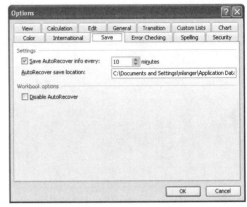

Figure 28 The default settings in the Save tab of the Options dialog.

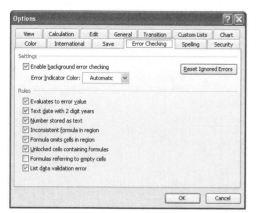

Figure 29 The default settings in the Error Checking tab of the Options dialog.

Error Checking Options

Error Checking options (**Figure 29**) enable you to fine-tune the way Excel's background error checking feature works.

Settings

Settings control basic error checking options:

◆ **Enable backround error checking** allows you to enable or disable the error checking feature.

◆ **Error Indicator Color** enables you to set the color of the tiny triangle that appears in each cell in which there might be an error. Use a menu similar to the one in **Figure 4**. Automatic sets the color to green.

◆ **Reset Ignored Errors** tells Excel to forget about any errors you told it to ignore.

Rules

Rules enable you to specify the types of errors Excel looks for and how some errors should be indicated.

◆ **Evaluates to error value** displays an error message as the result of a formula with an error.

◆ **Text date with 2 digit years** displays an error warning when a formula contains text formatted cells with years represented as two digits.

◆ **Number stored as text** displays an error warning when numbers are formatted as text or preceded by an apostrophe character when entered.

Continued on next page...

ERROR CHECKING OPTIONS

Continued from previous page.

- ◆ **Inconsistent formula in region** displays an error warning when a formula differs from other formulas in the same region of the worksheet.

- ◆ **Formula omits cells in region** displays an error warning when a formula omits certain cells.

- ◆ **Unlocked cells containing formulas** displays an error warning when a cell containing a formula is formatted as unlocked.

- ◆ **Formulas referring to empty cells** displays an error warning if a formula includes any references to empty cells.

- ◆ **List data validation error** displays an error warning if data in a list fails validation checks.

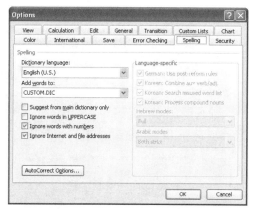

Figure 30 The Spelling tab of the Options dialog.

Figure 31 Use this drop-down list to select a language to use for spelling checks.

Spelling Options

Spelling options (**Figure 30**) control the way Excel's spelling checker works.

Spelling

Spelling options control the dictionaries and other spelling-related options for all languages.

◆ **Dictionary language** enables you to select the language of the dictionary that should be used for spelling checks. The drop-down list (**Figure 31**) includes all available dictionaries. Additional dictionaries are available from Microsoft.

◆ **Add words to** enables you to specify which dictionary new words should be added to.

◆ **Suggest from main dictionary only** tells Excel to suggest replacement words from the main dictionary—not from your custom dictionaries.

◆ **Ignore words in UPPERCASE** tells Excel not to check words in all uppercase characters, such as acronyms.

◆ **Ignore words with numbers** tells Excel not to check words that include numbers, such as *MariaL1*.

◆ **Ignore Internet and file addresses** tells Excel not to check any words that appear to be URLs, e-mail addresses, file names, or file pathnames.

◆ **AutoCorrect Options** displays a dialog you can use to set options for Excel's AutoCorrect feature.

Language-specific

Language-specific options become available when you choose certain languages from the Dictionary language drop-down list (**Figure 31**): German, Korean, Hebrew, or Arabic. If you work in one of these languages, explore its options on your own.

Security Options

Security options (**Figure 32**) help keep your workbooks and system secure.

File encryption settings for this workbook

File encryption encodes a file so it is impossible to read without entering a correct password. To use this feature, enter a password in the **Password to open** box. Clicking the Advanced button beside this option displays the Encryption Type dialog (**Figure 33**), which you can use to set advanced file protection options.

File sharing settings for this workbook

File sharing options protect a document from unauthorized modification.

◆ **Password to modify** enables you to specify a password that must be entered to save modifications to a file.

◆ **Read-only recommended** displays a dialog that recommends that the file be opened as a read-only file each time the file is opened. If the file is opened as read-only, changes to the file must be saved in a file with a different name or in a different disk location.

◆ **Digital Signatures** displays the Digital Signature dialog (**Figure 34**), which provides additional information about signatures attached to the document.

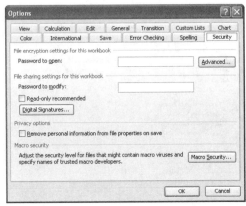

Figure 32 The Security tab of the Options dialog.

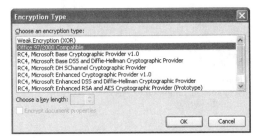

Figure 33 Use the Encryption Type dialog to set advanced document protection options.

Figure 34 The Digital Signature dialog displays information about digital signatures attached to a workbook.

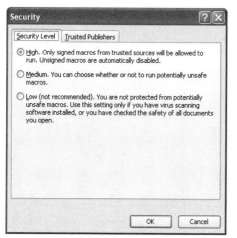

Figure 35 The Security Level tab of the Security dialog.

Figure 36 The Trusted Publishers tab of the Security dialog.

Privacy options

Excel offers only one Privacy option. **Remove personal information from file properties on save** removes user information from the file when you save it.

Macro security

The Macro security options enable you to protect your computer from viruses attached to macros that work with Excel or other Microsoft Office products. Clicking the Macro Security button displays the Security dialog with two tabs of settings. Although these advanced options are beyond the scope of this book, here's a quick explanation of each.

◆ **Security Level** (**Figure 35**) enables you to set a general security level for protecting your computer from macro viruses.

◆ **Trusted Publishers** (**Figure 36**) displays a list of the sources from which you have accepted files containing macros.

SECURITY OPTIONS

Menus & Shortcut Keys

Menus & Shortcut Keys

This appendix illustrates all of Excel's full menus for worksheets and charts and provides a list of shortcut keys you can use to access menu commands.

To use a shortcut key, hold down the modifier key (usually Ctrl) and press the keyboard key corresponding to the command. For example, to use the Save command's shortcut key, hold down Ctrl and press S.

✔ Tips

- I tell you more about menus and shortcut keys in **Chapter 1**.

- Throughout this appendix, when a menu or submenu has a different appearance for a worksheet and chart, both are illustrated, with the worksheet menu on the left and chart menu on the right.

File Menu

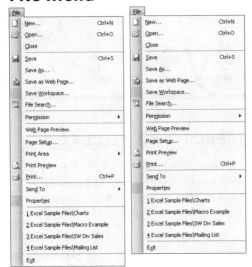

Ctrl N	New
Ctrl O	Open
Ctrl S	Save
Ctrl P	Print

Permission submenu

Print Area submenu
(worksheets only)

Send To submenu

Edit Menu

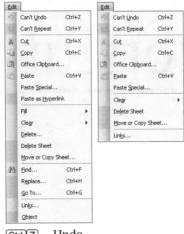

Ctrl Z	Undo
Ctrl Y	Repeat/Redo
Ctrl X	Cut
Ctrl C	Copy
Ctrl V	Paste
Ctrl F	Find
Ctrl H	Replace
Ctrl G	Go To

Fill submenu
(worksheets only)

| Ctrl D | Fill Down |
| Ctrl R | Fill Right |

Clear submenu

View Menu

Ctrl F1   Task Pane

Toolbars submenu

Insert Menu

Ctrl K   Hyperlink

Name submenu (worksheets only)

Picture submenu

Format Menu

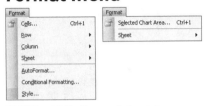

Ctrl 1   Cells (for worksheets)

Ctrl 1   Selected Chart
          Object (for charts)

Row submenu (worksheets only)

Column submenu (worksheets only)

Sheet submenu

Tools Menu

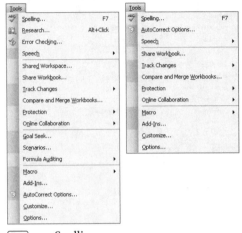

F7   Spelling

Alt   Research

Speech submenu

Track Changes submenu

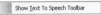

Protection submenu

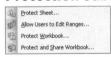

Online Collaboration submenu

Data Menu

Formula Auditing submenu

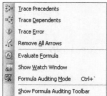

Ctrl ~   Formula Auditing Mode

Filter submenu

Macro submenu

Alt F8   Macros

Alt F11   Visual Basic Editor

Alt Shift F11   Microsoft Script Editor

Group and Outline submenu

Import External Data submenu

List submenu

Ctrl L   Create List

XML submenu

Chart Menu

Help Menu

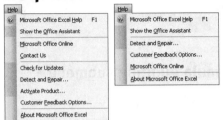

F1   Microsoft Office Excel Help

Window Menu

CHART, WINDOW, & HELP MENUS

Function Reference

Functions

Functions are predefined formulas for making specific kinds of calculations. Functions make it quicker and easier to write formulas. I tell you about functions in **Chapter 5**. In this appendix, I provide a complete list of every function installed as part of a standard installation of Excel 2003, along with its arguments and a brief description of what it does.

Financial Functions

DB(cost,salvage,life,period,month)	Returns the depreciation of an asset for a specified period using the fixed-declining balance method.
DDB(cost,salvage,life,period,factor)	Returns the depreciation of an asset for a specified period using the double-declining balance method or some other method you specify.
FV(rate,nper,pmt,pv,type)	Returns the future value of an investment.
IPMT(rate,per,nper,pv,fv,type)	Returns the interest payment for an investment for a given period.
IRR(values,guess)	Returns the internal rate of return for a series of cash flows.
ISPMT(rate,per,nper,pv)	Returns the straight-loan payment interest.
MIRR(values,finance_rate,reinvest_rate)	Returns the internal rate of return where positive and negative cash flows are financed at different rates.
NPER(rate,pmt,pv,fv,type)	Returns the number of periods for an investment.
NPV(rate,value1,value2,...)	Returns the net present value of an investment based on a series of periodic cash flows and a discount rate.
PMT(rate,nper,pv,fv,type)	Returns the period payment for an annuity.

PPMT(rate,per,nper,pv,fv,type)	Returns the payment on the principal for an investment for a given period.
PV(rate,nper,pmt,fv,type)	Returns the present value of an investment.
RATE(nper,pmt,pv,fv,type,guess)	Returns the interest rate per period of an annuity.
SLN(cost,salvage,life)	Returns the straight-line depreciation of an asset for one period.
SYD(cost,salvage,life,per)	Returns the sum-of-years'-digits depreciation of an asset for a specified period.
VDB(cost,salvage,life,start_period,end_period,factor,...)	
	Returns the depreciation of an asset for a specified or partial period using a declining balance method.

Date & Time Functions

DATE(year,month,day)	Returns the serial number of a particular date.
DATEVALUE(date_text)	Converts a date in the form of text to a serial number.
DAY(serial_number)	Converts a serial number to a day of the month.
DAYS360(start_date,end_date,method)	Calculates the number of days between two dates based on a 360-day year.
HOUR(serial_number)	Converts a serial number to an hour.
MINUTE(serial_number)	Converts a serial number to a minute.
MONTH(serial_number)	Converts a serial number to a month.
NOW()	Returns the serial number of the current date and time.
SECOND(serial_number)	Converts a serial number to a second.
TIME(hour,minute,second)	Returns the serial number of a particular time.
TIMEVALUE(time_text)	Converts a time in the form of text to a serial number.
TODAY()	Returns the serial number of today's date.
WEEKDAY(serial_number,return_type)	Converts a serial number to a day of the week.
YEAR(serial_number)	Converts a serial number to a year.

Math & Trig Functions

ABS(number)	Returns the absolute value of a number.
ACOS(number)	Returns the arccosine of a number.
ACOSH(number)	Returns the inverse hyperbolic cosine of a number.

ASIN(number)	Returns the arcsine of a number.
ASINH(number)	Returns the inverse hyperbolic sine of a number.
ATAN(number)	Returns the arctangent of a number.
ATAN2(x_num,y_num)	Returns the arctangent from x- and y-coordinates.
ATANH(number)	Returns the inverse hyperbolic tangent of a number.
CEILING(number,significance)	Rounds a number to the nearest whole number or to the nearest multiple of significance.
COMBIN(number,number_chosen)	Returns the number of combinations for a given number of objects.
COS(number)	Returns the cosine of a number.
COSH(number)	Returns the hyperbolic cosine of a number.
DEGREES(angle)	Converts radians to degrees.
EVEN(number)	Rounds a number up to the nearest even whole number.
EXP(number)	Returns e raised to the power of a given number.
FACT(number)	Returns the factorial of a number.
FLOOR(number, significance)	Rounds a number down, toward 0.
INT(number)	Rounds a number down to the nearest whole number.
LN(number)	Returns the natural logarithm of a number.
LOG(number,base)	Returns the logarithm of a number to a specified base.
LOG10(number)	Returns the base-10 logarithm of a number.
MDETERM(array)	Returns the matrix determinant of an array.
MINVERSE(array)	Returns the matrix inverse of an array.
MMULT(array1,array2)	Returns the matrix product of two arrays.
MOD(number,divisor)	Returns the remainder from division.
ODD(number)	Rounds a number up to the nearest odd whole number.
PI( )	Returns the value of pi.
POWER(number,power)	Returns the result of a number raised to a power.
PRODUCT(number 1,number2,...)	Multiplies its arguments.

MATH & TRIG FUNCTIONS

RADIANS(angle)	Converts degrees to radians.
RAND( )	Returns a random number between 0 and 1.
ROMAN(number,form)	Converts an Arabic numeral to a Roman numeral, as text.
ROUND(number,num_digits)	Rounds a number to a specified number of digits.
ROUNDDOWN(number,num_digits)	Rounds a number down, toward 0.
ROUNDUP(number,num_digits)	Rounds a number up, away from 0.
SIGN(number)	Returns the sign of a number.
SIN(number)	Returns the sine of a number.
SINH(number)	Returns the hyperbolic sine of a number.
SQRT(number)	Returns a positive square root.
SUBTOTAL(function_num,ref1,...)	Returns a subtotal in a list or database.
SUM(number1,number2,...)	Adds its arguments.
SUMIF(range,criteria, sum_range)	Adds the cells specified by a given criteria.
SUMPRODUCT(array1,array2,array3,...)	Returns the sum of the products of corresponding array components.
SUMSQ(number1,number2,...)	Returns the sum of the squares of its arguments.
SUMX2MY2(array_x,array_y)	Returns the sum of the difference of squares of corresponding values in two arrays.
SUMX2PY2(array_x,array_y)	Returns the sum of the sum of squares of corresponding values in two arrays.
SUMXMY2(array_x,array_y)	Returns the sum of squares of differences of corresponding values in two arrays.
TAN(number)	Returns the tangent of a number.
TANH(number)	Returns the hyperbolic tangent of a number.
TRUNC(number,num_digits)	Truncates a number to a whole number.

Statistical Functions

AVEDEV(number1,number2,...)	Returns the average of the absolute deviations of data points from their mean.
AVERAGE(number1,number2,...)	Returns the average of its arguments.
AVERAGEA(value1,value2,...)	Returns the average of its arguments, including text and logical values.

BETADIST(x,alpha,beta,A,B)	Returns the cumulative beta probability density function.
BETAINV(probability,alpha,beta,A,B)	Returns the inverse of the cumulative beta probability density function.
BINOMDIST(number_s,trials,probability_s,cumulative)	Returns the individual term binomial distribution probability.
CHIDIST(x,degrees_freedom)	Returns the one-tailed probability of the chi-squared distribution.
CHIINV(probability,degrees_freedom)	Returns the inverse of the one-tailed probability of the chi-squared distribution.
CHITEST(actual_range,expected_range)	Returns the test for independence.
CONFIDENCE(alpha,standard_dev,size)	Returns the confidence interval for a population mean.
CORREL(array1,array2)	Returns the correlation coefficient between two data sets.
COUNT(value1,value2,...)	Counts how many numbers are in the list of arguments.
COUNTA(value2,value2,...)	Counts how many values are in the list of arguments.
COUNTBLANK(range)	Counts the number of blank cells within a range.
COUNTIF(range,criteria)	Counts the number of nonblank cells within a range which meet the given criteria.
COVAR(array1,array2)	Returns covariance, the average of the products of paired deviations.
CRITBINOM(trials,probability_s,alpha)	Returns the smallest value for which the cumulative binomial distribution is greater than or equal to a criterian value.
DEVSQ(number1,number2,...)	Returns the sum of squares of deviations.
EXPONDIST(x,lambda,cumulative)	Returns the exponential distribution.
FDIST(x,degrees_freedom1,degrees_freedom2)	Returns the F probability distribution.
FINV(probability,degrees_freedom1,degrees_freedom2)	Returns the inverse of the F probability distribution.
FISHER(x)	Returns the Fisher transformation.

STATISTICAL FUNCTIONS

FISHERINV(y)	Returns the inverse of the Fisher transformation.
FORECAST(x,known_y's,known_x's)	Returns a value along a linear trend.
FREQUENCY(data_array,bins_array)	Returns a frequency distribution as a vertical array.
FTEST(array1,array2)	Returns the result of an F-test.
GAMMADIST(x,alpha,beta,cumulative)	Returns the gamma distribution.
GAMMAINV(probability,alpha,beta)	Returns the inverse of the gamma cumulative distribution.
GAMMALN(x)	Returns the natural logarithm of the gamma function.
GEOMEAN(number1,number2,...)	Returns the geometric mean.
GROWTH(knowy_y's,known_x's,new_x's,const)	Returns values along an exponential trend.
HARMEAN(number1,number2,...)	Returns the harmonic mean.
HYPGEOMDIST(sample_s,number_sample,population_s,...)	
	Returns the hypergeometric distribution.
INTERCEPT(known_y's,known_x's)	Returns the intercept of the linear regression line.
KURT(number1,number2,...)	Returns the kurtosis of a data set.
LARGE(array,k)	Returns the k-th largest value in a data set.
LINEST(known_y's,known_x's,const,stats)	Returns the parameters of a linear trend.
LOGEST(known_y's,known_x's,const,stats)	Returns the parameters of an exponential trend.
LOGINV(probability,mean,standard_dev)	Returns the inverse of the lognormal distribution.
LOGNORMDIST(x,mean,standard_dev)	Returns the cumulative lognormal distribution.
MAX(number1,number2,...)	Returns the maximum value in a list of arguments.
MAXA(value1,value2,...)	Returns the maximum value in a list of arguments, including text and logical values.
MEDIAN(number1,number2,...)	Returns the median of the given numbers.
MIN(number1,number2,...)	Returns the minimum value in a list of arguments.
MINA(value1,value2,...)	Returns the minimum value in a list of arguments, including text and logical values.
MODE(number1,number2,...)	Returns the most common value in a data set.
NEGBINOMDIST(number_f,number_s,probability_s)	
	Returns the negative binomial distribution.
NORMDIST(x,mean,standard_dev,cumulative)	Returns the normal cumulative distribution.

STATISTICAL FUNCTIONS

NORMINV(probability,mean,standard_dev)	Returns the inverse of the normal cumulative distribution.
NORMSDIST(z)	Returns the standard normal cumulative distribution.
NORMSINV(probability)	Returns the inverse of the standard normal cumulative distribution.
PEARSON(array1,array2)	Returns the Pearson product moment correlation coefficient.
PERCENTILE(array,k)	Returns the k-th percentile of values in a range.
PERCENTRANK(array,x,significance)	Returns the percentage rank of a value in a data set.
PERMUT(number,number_chosen)	Returns the number of permutations for a given number of objects.
POISSON(x,mean,cumulative)	Returns the Poisson distribution.
PROB(x_range,prob_range,lower_limit,upper_limit)	Returns the probability that values in a range are between two limits.
QUARTILE(array,quart)	Returns the quartile of a data set.
RANK(number,ref,order)	Returns the rank of a number in a list of numbers.
RSQ(known_y's,known_x's)	Returns the square of the Pearson product moment correlation coefficient. (If you know what that means, I hope you're making a lot of money.)
SKEW(number1,number2,...)	Returns the skewness of a distribution.
SLOPE(known_y's,known_x's)	Returns the slope of the linear regression line.
SMALL(array,k)	Returns the k-th smallest value in a data set.
STANDARDIZE(x,mean,standard_dev)	Returns a normalized value.
STDEV(number1,number2,...)	Estimates standard deviation based on a sample.
STDEVA(value1,value2,...)	Estimates standard deviation based on a sample, including text and logical values.
STDEVP(number1,number2,...)	Calculates standard deviation based on the entire population.
STDEVPA(value1,value2,...)	Calculates standard deviation based on the entire population, including text and logical values.
STEYX(known_y's,known_x's)	Returns the standard error of the predicted y-value for each x in the regression.

STATISTICAL FUNCTIONS

TDIST(x,degrees_freedom,tails)	Returns the Student's t-distribution.
TINV(probability,degrees_freedom)	Returns the inverse of the Student's t-distribution.
TREND(known_y's,known_x's,new_x's,const)	Returns values along a linear trend.
TRIMMEAN(array,percent)	Returns the mean of the interior of a data set.
TTEST(array1,array2,tails,type)	Returns the probability associated with a Student's t-test.
VAR(number1,number2,...)	Estimates variance based on a sample.
VARA(value1,value2,...)	Estimates variance based on a sample, including text and logical values.
VARP(number1,number2,...)	Calculates variance based on the entire population.
VARPA(value1,value2,...)	Calculates variance based on the entire population, including text and logical values.
WEIBULL(x,alpha,beta,cumulative)	Returns the Weibull distribution.
ZTEST(array,x,sigma)	Returns the two-tailed P-value of a z-test. Really.

Lookup & Reference Functions

ADDRESS(row_num,column_num,abs_num,a1,sheet_text)	
	Returns a reference as text to a single cell in a worksheet.
AREAS(reference)	Returns the number of areas in a reference.
CHOOSE(index_num,value1,value2,...)	Chooses a value from a list of values.
COLUMN(reference)	Returns the column number of a reference.
COLUMNS(array)	Returns the number of columns in a reference.
GETPIVOTDATA(data_field,pivot_table,field1,item1,field2,...)	
	Extracts data stored in a pivot table.
HLOOKUP(lookup_value,table_array,row_index_num,...)	
	Looks in the top row of a table and returns the value of the indicated cell.
HYPERLINK(link_location,friendly_name)	Creates a shortcut that opens a document stored on a network computer or the Internet.
INDEX(...)	Uses an index to choose a value from a reference or array.
INDIRECT(ref_text,a1)	Returns a reference indicated by a text value.
LOOKUP(...)	Looks up values in a vector or array.

MATCH(lookup_value,lookup_array,match_type)

    Looks up values in a reference or array.

OFFSET(reference,rows,cols,height,width)   Returns a reference offset from a given reference.

ROW(reference)   Returns the row number of a reference.

ROWS(array)   Returns the number of rows in a reference.

RTD(progID,server,topic1,topic2,...)   Retrieves real-time data from a program that supports COM automation.

TRANSPOSE(array)   Returns the transpose of an array.

VLOOKUP(lookup_value,table_array,col_index_num,...)

    Looks in the first column of a table and moves across the row to return the value of a cell.

Database Functions

DAVERAGE(database,field,criteria)   Returns the average of selected database entries.

DCOUNT(database,field,criteria)   Counts the cells containing numbers from a specified database and criteria.

DCOUNTA(database,field,criteria)   Counts nonblank cells from a specified database and criteria.

DGET(database,field,criteria)   Extracts from a database a single record that matches the specified criteria.

DMAX(database,field,criteria)   Returns the maximum value from selected database entries.

DMIN(database,field,criteria)   Returns the minimum value from selected database entries.

DPRODUCT(database,field,criteria)   Multiplies the values in a particular field of records that match the criteria in a database.

DSTDEV(database,field,criteria)   Estimates the standard deviation based on a sample of selected database entries.

DSTDEVP(database,field,criteria)   Calculates the standard deviation based on the entire population of selected database entries.

DSUM(database,field,criteria)   Adds the numbers in the field column of records in the database that match the criteria.

DVAR(database,field,criteria)   Estimates the variance based on a sample from selected database entries.

DVARP(database,field,criteria)   Calculates variance based on the entire population of selected database entries.

LOOKUP & REFERENCE, DATABASE FUNCTIONS

Text Functions

BAHTTEXT(number)	Converts a number to text.
CHAR(number)	Returns the character specified by the code number.
CLEAN(text)	Removes all nonprintable characters from text.
CODE(text)	Returns a numeric code for the first character in a text string.
CONCATENATE(text1,text2,...)	Joins several text items into one text item.
DOLLAR(number,decimals)	Converts a number to text, using currency format.
EXACT(text1,text2)	Checks to see if two text values are identical.
FIND(find_text,within_text,start_num)	Finds one text value within another. This function is case-sensitive.
FIXED(number,decimals,no_commas)	Formats a number as text with a fixed number of decimals.
LEFT(text,num_chars)	Returns the leftmost characters from a text value.
LEN(text)	Returns the number of characters in a text string.
LOWER(text)	Converts text to lowercase.
MID(text,start_num,num_chars)	Returns a specific number of characters from a text string.
PROPER(text)	Capitalizes the first letter in each word of a text value.
REPLACE(old_text,start_num,num_chars,new_text)	Replaces characters within text.
REPT(text,number_times)	Repeats text a given number of times.
RIGHT(text,num_chars)	Returns the rightmost characters from a text value.
SEARCH(find_text,within_text,start_num)	Finds one text value within another. This function is not case-sensitive.
SUBSTITUTE(text,old_text,new_text,instance_num)	Substitutes new text for old text in a text string.
T(value)	Converts its arguments to text.
TEXT(value,format_text)	Formats a number and converts it to text.
TRIM(text)	Removes spaces from text.
UPPER(text)	Converts text to uppercase.
VALUE(text)	Converts a text argument to a number.

Logical Functions

AND(logical1,logical2,...)	Returns TRUE if all of its arguments are TRUE.
FALSE( )	Returns the logical value FALSE.
IF(logical_test,value_if_true,value_if_false)	Specifies a logical test to perform and the value to return based on a TRUE or FALSE result.
NOT(logical)	Reverses the logic of its argument.
OR(logical1,logical2,...)	Returns TRUE if any argument is TRUE.
TRUE( )	Returns the logical value TRUE.

Information Functions

CELL(info_type,reference)	Returns information about the formatting, location, or contents of a cell.
ERROR.TYPE(error_val)	Returns a number corresponding to an error value.
INFO(type_text)	Returns information about the current operating environment.
ISBLANK(value)	Returns TRUE if the value is blank.
ISERR(value)	Returns TRUE if the value is any error value except #N/A.
ISERROR(value)	Returns TRUE if the value is any error value.
ISLOGICAL(value)	Returns TRUE if the value is a logical value.
ISNA(value)	Returns TRUE if the value is the #N/A error value.
ISNONTEXT(value)	Returns TRUE if the value is not text.
ISNUMBER(value)	Returns TRUE if the value is a number.
ISREF(value)	Returns TRUE if the value is a reference.
ISTECT(value)	Returns TRUE if the value is text.
N(value)	Returns a value converted to a number.
NA( )	Returns the error value #N/A.
TYPE(value)	Returns a number indicating the data type of a value.

LOGICAL, INFORMATION FUNCTIONS

Index

WWW.PEACHPIT.COM

Quality How-to Computer Books

About

News

Books

Features

Resources

Order

Find

Welcome!

Visit Peachpit Press on the Web at www.peachpit.com

- Check out new feature articles each Monday: excerpts, interviews, tips, and plenty of how-tos

- Find any Peachpit book by title, series, author, or topic on the Books page

- See what our authors are up to on the News page: signings, chats, appearances, and more

- Meet the Peachpit staff and authors in the About section: bios, profiles, and candid shots

- Use Resources to reach our academic, sales, customer service, and tech support areas and find out how to become a Peachpit author

Peachpit.com is also the place to:

- Chat with our authors online
- Take advantage of special Web-only offers
- Get the latest info on new books